HOUSE TO HOUSE

HOUSE

An Epic Memoir of War

TO HOUSE

Staff Sergeant David Bellavia

With John R. Bruning

POCKET
BOOKS

LONDON • SYDNEY • NEW YORK • TORONTO

First published in Great Britain by Simon & Schuster UK Ltd, 2007
This edition first published by Pocket Books, 2008
An imprint of Simon & Schuster UK Ltd
A CBS COMPANY

3 5 7 9 10 8 6 4 2

Simon & Schuster UK Ltd
Africa House
64–78 Kingsway
London WC2B 6AH

www.simonsays.co.uk

Simon & Schuster Australia
Sydney

A CIP catalogue for this book is available from the British Library.

ISBN: 978-1-84739-118-6

Designed by Erich Hobbing
Printed and bound in Great Britain by
Cox & Wyman Ltd, Reading, Berks

For the Ramrods of the
2nd Battalion, 2nd Infantry Regiment

Noli Me Tangere
"Do Not Touch Me"

Contents

CONTENTS

Author's Note

This is a work of nonfiction. Events, actions, experiences, and their consequences have been faithfully retold as I remembered them and based on interviews with a number of the participants. Events to which I was not an eyewitness have been recounted based on documented accounts and interviews. Every event within the book took place, but a few have been reordered or combined for narrative clarity. Conversations presented in dialogue form have been re-created from my memory of them but are not intended to represent a word-for-word documentation; rather, they are intended to invoke the essence of what was said.

HOUSE TO HOUSE

The Coffins of Muqdadiyah

April 9, 2004
Diyala Province, Iraq

Dust cakes our faces, invades our sinuses, and stings our eyes. The heat bakes the moisture from us with utter relentlessness. Our body temperatures hover at a hundred and three. Our ears ring. On the edge of heat exhaustion, we get dizzy as our stomachs heave.

We have the spastic shits, with stabs of pain as our guts liquefy thanks to the menagerie of local bacteria. Inside our base's filthy outhouses, swarms of flies crawl over us. Without ventilation, those outhouses are furnaces, pungent with the acrid smell of well-cooked urine.

All this, and we get shot at, too.

Welcome to the infantry. This is our day, our job. It sucks, and we hate it, but we endure for two reasons. First, there is nobility and purpose in our lives. We are America's warrior class. We protect; we avenge. Second, every moment in the infantry is a test. If we measure up to the worst days, such as this one, it proves we stand a breed apart from all other men.

Where we work, there are no cubicles. There are no break rooms. Ties are foreign objects; we commute in armored fighting vehicles.

Our workplace is not some sterile office or humming factory. It is a stretch of desolate highway in a vast and empty land. A guard tower burns in the background. Shattered bodies litter the ground around us. Vacant corpse eyes, bulging and horror-struck, stare back at us. The stench of burned flesh is thick in our nostrils. This was once an Iraqi Civil Defense Corps (ICDC) checkpoint, designed to regulate traffic in and out of Muq-dadiyah, one of the key cities in the Diyala Province. Thanks to a surprise attack launched earlier in the morning, it is nothing more than a funeral pyre. We arrived too late to help, and our earnest but untrained allies died horribly as the insurgents swept over them. One Iraqi soldier took a direct hit from a rocket-propelled grenade (RPG). All that's left of him are his boots and soggy piles of bloody meat splattered around the guard tower.

This is our workplace. We began to acclimate to such horrors right after arriving in the country. While on our second patrol in Iraq, a civilian candy truck tried to merge with a column of our armored vehicles, only to get run over and squashed. The occupants were smashed beyond recognition. Our first sight of death was a man and his wife both ripped open and dismembered, their intestines strewn across shattered boxes of candy bars. The entire platoon hadn't eaten for twenty-four hours. We stopped, and as we stood guard around the wreckage, we grew increasingly hungry. Finally, I stole a few nibbles from one of the cleaner candy bars. Others wiped away the gore and fuel from the wrappers and joined me.

That was three weeks ago. We're veterans now, proud that we can stomach such sights and still carry out our job. It is this mis-ery that defines us, gives us our identity. It also cleaves infantry-men apart from everyone else in uniform. Some call it arrogance. So be it. We call it pride since we believe fervently in what we are doing.

"Check it out," calls Staff Sergeant Colin Fitts. He points to a Humvee rolling up the highway toward our battlefield.

The two of us pause and watch the rig approach. Fitts is a Mississippian with a gravelly voice and intense eyes. We're so close that long ago I learned to tell every entertaining story from his life in more detail than he can, and he can do the same with mine.

The Humvee screeches to a stop a short distance from us. In the right seat sits a clean-cut major. With his tiny, wire-rimmed glasses, he looks like an accountant in Kevlar. He's so clean that I doubt he's more than a few hours removed from his last shower. I can't even remember when I last had one. We've been making do with whore's baths—baby wipes to the armpits and private parts—since running water is a luxury not bestowed upon the infantry.

Right here we have the dichotomy that defines our military. We all wear the same uniform, but we might as well be from two different armies. We're the frontline bullet-chewers. This officer embodies all that we despise about the other half. He is scrubbed; we are filthy. His skin has rarely seen the sun. We are sunburned and leathery. He is well fed and a bit on the pudgy side. Most of our platoon has lost over ten pounds since getting to Diyala. Maybe that's because when we get a chance to eat, the appetite doesn't stick around long. Our mess hall is an abandoned Iraqi morgue.

"Boys," the major says, "Go tell your sergeant that Quarter Cav is here!" The major obviously thinks he has a flair for drama. He doesn't realize that he's just insulted both of us. Fitts and I are both staff sergeants; our rank insignia are not easily missed. Fitts turns bright red.

In our world, the world of the infantry, this major is a wannabe. He sits safe behind the wire, but tries to act the part of a combat leader. Most of the time we must simply suffer fools like him as we go about our business.

I'm prepared to do just that. Fitts, on the other hand, has no inner censor. He's allergic to bullshit and fears nobody. He's made plenty of enemies in our battalion for this, but you have to admire a man who reacts with pure honesty to every situation and never, not once, considers the consequences to his career. It has cost him, too. Several times he has lost rank, but he always earns his stripes back.

Fitts nods to the major and shouts across the road to his A Team leader, "Hey, Sergeant Misa! The Quarter Cav is here. What's that? You don't give a fucking shit either? Well, that makes two of us, two hundred-fifty thousand if you count the whole sector."

My jaw drops. Fitts has just emasculated a major the same way he would a private. I wait for the fallout.

The major stammers, pushes his glasses up on his nose, turns to his driver and says, "Move on."

The Humvee speeds up the highway for the safety of Forward Operating Base Normandy. The fact that we are willing to submit ourselves to filthy conditions and brutal fighting sometimes gives us a free pass with the other half of the army. It is the one card that saves our asses from charges of insubordination.

Sergeant Warren Misa steps over a rag-dolled Iraqi corpse and approaches Fitts. A muscular, Cebu-born Filipino who grew up in Cincinnati, Misa is the only man I've ever met who speaks Tagalog with an Ohio accent. We can barely understand him.

"Sergeant Fitts?"

"Yeah, Misa?"

"They are trying to get you on the radio. There's trouble in Muqdadiyah again."

We head for our Bradley Fighting Vehicles and pile inside. The interiors of these armored troop carriers are like mobile ovens in the Iraqi heat. In our fifty pounds of full battle rattle—Kevlar, body armor, ammo, weapon, water, and night vision—we sweat pounds off on every drive. It makes us long for the less terminal heat of the FOB outhouses.

The Brads lurch forward, leaving the shattered checkpoint in their dust. A short ride later, we reach downtown Muqdadiyah. It was here the day before that our platoon saw the heaviest fighting of its short combat career.

"Holy shit," comes the voice of our platoon sergeant, James Cantrell, over the Bradley's internal speaker. I peer out the viewing port and gasp.

We're surrounded by coffins.

Fresh wooden ones line both sides of the street. In places they're piled two and three high. Nearby, an old man stoops over two boards as he swings a hammer. I realize he's building a coffin lid. More lids lie scattered on the street around him, blocking our path ahead.

Cantrell orders us to dismount. Our vehicle's ramp flops down and clangs onto the street. We sprint out into the brutal morning sun. Buildings still smolder. A battle-damaged house has already been gutted by men wielding sledge hammers. All around us, interspersed among the coffins, women cry and children stare into space. Old men, survivors of Saddam's reign of violence, the war with Iran, and Gulf War I, regard us with hollowed eyes.

We slowly make our way past the house we used as our casualty collection point the day before. Stacked out front are three caskets. I wonder if one of them houses the teenaged kid I had to shoot.

In the middle of yesterday's fight, my squad reached a gated and walled house. Sergeant Hugh Hall, our platoon's stocky, door-crushing bruiser, smashed the gate and led the way into a courtyard. Just as we got inside, the face of the house suddenly exploded. A chunk of spinning concrete slammed into Hall and sent the rest of us flying for cover. A sudden barrage followed as three Bradley armored vehicles opened up with their 25-millimeter Bushmaster cannons in response to the explosion of the enemy rocket. As the high-explosive rounds tore up the area outside of the house, the din was so intense I could hardly hear.

Over the radio, I made out Cantrell yelling—"Bellavia, give me a fucking SITREP." Cantrell's voice is the only thing that can rise above the cacophony of a firefight. He has a real gift there.

Confused and dazed, I initially failed to respond. Cantrell didn't like this. "BELLAVIA, ARE YOU FUCKING OKAY?"

I finally found the wherewithal to respond. All I had heard was the Bradley fire, so I finally screamed back, "Stop shooting! You're hitting our location."

"Hey asshole, that wasn't us. That was a fucking RPG," Cantrell's voice booms through the radio. "And here comes another."

The top of a large palm tree in the courtyard suddenly exploded overhead. Cantrell and the other Bradleys immediately returned fire. Bits of wood and burned leaves rained down on us. Hall, already covered with concrete dust, dirt, and blood, blurted out, "Would they kill that muthafucka already?"

"Get inside and take the roof," I holler over our Bradley's fire.

The men moved for the door. As they forced their way inside, I peered around the corner and caught sight of a gunman on a nearby rooftop. I studied him for a moment, unsure whose side he was on. He could be a friendly local. We'd seen them before shooting at the black-clad Mahdi militiamen who infiltrated this part of the city earlier in the fight. Not everyone with a rifle was an enemy.

The gunman on the roof was a teenaged boy, maybe sixteen years old. I could see him scanning for targets, his back to me. He held an AK-47 without a stock. Was he just a stupid kid trying to protect his family? Was he one of Muqtada al-Sadr's Shiite fanatics? I kept my eyes on him and prayed he'd put the AK down and just get back inside his own house. I didn't want to shoot him.

He turned and saw me, and I could see the terror on his sweat-streaked face. I put him in my sights just as he adjusted his AK against his shoulder. I had beaten him on the draw. My own rifle was snug in my shoulder, the sight resting on him. The kid stood no chance. My weapon just needed a flick of the safety and a butterfly's kiss of pressure on the trigger.

Please don't do this. You don't need to die.

The AK went to full ready-up. Was he aiming at me? I couldn't be sure, but the barrel was trained at my level. Do I shoot? Do I risk not shooting? Was he silently trying to save me from some unseen threat? I didn't know. I had to make a decision.

Please forgive me for this.

I pulled my trigger. The kid's chin fell to his chest, and a guttural moan escaped his lips. I fired again, missed, then pulled the trigger one more time. The bullet tore his jaw and ear off. Sergeant Hall came up alongside me, saw the AK and the boy, and finished him with four shots to his chest. He slumped against the low rooftop wall.

"Thanks, dude. I lost my zero," I said to Hall, explaining that my rifle sights were off-line, though that was the last thing going through my mind.

Now a day later on a street surrounded by coffins and mourning families, their grief is too much for us to witness. These poor people had been caught in the middle, abused by the fanatics who chose to fight us. Muqtada al-Sadr's Mahdi militiamen are the foot soldiers of the Shia uprising. They're the ones who have created this chaos in Muqdadiyah. They use innocent people's homes and businesses as fighting positions and ambush points.

The angst-filled scenes on the street cannot compare to what we find inside these battle-scarred houses. Yesterday, my squad kicked in one door and stumbled right into a woman wearing a blood-soaked apron. She was sitting on the floor, howling with grief. She looked to be in her mid-forties and had Shia tattoos on her face. When she saw us, she stood and grasped Specialist Piotr Sucholas by the shoulders and gave him a kiss on his cheek. Then she turned and laid her head on Sergeant Hall's chest, as if to touch his heart.

I stepped forward and said in broken Arabic "La tah khaf madrua? Am ree kee tabeeb. Weina mujahadeen kelp?" *Do not be afraid. Injured? American doctor. Where are the mujahadeen dogs?*

She bent and kissed my wedding ring. "Baby madrua. Baby madrua." The despair in her voice was washed away by the sound of a little girl's laughter. When the giggling child came in from the kitchen and clutched her mother's leg, we immediately realized she had Down's syndrome. I was struck by the beauty of this child. Specialist Pedro Contreras, whose heart was always the biggest in our platoon, knelt by her side and gave her a butter-scotch candy. Contreras loved Iraqi kids. He had a six-year-old nephew back home, and seeing these little ones made him ache for the boy.

We didn't see the injured baby at first—we still had a job to do. I moved upstairs, searching for an insurgent who had been shooting at our Bradleys. Halfway up, I discovered a smear of blood on the steps. Then I found a tuft of human hair. Another step up, I saw a tiny leg.

Baby madrua.

Ah, fuck. Fuck.

The child was dead. She was torn apart at the top of the

stairs. Specialist Michael Gross had followed me partway up the stairs. I turned to him and screamed, "Get back down! I said get the fuck back down!" Gross stopped suddenly, then eased off the stairs, a wounded look on his face. I was overly harsh, but I didn't want him to see what was left of this dead child.

Leaving the squad on the first floor, I went to clear the roof alone. Three dead goats lay bleeding on the rooftop next to a dead Mahdi militiaman dressed in black with a gold armband. He had died with an AK in hand, a rocket-propelled grenade launcher leaning against the wall at his side. My stomach churned. Was this the woman's husband? Had he really endangered his family by shooting at us from his own rooftop? What kind of human does this? Revolted, I fled downstairs. The rest of the squad had found shell casings in the children's bedroom. The Mahdi militiaman had been shooting from the window there as well.

I'll never forget that house. The woman kissed each of us good-bye. As she touched her lips to my cheek, I pointed to my wedding ring and asked her where her husband was.

"Weina zoah jik? Shoof nee, shoof nee." *Where is your husband? Show me, show me.*

She spat onto the floor and cried, "Kelp." *Dog.* I guessed he was the corpse on her roof. I touched my heart and tried to convey my feelings, but the language barrier was too great.

Her surviving daughter giggled and waved good-bye.

Now I wonder if the woman is among the crowd around the coffins. If I saw her, what would I say?

Cantrell orders us back into our Bradleys. I climb inside. The ramp closes behind me. We move out. Over the radio, we hear that our battalion commander, Lieutenant Colonel Peter Newell, and his security detail have made contact with insurgents. We race off to support him.

Newell's Humvee has a .50-caliber M2 machine gun in its turret. When we arrive, his gunner, Sergeant Sean Grady, is busy

hosing down a grove of trees the insurgents are using for concealment. In response, a trio of rocket-propelled grenades land in
front of his Humvee. Our battalion commander ignores the
incoming and from the right seat he coordinates the fight with a
radio in each ear. He is unflappable.

The radio chatter makes us tense and anxious to get into the
fight.

Newell's two-rig convoy takes fire from both sides of the highway. The volume swells as more rockets streak across the road.
Suddenly, a small boy of perhaps five or six steps out into the
street. Standing next to Newell's Humvee, the kid holds up first
two fingers, then five fingers.

Sergeant Grady swings his machine gun around. It is obvious
that the boy is signaling to the Mahdi militiamen how many
American vehicles and soldiers are present.

As Grady racks the bolt on his machine gun, Newell realizes
what his gunner has in mind. "Don't shoot the child," he orders.

"Sir, the kid is giving our position away," says Grady, his voice
nearly drowned out by the swelling volume of incoming fire.

"Don't shoot the child," Newell reiterates, his voice stern.
Grady gets the message. Our colonel possesses a black-and-
white sense of morality. The kid, no matter what he's doing, will
not be targeted. At times, our battalion commander's adherence
to such niceties frustrates us, but I know in time we will thank
him. Nobody wants a child on his conscience.

From the backseat of the Humvee, the Iraqi Defense Corps
officer accompanying Newell leans forward and says, "Those
men out there, sir, they are mine."

Never intimidated, Newell ignores the Iraqi colonel and
remains focused on fighting his task force. The Iraqi colonel
falls silent and turns to look out his window. Grady sees him
smiling. Is he a Mahdi militia sympathizer, too?

By the time my Bradley reached the fight and dropped its

ramp, Staff Sergeant Colin Fitts is on the ground ahead of me, with his entire squad and my B Team. They're advancing eastward under heavy fire. We've got to catch up with them and give him support. We sprint across open ground, making a mad dash through heavy but poorly aimed machine-gun fire. The professional in me derides their skill.

These bastards could kill us all if they'd just give us a two-finger lead.

The heat of the morning is already intense. By the time we reach a cluster of buildings, I am lightheaded and a bit fuzzy from the near-brush with heat exhaustion.

Assault rifles bark. Bullets ping around us. We run along a wall, turn into an alley, and start weaving around houses and shacks. Every doorway, window, and rooftop is a potential threat. We keep our heads on a swivel as we run, looking for shooters.

We cross through two alleys before a wave of small-arms fire bursts in front of us. The rapid metallic bangs of Fitts's M4 rifle follow hard on the heels of the lighter cracks of AK-47 fire. Fitts and a dozen good men, his nine-man squad and three from my squad, are out there unsupported. I've got to get to them. We home in on the sound of battle.

We cross more alleys, pass more houses. Ahead a few blocks, I catch sight of three of Fitts's men hugging a wall and blasting away with their rifles. Where's Fitts? I turn and lead my men up an alleyway. I intend to move parallel to his squad's position with the intent to envelope the enemy that Fitts has encountered.

Behind us, an M4 rifle barks. I spin around and see Lieutenant Christopher Walls, our platoon leader, on the trigger. In the maze of alleyways, I know he'll have a hard time finding us as we continue to advance. I tell Specialist John Ruiz, Private First Class Raymond Cullins, and Sergeant Alan Pratt to hang back and wait for him while I move forward to find Fitts and figure out how we can consolidate both squads.

I reach a corner, peer around, and finally spot Fitts and the rest of First Squad. They've taken cover up a small side street about a football field away from me. They're twenty meters from a walled compound.

Inside the compound sits a small house with a sandbagged machine-gun nest in one window. The nest looks empty, and the gun's barrel points skyward. Yet many of the rockets and much of the small-arms fire sizzling our way seems to be coming from this area.

Fitts is taking fire from his rear, too. Black-hooded insurgents slash through the alleys all around Fitts's squad. Rockets zip and explode over low-walled compounds. Machine guns chatter. I can see clearly that Mahdi militia have surrounded First Squad. There's only one option for Fitts: get his men inside a house and seize a rooftop that can be used as a defensive position. The nearest house is the one inside the walled compound. That's the one he'll take down. Fitts and I think alike. He doesn't see me, but I know what he's doing. If Fitts is able to seize that defensive position inside the compound, he'll gain a solid foothold in this neighborhood and a position that can weather the cross fire his squad is now in. I prepare to maneuver my A Fire Team to support him.

Pratt, Collins, and Ruiz advance toward me, only to take fire from an alleyway. They stop to return fire, embroiled in a fight of their own. I realize my team won't be able to support First Squad. We're strung out over about fifty yards of enemy-infested urban jungle and preoccupied with our own survival.

Up the alley, I see Fitts gathering his men in a wedge formation to move on the compound and escape the crossfire. He leads them forward, opening into a reverse-horseshoe formation. Fitts is doing it by the book. As they reach just outside the compound's wall and move toward the front gate, multiple machine guns unleash a torrent of fire at them from the upper stories of another fortified complex about three hundred meters away.

Desperately, I scan for targets. Fitts needs me to put suppressive fire on that complex, but the buildings near me mask my view. I can't see anyone to shoot.

Fitts leads the men forward even as Misa and others loft a volley of 40mm grenades toward the fortified complex. They boom in the distance, but the incoming fire doesn't diminish.

As Fitts's squad approaches the compound's entrance, they enter hell. Bullets smack around them on the street, coming from every point on the compass. Insurgents are firing from everywhere. First Squad is caught in a triple crossfire. Their only hope is to get inside the building.

As a rash of bullets tear the ground around Gross and Contreras, Fitts never hesitates. His M4 blazing, Fitts leads his squad and my B Team in a dash for the house. Tracers whiz past them like hot embers from a windblown bonfire. I seethe. I can't see anyone to shoot. I can't help. My first instinct is to run into the open and give our enemy someone else to shoot at.

I'm just about to move when it happens. Fitts is crouched and shooting into the other side of the compound when his right forearm snaps back violently. A spray of blood fills the air. He doesn't break stride. He takes two more steps, switches his rifle to his left hand and braces it under his armpit. He fires it like a child's toy with his one good arm.

Then his left arm jerks and slumps as another bullet strikes him in the left bicep, right above the elbow. His rifle tilts to the ground and he triggers several rounds into the dirt. He staggers, drops his rifle, and falls down.

Ten feet behind Fitts, Specialist Desean Ellis spins backward and screams. Even from my distant vantage point, almost a hundred meters away, I hear a terrible ripping sound, like denim jeans being torn apart. A bullet has hit him in the right quadri-cep. As he spins I can see a crimson stain on Ellis's pants. He crumples to the ground.

Summoning reserves of strength, Fitts retrieves his M4 rifle and regains his feet. He pumps four or five quick shots into the house as he stumbles forward. Behind him, his men go "cyclic" with their automatic weapons' rate of fire. Properly trained infantry-men don't do that in close combat except in desperate circum-stances. Faced with the loss of their leader, they have no choice but to turn their weapons into lethal showerheads.

A shape appears in the doorway. Fitts fires at the insurgent, triggering his weapon now with his thumb and the ring finger of his opposing hand. Sergeant Hall unleashes a volley as well. The enemy collapses in the doorway. Seconds later, another takes his place. Contreras shoots him dead with two well-placed rounds.

The abandoned machine gun in the second-story window sud-denly tilts down. I see the movement and realize what it means. Somebody is manning the weapon now, and our men are in the open. I still have no clear shot. I can't help. My stomach churns. I rage against my own helplessness.

The gun barks. Bullets erupt all around the squad. The men scramble for their lives. Fitts has no chance. I see him double over as blood fountains from his right knee, his third hit. He sags into the dirt, blood pooling around him.

I cannot believe what I'm seeing. Fitts, my closest friend, has been shot three times, and I'm powerless to help. Searing heat ripples down my spine. I lose feeling in my legs. I can't move. I can't think. All I can do is watch in horror. I think of Fitts's wife. She's back home pregnant with their third child. How am I going to explain this day to her?

I can't look, but I have to.

Fitts is lying facedown in the dirt about ten meters from the house's front door. Misa launches another 40mm grenade into the machine-gun nest overhead just as two men charge out the front door.

To my amazement, Fitts grasps his M4 again and opens fire. He still has plenty of fight left in him.

Specialist Michael Gross kills the first man out the door. The second, a thin man with a dark beard, bolts through the doorway and passes straight into Private First Class Jim Metcalf's line of fire. He and Specialist Lance Ohle squeeze off several rounds and the thin man dies only a few steps from Fitts. Simultaneously two more militiamen duck out of a neighboring house. Specialist Jesse Flannery cuts them down as Contreras sprints to Fitts, picks him up, and starts to drag him backward toward the refuge of a walled compound.

"Get the fuck off me and grab security in that shack back there," orders Fitts. Behind the squad sits a tiny shack against the interior of the compound wall. Aside from the house itself, it is their best hope. The house seems to be clear of enemy fighters. The danger lies in the incoming fire from the neighboring buildings. In the middle of the compound, Fitts and Contreras are sitting ducks.

"I'm not leaving you here," argues Contreras.

"Get the fuck off me. Leave me here."

Reluctantly, Contreras drops Fitts just as another burst of fire laces the squad from their left. Contreras drops to one knee, turns, and drains his magazine in the direction of the incoming. He's exposed, but he doesn't care. He keeps banging away at targets I can't see. Empty shell casings fly through the gun's ejection port and tumble down on top of Fitts, who has started to crawl forward toward the enemy.

I hear a rifle bark from somewhere in front of me. I catch sight of a dark-faced Iraqi in Ray-Bans. He's on a roof using an Iranian-made rifle. I can't tell if he's on our side or not, but he seems to be suppressing the enemy around Fitts and the rest of First Squad. Not far from the compound, a rocket-toting militiaman breaks cover. Mr. Ray-Ban on the roof drops him with a series of well-placed shots.

I am so fucking confused right now.

Fitts rises to his feet. Using his rifle as a cane, he about-faces and limps the rest of the way to the compound wall without assistance. Hall moves toward Fitts, but I see him suddenly jerk and spin. A geyser of water shoots out of his CamelBak hydration pack.

"Hall, you hit, man?" shouts Misa.

"I know. I know, dude." Hall never slows, though three bullets have just hit him in the back. Only his body armor saved him.

The squad takes cover against the inside of the compound wall. Seconds later, a rocket-propelled grenade meant for Staff Sergeant Cory Brown's Bradley sails high and explodes against the outside of the wall.

A militiaman pops up on a rooftop, looking for a new angle from which to fire into the trapped squad. He's the first real target I've had, and I unload on him. He ducks and disappears, and I fume at myself for missing him.

My zero is off.

Behind me, Pratt and Ruiz are still battling by the alleyway. Insurgents take shots at them from between two buildings. They're in no position to help us. Bullets strike around them with high-pitched zips and whines.

I decide I need to move. I get to my feet and zig down an alleyway, then turn a corner. I stop short. I've come right up behind a man smoking a cigarette. His golden armband denoting membership in the Mahdi militia has fallen around his wrist.

He doesn't notice me. He's preoccupied with Mr. Ray-Ban on the roof only a few meters away. His back is to me. He casually continues to smoke, with his AK strapped over his right shoul-

der. At first I think I'm hallucinating. Does this jackoff think
there are unionized smoke breaks in battle?

My weapon comes up automatically. I don't even think. In the
second it takes to set the rifle on burst-fire, my surprise gives way
to cold fury. The muzzle makes contact with the back of his
head.

Fuck a zero. I can't miss now.

My finger twitches twice. Six rounds tear through his skull.
His knees collapse together as if I'd just broken both his legs. As
he sinks down he makes a snorting, piggish sound. I lower my
barrel and trigger another three-round burst into his chest, just
to be sure. He flops to the ground with a meaty slap.

His head bobbles back and forth. He snorts again. I convince myself that this is the man who shot Fitts, and I am roused
to a full fury. His face looks like a bloody Halloween mask and
I stomp it with my boot until he finally dies. While I spike his
weapon, bending the barrel to assure that anyone who uses it
again will only hurt themselves, I notice my entire boot is
bathed in blood and gore.

Rockets fly. Our gunners in the Bradleys have a bead now.
Specialist Shane Gossard, Staff Sergeant Brown's Bradley gunner, blasts away at insurgent positions as they make their way to
Fitts's squad. Cantrell's gunner, Sergeant Chad Ellis, kills two
men running with bags of rockets on their backs. In the cover of
this chaos, my men run and shoot their way into the compound.
Finally, I get through the gate and rush to Fitts.

He's lying on his back, his face waxen. I can tell he's in
shock.

"How you doing, bro?"

"Been better. This fucking smarts."

That's all he'll say, despite taking three bullets from three different weapons.

I call Cantrell to bring in a medevac and get Fitts and Ellis out. When our platoon sergeant realizes two of his men are hurt, he goes ballistic. He speeds his Bradley to our rescue. Initially, he can't find us, and his wrath swells until I fear he's on the verge of an aneurism. He bellows repeatedly over the radio.

I strip Fitts of his weapon, magazines, night vision, and tools. He understands. He's in no condition to fight, and we'll need everything for what's ahead. I take everything off him but his can of Copenhagen dip.

Cantrell's Bradley arrives. Quickly, we load Fitts and Ellis aboard. Even as the ramp is raised, I hear Fitts giving orders to his men while Ellis screams for home.

The Bradley lumbers away, my best friend bleeding inside.

Moments later, we wade back into the fight. We battle from building to building. The killing continues unabated as darkness approaches. After dark, the advantage will be ours. With our night-vision equipment, we own the night. The Mahdi militiamen are fanatical but ill-trained. They only know how to die.

An Air Force F-16 jet arrives to fly back and forth overhead, bombs slung on the weapon pylons under each wing. They stay on those racks.

The pilot isn't allowed to drop his ordnance. Division doesn't want to have to rebuild the damage his bombs will cause. Apparently, we're fighting a kindler, gentler war.

Welcome to the infantry. Where hajji buildings are worth more than our lives. Fine, we'll live with the burden. It is just another test, another measure that sets us apart from the likes of that Quarter Cav major.

In Diyala, on April 9, 2004, we're in full battle rattle. The high-intensity urban fighting we've practiced since basic training is now finally allowed to be unleashed on our enemy. There is no weak-stomached four-star general to hold back on our reins. We are again the First Infantry Division of Vietnam and the beaches of Normandy. We pour through compound gates, rifles shouldered, targets falling as we trigger our weapons. Mahdi militiamen sprint from corner to corner, but we are quick and accurate with our aim. We knock them right out of their shoes. Our Brads are rolling, unleashing volley after volley from their Bushmasters into the nearby buildings. Yet the militiamen refuse to give up the fight. Tracers from unseen enemy positions spiderweb overhead. They make us earn every house and every inch.

This is our war: we can't shoot at every target, we can't always tell who *is* a target; but we look out for one another and we don't mind doing the nation's dirty work. Air Force pilots and Army majors expert in Microsoft PowerPoint have a perfectly clean view of it. We won't get support if it makes a mess.

Bring it.

We're the infantry.

War's a bitch, wear a helmet.

CHAPTER ONE

In the Shit

November 2, 2004
Diyala Province
Our last mission before Fallujah

Seven months later, by the light of a full moon, we wade through chest-high sewage. We inch along, arms above our heads to hold our weapons out of the muck. The sludge that bathes us is exquisitely rank. Gnats swarm. Mosquitoes feast and flies crawl. If my first day in the army had been like this, I'd have gone AWOL.

Behind me, I can sense my men are pissed off. We have a mission, but some of them question it. What's beyond question is the fact that I've made them come out here in the middle of the night to wade through a trench of human excrement. I glance behind me just in time to see Piotr Sucholas nearly take a header into the filth. John Ruiz slops an arm out of the sewage and catches Sucholas before he goes under. The two of them spit funk out of their mouths, then make eye contact with me for a nanosecond.

Part of me feels guilty for their plight. Knowing they're angry with me makes it even worse. Call that my human side. At the same, the professional in me, the NCO side of my brain, gives exactly two-fifths of a fuck about how my men feel. This inner conflict doesn't usually last. The NCO in me beats the ever-loving shit out of my human side. The mission is what counts.

But tonight I just can't seem to help myself.

Voice barely a whisper, I ask, "Hey, you guys alright?"

Ruiz and Sucholas nod. So does Hugh Hall who is next to Ruiz.

"Pull your nuts out. You might just die at the end of this bitch."

They stare at me without expression, streaks of shit water running down their faces. Sucholas spits again, but does so quietly. They get the point.

The fact that my men don't say a word in response shows discipline. They are angry and miserable, but they don't display it. We both play the game, soldiers and NCOs. I'm proud of their discipline, yet at the same time I am hyperalert for the first one to break the rules.

I have pushed my squad so hard in the ten months we've been in Iraq, the men must despise me. Back at base, there is a long-standing rumor of a sock full of five-dollar bills the platoon has collected, a little wager over which of their three leading sergeants will get fragged first: Fitts, Cantrell, or me.

We push along the trench. We have almost two more kilometers to go. The moonlight leads the way; it is so bright, we don't bother with our night-vision goggles. We slop our way slowly toward a large pipe that crosses the sewer trench right at head level. It is old and rusted and looks unstable. I turn around and motion to Staff Sergeant Mike Smith. Smitty edges past me in the trench and swings a leg up onto the pipe.

A metallic groan echoes through the night. Smitty tries to shift his weight and the pipe whines in protest. It starts to buckle, and a good-sized chunk falls off, leaving a gaping hole in one side. The palm groves around us are full of chained watch-dogs—the hajji version of an ADT security system. They hear the noise and bark viciously in response. The barking grows frantic. Smitty eases off the broken pipe. We can't get over it, and now we risk detection, thanks to the dogs. The whole squad freezes. I grow tense. The mission is on the line here.

We are after Ayub Ali again, the terror-for-hire arms broker who has sewn so much misery in the Diyala Province since the Shia uprising began in April. When we first arrived in country, we had no idea who he was. Gradually, through the summer, we picked up bits of intelligence that suggested there was a network providing weapons and explosives to both the Mahdi militia and the Sunni insurgents. Ayub Ali sits atop this shadowy group.

We've tried to catch him several times already, but his luck ran strong and he evaded us at every turn. The more I learn about him, the more I want him dead. He's no ideologue or jihadist, he's just a criminal selling the tools of death to the highest bidder. He helps blow up women and children for profit. Taking Ali down will save countless innocent lives.

Tonight, we are on a sneak-and-peak mission to find his latest hideout. Intelligence reports suggest Ali has moved into a horse farm in the countryside outside Muqdadiyah. Our job is to get as close as we can, get a good look at the place, and confirm he's there. The shit trench offered the surest way to approach unde-tected by those vicious mutts.

Now stuck at the pipe crossing our trench, we face the possi-bility of blowing the op altogether. In the satellite photos I received before the mission, this pipe could not be seen. Now I have to act like I expected it. We cannot backtrack. If we do, it will be the admission of a mistake, and NCOs never make mis-takes. We lie like professionals to protect that image of infallibil-ity because that is what cements us to our men.

If they believe in you and the example you set, these men will do whatever is asked of them. This connection between soldiers is a deep bond. It is the root of what it means to be an infantryman. In this cruel here and now, it is what gives my life value and meaning. That doesn't mean my men won't despise me. The nature of soldiering brings ultra-intensity to every emotion, especially in combat. We love, hate, and respect one another all at the same time, because the alternative is the bland oblivion of death.

I look at the pipe and utter a silent curse. The men are going to have to take a bath. It is the only way to continue the mission.

I had handpicked these men for this mission. I chose Specialist Lance Ohle for his mastery of the SAW light machine gun. In a firefight, Ohle on his SAW is an artist at work. He talks like a gangsta rapper but wears cowboy hats and listens to Metallica. Neither the Army nor any of those other worlds he has occupied has prepared him for this. He moans a protest about the breaststroke confronting us.

"Oh. Oohh."

"Shut the fuck up," Hugh Hall hisses.

Staff Sergeant Mike Smith stands beside me. He's our land navigation guru, though he's usually a Bradley commander, not a dismount. I nod to him and point downward, and he grimaces before taking a deep breath. An instant later, he descends into the sewage and swings around the bottom of the pipe. I hear him break the surface on the other side and exhale. Somebody hands him his weapon.

Sergeant Hall goes next. He doesn't hesitate, and I'm not surprised. I consider him one of the best soldiers in Alpha Company. He dips under the filth and pops back up on the far side of the pipe. The moonlight betrays Hall's misery. He's slick with sewage; the ochre slime drips from his Kevlar. John Ruiz sees his condition but doesn't flinch. He ducks under the pipe and breaks the surface next to Hall a second later.

I'm next. I close my eyes and hold my nose. Down into the filth I go, feeling my way under the pipe. Then I'm out the other side. Misa, Sucholas, and Sergeant Charles Knapp follow me.

We continue along the trench, more concerned about watchdogs than gunfire. Finally, we come to a stretch of palm grove that seems to be free of hajji dogs. We crawl out of the sewage and move through the grove. By now, it is 0300, and the night's chill has set in. Soaked to the bone, we start to shiver. I almost wish I was back in the shit trench. It was warmer.

We creep to a barn about 350 meters from Ali's main compound. The squad sweeps through it, hoping to find somebody to detain, but it's empty. We maneuver toward the compound. Our job is to get within view of the place, to study its layout and defenses. If possible, battalion wants us to try and flush people from the compound. If they bolt in vehicles, we can call helicopters down to follow them and others will trap them with Bradleys. Taking down these guys on the road while they're inside their cars will be easier than storming a fortified and defended compound.

On our bellies, we snake forward, bodies still shivering from the cold night air. We're just about to reach a good vantage point a hundred meters from the compound when the roar of engines shatters the stillness of the night. The cacophony grows deafening. Around us, the guard dogs howl with rage. I look over my shoulder in time to see a pair of Blackhawk helicopters thunder right over us. They hug the ground, then hover over the compound.

I hear men shouting in Arabic. A shaft of light spears the night, then another. Ali's guards are turning on searchlights. Soon the entire compound is ablaze, and the searchlights probe around us.

The birds have inadvertently compromised our mission. Cursing, we pull back to the barn, then dash into the palm grove. Behind us, the compound is fully alerted now. The guard dogs growl. The searchlights snoop. We cannot stick around. The Blackhawks dip and slide overhead. Their spinning rotors blast the buildings with mini-hurricanes of wind and dust. What was silence is now total chaos.

We hike the four kilometers back to our Brads without a word between us. This had been a perfect op until it was ruined by miscommunication with a pair of helo pilots. Stinking, frustrated, and ill-tempered, we mount up into our vehicles. We know this was our last shot at finding Ali. This mission is our swan song in the province.

Our unit is set to head out to Fallujah, a city of about 350,000 in the restive Anbar Province, along the Euphrates River. Fallujah has been under total insurgent control since April, when Operation Vigilant Resolve, a Marine offensive planned in response to the ghastly and well-publicized hanging of four U.S. contractors, was canceled for political reasons. The jarheads just loved that. All they wanted to do was finish the insurgents off once and for all. Marines. They may all be double-barreled and single-helixed. They may just be the worst historical revisionists of all time. But at their core they are fiercely proud and spoil for an unfair fight. God love 'em all.

In two days, Diyala's miseries will be behind us—the IEDs on the local highway, the Mahdi militia around Muqdadiyah, and the house-to-house firefights downtown. We can't yet know how much we'll miss them. We are leaving the good life, and heading into the mother of all city battles.

I lean back against the Bradley's bulkhead, my uniform still wet. My boys shiver violently from the cold. A few wipe their faces with rags. Piotr Sucholas, my new Bravo Team Leader, sits next me, weapon between his legs, barrel touching the Brad's floorboards. I half expect for him to start riffing on the evils of President Bush again. Sucholas is our platoon liberal. He fell in love with Michael Moore after watching a bootlegged DVD of *Fahrenheit 9/11*. Fortunately, his flaky suspicions that President Bush is out to conquer the world don't have the least effect on his willingness to do battle. When the shooting starts, he thinks only of killing the other guys and saving his men. That's why I love Piotr Sucholas.

Now he sits quietly next to me. The news that we are going to Fallujah has made everyone introspective. Sucholas has ice water for blood. In a fight, he is utterly calm, but even he is uneasy at the thought of what we will soon face.

The Brads carry us back to base. We pile out and head for our isolated, three-story barracks building. From where we live, it's a twenty-five minute walk just to reach a telephone. The battalion operations center is over a kilometer away. Even the former Iraqi Army morgue that serves as our chow hall is half a kilometer from us.

Our uniforms are filthy. Cleaning them is no easy chore. We have a couple of Iraqi washing machines, but we currently don't have electricity in our building. We'll have to do our wash by hand. Fitts and I order the men to round up as many spray bottles of Simple Green cleaner as they can find. We have no running water either, so the shower room on the first floor of our barracks serves mainly as a storage area.

In the darkness, we peel off our filthy uniforms and get to work. Soon, we're all freezing cold and shaking uncontrollably as we scrub our uniforms and wash them with bottled water. When they're as clean as we can manage, we take bottled-water showers and lather up with the leftover Simple Green. The muck of the sewage trench dribbles off us as the frigid water hits our bodies. It takes us until dawn to smell semihuman again.

Once my squad is squared away, I collapse into my cot in

hopes of a quick catnap. Sleep does not come easily, despite my fatigue. My mind refuses to shut off.

Fallujah.

When I first learned we will be redeployed to Fallujah, I pumped my fist and shouted with excitement. *Finally.* We'd been stuck in the backwater of the war, chasing shitheads like Ayub Ali across palm and dale without luck. We'd missed out on the Battle of Najaf in August that wiped hundreds of Mahdi militiamen and crippled al-Sadr's street army—at least for the moment. Perhaps now we'll have a chance to take part in something truly decisive. My adrenaline is already flowing.

Later that morning, we head out of the barracks to blow up our own equipment. Intelligence reports tell us that the defenders of Fallujah, who may number as many as three thousand Sunni and foreign fighters, are heavily armed—with our own weapons. Aside from the standard AK-47s, PKM machine guns, and rocket-propelled grenades, the Sunnis and foreign fighters in the city have acquired American weapons, body armor, uniforms, and Kevlar helmets. They've also used stolen Texas barriers to fortify the roads leading into Fallujah. Texas barriers are five-ton, reinforced concrete barricades that will hamper the movements of our vehicles.

We're not sure how to destroy Texas barriers, and we've never faced our own defenses and weapons before. John Ruiz, who has written the message "fuck you" on his knuckles in honor of our Fallujah vacation, wondered aloud during one meeting if our SAWs can penetrate our own body armor.

Today, we will find out. Our Brads deliver us to our firing range, just outside the wire. Usually, we shoot at pop-up targets, human silhouettes that allow us to hone our marksmanship and zero our weapons, making sure our gunsights are accurately adjusted. Not today. We pull out a couple of plates from our body armor and set them up at various intervals on the range. The plates hold up well, even against our armor-piercing rounds. This is good news and bad news. Our equipment is world-class, but some of our enemies will be wearing it.

Finally, with our SAWs, we discover a weakness. If we hit the plates with multiple concentrated bursts of fire, our rounds will penetrate the slab of armor that protects a soldier's heart and lungs. When we're done, the plates look like sieves. And this discovery, too, has a dual effect on morale—the enemy has captured our SAWs. We're in an arms race with ourselves—we know how to kill our enemy, but he can kill us in the same way.

Next, we work on ways to blow up Texas barriers. We operate with Bradleys and tanks for this exercise, and discover that a main gun round from an Abrams tank is the best option. The 120mm shell demolishes even the thickest concrete barrier. As yet we have no reason to believe the insurgents have captured any tanks.

After lunch, our battalion Command Sergeant Major, forty-six-year-old Steve Faulkenburg, shows up with a cache of left-over Eastern bloc goodies. He arms himself with RPGs and AK-47s and takes aim at a couple of wrecked Humvees that were dragged onto the range. He blasts the vehicles with rockets and small-arms fire, pausing every few minutes to inspect the damage. He searches for weak spots in the armor system. All afternoon, he goes about this chore and takes copious notes. Finally satisfied, Faulkenburg sets off to design extra pieces of "hillbilly armor" to cover our vulnerable spots.

We move to the vehicle range and work with the Bradleys and M1A2 Abrams tanks, practicing our breaching techniques on fortified houses. For weeks now, we have been working around the clock. Day after day, night after night, the manic routine grinds us down. We rehearse our breaching roles, refine our room-clearing fundamentals. Every mission into Muqdadiyah serves as an operational training exercise. We polish our tactics; we cross-train on different weapons systems. Every man in the platoon is now intimately familiar with everything in our arsenal. Every man can drive a Bradley and work a radio. Every man in my squad goes through combat lifesaver medical classes. I tell them they must be their own medics.

At the same time, we carry on with our twelve- to fifteen-hour combat patrols around Diyala. We're training for a fight while continuing to be in one. It leaves us brittle and bone-weary.

Toward sunset, we finally knock off. The tanks roll back across the road into the base. My platoon stays behind, tasked with guarding the sandbags and pop-up targets from marauding Iraqi thieves. The locals will steal anything.

It is easy duty, and I stretch out on the ramp of one of our Bradleys. Fitts limps over and sits down next to me. With Sergeant Cantrell on leave, Fitts is our acting platoon sergeant.

"Not to alarm you, but I am beginning to develop early stages of pretraumatic stress disorder. I want to officially go on the record to say that I am pretty sure we're all gonna die, dude," I say with as much sarcasm as I can muster.

Fitts grins. "You know, you are a difficult subordinate."

"Maybe you just can't handle me as a subordinate," I shoot back. He has already reorganized the platoon, which is sure to piss off Cantrell when he returns.

As the two of us smoke and joke, watching the Iraqi sun sinking on the horizon, Captain Sean Sims, our company commander, appears and steps past us to climb inside our Bradley. He sits down and props his feet up. He's been tense and short-tempered ever since we got the orders for Fallujah. I've also seen him head to the call center almost every night to talk with his wife. Prior to October, he rarely did that.

"Staff Sergeant Fitts and Staff Sergeant Bellavia. How are you two gentlemen doing?"

I am a little surprised by Sims's friendly tone. When Fitts returned to us over the summer, his wounds only half-healed, our captain tried to kick him out of the company. Fitts had pissed him off by bashing a hostile Muqdadiyah police officer in the face with his Kevlar helmet. Staff sergeants often piss off the higher-ups, but Fitts was particularly good at it.

"We're good, sir. You?" Fitts replies cautiously.

Captain Sims and I also have a tense relationship. In April during the house-to-house fighting in Muqdadiyah, we fought as disparate squads with little overall coordination. I later heard that Sims never left his Bradley during the fight. A commander who leads on the ground is always more desirable than one who stays in an armored vehicle. After that, I questioned his judgment on the battlefield. Later, our relationship almost fractured after I had my squad shoot three IED-laying Iraqis who turned out to be the nephews of a local good guy, an Iraqi security officer. Instead of believing my version of the events, he took sworn statements from my men and even considered opening a formal investigation. Sims dropped it at the urging of our company executive officer and other elements of our company leadership, but the incident created an uncomfortable rift between us.

Captain Sims watches the sunset in silence. Not sure he had heard us, I ask, "How are you, sir?"

"I have been better."

We can tell. He looks exhausted, and he has a quarter-sized stress zit marring his face. Since the news broke, Sims has worked relentlessly. He rarely sleeps. Instead, he pores over incoming intel reports, studying and restudying the plans the battalion staff produces. He sat for hours at night with Captain Doug Walter, our previous company commander, discussing details and working through new ideas.

Captain Sims even wanted to use Muqdadiyah for a final

dress rehearsal before Fallujah. He proposed that the full task force do a cordon and search of the city, clearing every room and every house. I thought this was a brilliant idea, and it showed Sims had a lot of nuts to even pitch it. Of course, battalion command nixed the idea, afraid that such a heavy hand would stir up the locals. Nevertheless, the fact that he wanted to do it gave us newfound respect for our commander. We don't give a shit about stirring up the locals; as far as we're concerned, they're already stirred up. Using maximum force is exactly what we want to do.

Captain Sims takes his eyes off the sunset and turns to us. "What do you think about the training?"

Neither Fitts nor I hesitate. We give him some input, and he takes notes. I am astonished. He's never listened to me like this before.

We talk shop as dusk overtakes us. It is clear that Captain Sims genuinely wants our opinion. Eventually, the conversation takes another turn.

"Where are you both from?" Sims asks.

"Randolph, Mississippi," replies Fitts.

"Buffalo, New York," I answer.

"Why'd you two join the infantry?"

I reply first, "Stephen Sondheim."

"What?"

Both Fitts and Sims stare at me.

"Stephen fucking Sondheim."

"You mean the composer?" asked Sims.

"What the fuck are you talking about, bro?" says Fitts. So there's one thing about me the guy doesn't know.

"I was a theater major," I begin to explain.

"No fucking way."

"Sure. Musical theater direction and stagecraft. I ended up starting my own theater company in Buffalo. Sondheim, well, I loved his work. He was my idol, man."

"This is a very different side of you, Sergeant Bellavia."

"He wrote a musical called *Assassins*. Basically disenfranchised Americans kill presidents, except that he got his history all screwed up. John Wilkes Booth commits suicide, Leon Czolgosz kills McKinley over a girl, Lee Harvey Oswald actually shoots JFK—shit like that."

I take a drag on my cigarette. Both Fitts and Sims are just staring at me. I guess a grizzled infantryman who loves Sondheim is more shocking than one who loves Michael Moore.

"Okay, so I rewrote it to make it historically accurate and show why these losers killed our presidents. When my theater company put it on, Sondheim stopped my show and threatened to sue me. I called his bluff. Only he wasn't bluffing.

"Next thing I know I'm field-dressing machine guns."

Sims and Fitts burst out laughing.

I ask Captain Sims, "What made you go infantry, sir? How'd you end up here?"

"My dad was a colonel in Vietnam. I went to Texas A&M. Married the love of my life, decided to join the army. My dad told me that I could be whatever I wanted to be, but nobody would respect me unless I started out in the infantry. And I loved it, so here I am."

He paused, then added, "I have a little boy. Sergeant Fitts, you have two children, right?"

"Three kids now, sir. Two boys and a two-year-old she-devil who runs my life."

"Are you married, Sergeant Bell?" Sims asks.

"I am. We have a four-year-old boy, Evan."

Sims looks off in the distance again. The sharing of personal details strikes me as almost unprofessional, until it dawns on me that Captain Sims is trying to do something here. He is breaking bread with us, making peace. Settling our differences.

"How are your men doing?" Sims asks.

"They're great. They're all great kids," says Fitts.

"We're lucky, sir."

"How do they feel about the intelligence reports?"

"Well," I begin, "I painted a green arrow in our living area. It points east. I figure we might as well get them used to praying six times a day now."

I know the men are ready, but they are also tense. In recent days, all the typical bitching and bickering common among infantrymen has evaporated. Those with grudges have made peace with one another. Even Cantrell did that before he left on leave earlier in the month.

One night, Cantrell was walking back to the platoon area when Sergeant Major Steve Faulkenburg spotted him and drove up in a Humvee. He told Cantrell to climb aboard. The two men seemed to detest each other. It hadn't started that way, but conflicts early in the deployment had hurt their relationship. Here was the opportunity to bury the hatchet. When Faulkenburg said good-bye to Cantrell, he looked him in the eye and remarked, "You know, we won't be able to bring them all back."

Our platoon sergeant nodded grimly. "I know, but we'll handle it head on."

The same spirit of reconciliation drove Captain Sims to share this sunset with us. Already the past weeks have changed my view of him. Uncertain in battle, perhaps, Sims is in his element when planning and preparing for a set-piece event. He has no ego invested in his ideas, and he genuinely seeks input to make the company even more capable, even more fierce.

"You know what, sir?" I finally say, "we're gonna be all right."

Fitts looks around, spits chaw in the dust near the ramp. "The way I figure it, sir, Fallujah can't be worse than hearing Sergeant Bell bitch at me every five seconds for not having enough batteries or forty-millimeter rounds. This guy is unbelievable. What a pain in the ass."

"Sergeant Bell, are you demanding?" Sims said in mock astonishment.

"I have needs, sir," I explain. "Sergeant Cantrell met those needs. This new guy you brought in—he's such a dick. Doctrinally proficient, sure. But he's just not a people person."

Fitts scoffs, "People person."

Sims chuckles, but soon grows contemplative again. He's not finished with us. After another long pause, he asks, "Did you know Staff Sergeant Rosales well?"

Rosales was killed during an engagement on our way to Najaf in the spring. His vehicle had been targeted, and he'd been hit. Despite his wounds, he stayed in the fight, shooting his weapon until he died. He never once let anyone know he'd been wounded.

"Yeah, sir, I knew him. We all did," I explain, "He was a great guy. His wife was over in finance, so they deployed together. They had a little boy."

We had named our makeshift shooting range after Rosales, but Fitts seemed bitter about it. "And what do we give him? This piece of shit range in his honor."

I nod my head. "Yeah. When people die in the army, it isn't like the real world. They die and it's just like they went on leave or went to a new station. It isn't real till it's over, I guess."

Sims nods his head, "It sure seems that way, doesn't it."

"When you get home, sir, sit your little boy down with your dad. You tell him about us, okay? Our war. The way we fought. They can't touch us. They'll never touch us. We're gonna be all right."

"Spoken like a man who has never been shot repeatedly."

Fitts has been throwing that down a lot recently.

"Dude, I gotta hear this story again?"

Sims grinned, "It gets better every time I hear it."

"April 9, 2004. We face a company-sized element."

"Bullshit, it was a twelve-year-old with a .22 rifle."

Fitts shrugs, "Well, that little fucker could shoot."

Fitts hikes up his pant leg and sleeves, and we see the damage. The scars of that day in Muqdadiyah will always mark him, like bad tattoos.

The sight of them sobers Captain Sims. He slides off the bench inside the Bradley and jumps to the ground next to the ramp. Turning, he makes eye contact with us both.

"You two are the best squad leaders in the battalion. Everyone knows that. And everyone looks to you two to set the example." The compliment catches both of us off guard. "We're going to lose people."

"We know, sir."

"We're going to be tested. We will all be tested."

Silence. We wait.

"The only way we'll make it through this is to stay together."

We nod our heads. Sims is speaking from his heart.

"I am proud of the men," he manages. "I am proud to lead Alpha Company into the fight."

"Hooah, sir."

"Thank you, sir."

I needed him to say all this. As I watch Captain Sims move off into the growing darkness, my entire view of him has changed in less than twenty minutes.

I'd die for this man.

Fitts and I stay on the ramp, the silence between us like a cocoon. The sun is long gone, and we stare into the blackness.

CHAPTER TWO

Beyond Redemption

November 4, 2004

The night grows cold, but we don't move. Fallujah weighs on our minds. Fitts doesn't speak, but I know his thoughts are the same as mine. We will face the challenge of our lifetimes in Fallujah. I'd be more worried, but with Fitts back in the platoon, I have the sense that we will get through this.

By all rights, Colin Fitts shouldn't even be in Iraq. Three bullet wounds is usually a ticket to a medical retirement and a disability check. Not for Fitts. He flowed through the casualty pipeline from Diyala and Baghdad through Germany before landing at Walter Reed Army Medical Center in Washington, D.C. He stuck around stateside long enough to see his third child born, then bullied his way back to Germany where a friendly sergeant gave him a pass on his PT test.

One summer day, he showed up again. There was no fanfare, but I'll never forget him limping back into the company area. My morale soared. Lieutenant Colonel Newell even decorated him with the Bronze Star for valor.

The truth is Fitts should not be back with us. His body has not healed completely. He walks with a limp. His arms ache. His leg is always stiff, and there are times I find him in great pain.

It is hard not to love a guy who will sacrifice this much for you.

We make small talk on the ramp for about an hour before we are cleared to go home. We pack up and our Brads drive us back to our barracks, where we discover dozens of Het and Heminit tractor trailers parked next to our company area. These are the huge rigs used to move our tanks and Bradleys over long distances. The transportation guys have practically taken over all the open ground. Scattered around their gigantic trucks are sacks of laundry, overstuffed rucksacks, and piles of gear. Their arrival confirms that big plans are afoot. Fallujah is a go.

We stow our gear and head off for chow. As Fitts and I approach the mess hall, we catch sight of Lieutenant Colonel Peter Newell. He is surrounded by concentric circles of reporters and cameramen. They jostle each other to get closer and compete to ask questions. It's surprising to find such a commotion here, in the war's backwater. Even during the Shia uprising last spring, there have been few reporters out here in Diyala. The journalists have come to FOB Normandy to ride with us into Fallujah. It is clear now. Unlike last April, there will be no stand-down on this one.

The sight of so many media types puts us in a foul mood. Good infantrymen have no interest in playing nursemaid to reporters in the midst of combat.

Fitts opens the mess hall door. As we step inside, I nearly fall on my ass. To our astonishment, the place has been spruced up just in time for the reporters. Instead of the packed dirt and concrete floor, the mess hall now sports faux-marble tiling. Trouble is, whoever dreamed this up forgot to factor in how slippery it would be, especially to Joes wearing sand-speckled boots.

Making our way to get our dinner trays is like trying to walk across an ice rink. On the far side of the tables, I watch as a young private slips and falls. He crashes down on his back, food, silverware, and dishes flying in all directions.

Reporters are everywhere. They've taken over the mess and now they huddle around us and gawk. These journalists are spotlessly dressed in designer khakis from Banana Republic. It is hard not to be nauseated.

Another Joe slips and falls flat. The reporters take this all in but make no comments. The soldiers, embarrassed, pick themselves up.

Right outside the chow hall, a reporter hands a smoke to a soldier and lights it for him. All of a sudden, the rest of the herd has the same idea. Hands reach into pockets and thumbs flick a dozen smokes in front of the weary Joes.

"This is going to be so fucking stupid," I say to Hector Diaz, Alpha Company's supply sergeant.

Sergeant Cory Brown, a hulking Montanan, grabs a tray next to us and gets in line next to Fitts. He's our most experienced Bradley commander, but isn't exactly a rocket scientist, and I'm in the mood to stir the pot a bit.

"Diaz. Check this shit out," I whisper as I turn to Brown.

"Hey Grizzly," I say, "these fucking reporters ate the last steak, man. Dude picked it up, took a bite out of it, and then spit into the trash can. Can you believe that asshole? Fucking Reuters. I would take that from an AP guy, but fucking Reuters? Are you serious?"

Brown goes from zero to pissed in a heartbeat. "What's his name? Rory Turds? Royters? HEY, WHO IS REUTERS?!"

Fitts grabs his arm, "Brown, he's just fucking with you, dude. Reuters is a press service."

"I don't give a fuck who he is! He spit a good steak in the trash, and I'm going to beat his dumb ass."

Diaz and I break out laughing. Alpha Company's First Sergeant, Peter Smith, storms over. Raised in Germany by an

American father and a German mother, his accent is so thick it could repel grenade shrapnel. Though he might feel more at home at Oktoberfest than a Fourth of July parade, our senior enlisted man in Alpha Company is a brilliant soldier.

"Bellavia and Fitts," he says, "Get a hold of Mongo. I don't need his dumb ass making a fucking scene in front of the press corps."

I try to act indignant, "First Sergeant, what am I, the Retard Whisperer? I can't control this dude. That's Fitts's job."

"I don't give a fuck whose job it is. Do it or Cory'll end up wearing corporal rank and a lacrosse helmet to work."

Fitts and I try to calm down Brown, who still seems to be looking for the reporter who spit out the steak.

As we sit down to eat our chow, Lieutenant Ed Iwan walks over to us with a journalist who has been shadowing him. Iwan, our husky red-headed Executive Officer, has had the job for all of four months. Much to his disgust, Iwan had been conducting an impromptu interview with this reporter from the chow line through to the salad bar and now in front of our table. Iwan rests his tray down as he applies dressing to his salad. Iwan squints with an ersatz concern that would rival the best-trained Julliard graduate. He smiles politely to the most ridiculous questions regarding the upcoming Fallujah operation.

"Oh, I don't know much about nuclear weapons or the space program. I think that is way above the pay grade of a junior army infantry officer. But Staff Sergeants Fitts and Bellavia could answer this probably better than I could." Iwan gives us a deliberate eyebrow raise as he warmly shakes the reporters hand.

Fitts and I stare at each other as the reporter fires questions at us without a proper introduction. Iwan darts away into the mass of strangers loitering about in our new dining facility.

"How would you describe combat to average Americans back home?"

"Combat? You ever play paintball, sir?" I ask him with complete seriousness.

"No, but I am aware of the sport."

"Tell America that combat is like paintball. With the exception that the enemy is motivated by fanatical devotion and uses bullets as they attempt to kill you. But basically it's the same thing."

"Make sure you get that 'killing with bullets' part," Fitts adds.

"Do either of you fly helicopters?"

Iwan comes back to our table this time with two other reporters. He takes the now confused journalist away from us and drops off our platoon's embedded reporters for Fallujah. Fitts and I shake hands with Michael Ware and his photographer, a scowling Russian named Yuri Kozyrev. These two stand in stark contrast to their brownnosing and perpetually confused cohorts. No starched Banana Republic garb for them. Bandoliers of camera batteries crisscross their chests. They wear green cargo pants that are quite possibly filthier than anything Specialist Tristan Maxfield wears. Maxfield is one of my best soldiers, but he emphatically refuses to practice even the basics of personal grooming. His stench has long since become the stuff of legend and earned my squad the sobriquet "The Dirty Boys."

Ware and Yuri eat like us, too. They don't bother with silverware, napkins, or table manners. They just dig in with their hands, soaking up gravy with swift swipes of bread across their plates, as if they don't know how long they will have to eat or when they'll get another meal. They devour everything. In any restaurant back home, they'd be asked to leave, but I'm warming up to them. Their manners are strangely appropriate for this room that formerly hosted autopsies.

I've heard of Michael Ware. He's a *Time* magazine journalist who developed deep ties to the insurgents in Baghdad. He embedded with the Mahdi militia during the summer 2004 offensive in An Najaf. On several occasions, he was nearly killed by American tank fire. Al Qaeda passed him beheading videos until he stopped accepting them in September. He also wrote a heart-stopping piece about a pitched firefight in Samarra. He is the face of Western journalism to the jihadists. He's also an Aussie, a fact that he periodically plays up by emphasizing his accent.

Around us in the chow hall, two worlds collide. Infantrymen suck their dinner-soiled fingers clean while elitist journalists fastidiously wield silverware and dab the corners of their mouths with napkins. It is too much for me. I dump my tray and flee into the safety of the night.

In the darkness, I light a smoke and take a long drag. I pass a small courtyard and spot Chaplain Ric Brown with a halo of soldiers around him. They're praying.

At first, I can't tell who is in the group. But as my eyes adjust to the darkness, I make out a few faces. One soldier has his head bowed, with a copy of the New Testament tucked under one arm.

I find a wall and perch on it. The night swallows most of Chaplain Brown's prayer, but I do catch a snippet or two. He is earnest, a good man who seems to rise above all the depravity we face outside the wire. We all respect him. Once, a couple of Georgian (former Soviet republic) soldiers started to rough him up after he ordered them to remove pornography from their computers. Every American in the area charged over to Chaplain Brown's rescue.

The prayer ends, and the men begin to drift away. I smoke in silence, thinking about my own faith, or what's left of it. I have three brothers, two of whom graduated from seminary. One became a minister. When I was five, my two oldest brothers got into a wrestling match and one suffered a neck injury. I remember seeing him lying on the floor, choking and gagging as foam flecked his lips. I fell to my knees and prayed for him with everything I had. I didn't know what else to do.

A few minutes later, he opened his eyes. After that, throughout my childhood, I actually believed that I could save people with the power of my prayers. Later, when a family friend I prayed for died, I blamed myself for not praying hard enough. I had nightmares about those I had failed to save by somehow not praying with complete devotion. The guilt assailed me for months each time this happened.

I take another drag from the cigarette and begin to walk again. I make a detour and head for the latrines. Just as I get there, a hand reaches out of the night and grabs my arm.

"Sergeant Bellavia," says the gentle voice of Chaplain Brown, "would you like to pray with me?"

I am a Christian, but my time in Iraq has convinced me that God doesn't want to hear from me anymore. I've done things that even He can never forgive. I've done them consciously; I've made decisions I must live with for years to come. I am not a victim. In each instance, I heard my conscience call for restraint. I told it to shut the fuck up and let me handle my business.

All the sins I've committed, I've done them with one objective: to keep my men alive. Those kids in my squad, those kids of mine, they are everything. My wife doesn't understand this job or why I do it. My son is too young. My dad wouldn't get it if I tried to explain. My mom would have a heart attack. The need to keep my men alive makes everything else negotiable, and everyone and everything a potential threat.

My mind flashes to April 9 again, when we burst into a house full of men, women, and children. I separated the men. The children screamed. The women sobbed hysterically. My squad found AKs and an RPK machine gun in closets around the house. They were still warm, and the men reeked of gunpowder. They laughed at our situation as our Bradleys fired and rockets boomed outside.

One man waved his finger and mockingly lectured me, "Geneva conventions. You must do good, Amreekee. You good Amreekee."

I couldn't leave them in the house with one of my soldiers as a guard, as we were already short of men. I couldn't leave them alone either. They would have shot us in the back as we left. I decided to flex-cuff them to their front gate, and return for them after the fight ended. But as we left the house and advanced up the street, a wave of machine-gun fire ripped over us. I looked back. The four men had somehow broken loose from the gate and were running for it in all directions. A Bradley cut one down, and as the 25mm shells hit him, he exploded. His flex-cuffed arms spun across the street and smacked to the pavement.

One bound insurgent started to crawl back to his compound. A bearded man from another house ran out to cut his flex-cuffs loose with large pruning shears. I moved into the open danger area and shot the rescuer repeatedly. My rounds sparked off his shears as they shattered into pieces.

Machine-gun fire raked the ground around us. The flex-cuffed insurgent doubled over, hit by an errant enemy bullet. Writhing in pain, he began to scream only feet away from his own house. His family heard him, and two sobbing children came out to see what had become of their father. I tossed a smoke grenade that scattered the children back to the safety of their home. I did it to keep the kids from getting harmed, but also to deny their father a chance to say good-bye. My brothers who died in the field got no such opportunity to say good-bye to those they loved, and I will afford none to this man. I wanted him to die alone, shrouded in smoke, choking on his own blood.

Their father, utterly despondent, stared at me with pleading eyes as the white smoke filled the air around him. He died without another chance to see his children. I robbed him of his final earthly joy. I delighted as I watched his life ebb away. It felt just.

What have I become?

As the youngest of four boys in our devout family, I was once considered the weakest link. Every son had at least a master's degree, some had two. I struggled through most of college but failed to graduate. I was the son who had to be sheltered and protected.

That came to a boiling point shortly after my twenty-third birthday when I moved back home. I was out in my parents' backyard when I heard a commotion inside the house. When I went to investigate, I ran right into a pair of crack-addled burglars ransacking the living room. My mother had just returned home after a serious surgery and was unable to move out of bed. My father stayed in the doorway to the bedroom, ready to protect her.

The hoods jeered and laughed, seeing me as no threat at all. I fled downstairs to the basement and found my father's shotgun. I held the weapon, but realized I was not prepared to use it. I didn't even know how. I stood there, shotgun in hand, unable to move from the basement as the two hopheads terrorized my parents and robbed us. Slowly, I put the weapon away. I didn't know how to use it, and I would probably be a danger to my own family with it. Instead, I found a baseball bat.

When I reappeared, the hopheads howled with derision as they carried off our valuables. One of them held a knife in his hand. He cut cables from the back of the entertainment center and picked up equipment to take to his car. I couldn't intimidate them, and I could not find the strength to attack them. As they made one more circuit through the house to look for valuables, they ignored me completely. I stood paralyzed with fright and watched them.

As they got into their car outside, my father came out of the bedroom and stared at me with a mixture of disgust and pity. I was still the timid little boy he and my mother had had to shelter from the real world. I was not yet a man, even at twenty-three.

I tried to rally. My legs broke free of their paralysis and I found myself in the front yard, chasing the burglars as they began to drive away. I took one swing with the bat and splintered their windshield. But then they were gone, their stoned laughter lingering behind them.

I could hardly face my family. I was a coward that day. I had let everyone down and proved that I couldn't take care of myself, let alone protect the ones I loved the most.

I joked that Steven Sondheim was the reason why I joined the army. In my most honest moments, I have to confess that it was the look on my dad's face that day. That look shamed me, and the humiliation drove me to join the army in search of the heart and spirit I so desperately lacked. I needed to understand courage. I needed to become a man.

Six years later, the boy who failed his family that day is long dead. The man who replaced him is at ease with fear. It is his motivation. Anger, aggression, hate—they have smothered that timid disposition. In a matter of days, I will be the home invader this time, only those I find inside Fallujah's houses will not be high-strung boys paralyzed by fear. They will be cold-hearted killers stoked by religious fervor, soaked in adrenaline and dope.

That's fine.

I am a killer now, too. I want to kill. I *yearn* to kill my enemies. *Am I beyond redemption?*

"Sergeant Bellavia?" Chaplain Brown now prompts again.

I don't know what to say. He moves closer to me, and I see the sincerity on his face. It rattles me. I start to laugh to break his focus, but he stares right back at me. My faith is being tested, and I know I do not measure up to what He wants from me. That is hard to face.

I want to ask Chaplain Brown how God will forgive such things. But he is too good of a man to burden with a replay of the horrors I've perpetrated—my arrogance and lack of mercy. I want to tell him that I am not like those other scared kids. I do have faith, but I don't want to talk to God after the things I've done. I don't know how.

Chaplain Brown, there have got to be other people who need you more. Go talk with those who can be saved.

I cannot verbalize any of these thoughts. All I can do is bow my head as Chaplain Brown takes my hand.

"Lord, give this young man the strength and wisdom to protect his soldiers. Give him the courage and conviction to deliver them from the unknown. Give him the faith and guidance to know your path, Lord. Give him the perseverance to stay on it. In Jesus's name, we pray. Amen."

I know, when I return home, I will be an alien amid tranquility.

Chaplain Brown's prayer makes me think of my future. It leaves me cold with fear. I feel alone. The chaplain stands beside me, his hand in my hand. The silence is a gulf between us.

Chaplain Brown squeezes my arm and departs, unaware of his impact on me.

Give him the courage and conviction to deliver them from the unknown.

An hour later, I meet with Sims, Iwan, and Fitts for a final briefing. We'll roll out in the morning, and our mission is now defined. Sims details the assault plan, and explains our job with step-by-step precision. Each platoon will play a different part in the initial attack.

Fallujah is a city designed for siege warfare. From the studs to the minarets, every goddamned building is a fortress. The houses are minibunkers with ramparts and firing slits cut into every rooftop. The mosques are latter-day Persian castles with concrete walls three feet thick. Within those walls, the courtyards offer perfect ambush points from every window. Even the shops and the local markets are fortified. Block after block, Fallujah is a sophisticated deathtrap.

Architecture aside, the insurgents have had months to prepare for this battle. They've dug fighting positions, mined the streets, booby-trapped the houses, built bunkers, and cleared fields of fire. Every road into the city is strong-pointed, mined, and blocked with captured Texas barriers. Fallujah is shaping up to be the Verdun of the War on Terror. We face a battle of attrition fought within a maze of interlocking fortresses. Attrition is such a sterile word. We'll be trading our lives for theirs.

Sims makes it clear that our initial objectives will be heavily defended. The insurgents have deployed foreign fighters on the city's approaches. They form the outer crust of their defense-in-depth, so we will face them first. Intelligence reports tell us we'll face Syrians, Iranians, Saudis, Filipinos, even Italians and Chechnyans. They're well trained, ideologically motivated, and armed with ample ammunition and equipment. They've trained for years to kill us infidels. Some have cut their teeth in Chechnya, Afghanistan, and Somalia. They are veterans just like us— a regular Islamist all-star team.

"We can expect possibly thirty-percent attrition at an urban breach like this," Sims tells us.

I've been writing down everything Sims has said. Now I pause and stare at the initial casualty estimate.

Thirty percent just to get into the city? There is no way we can keep everyone alive.

"Once inside the city, obviously we will not use the main roads. They are all heavily IED'd. Our lead tracks must create their own paths with the help of the engineers. Look over the maps; we'll have to improvise most of these routes."

Captain Sims flicks open a nearby laptop and shows us a gun-camera video shot by an Air Force F-16C.

"This is the neighborhood we'll be in. The Askari or Soldier's District," he says as he runs the video.

The F-16 drops a 500-pound satellite-guided bomb. It falls onto one of the main roads into Fallujah—a street we will have to use during our advance. A cloud of smoke and flames mushrooms from the impact point. A split-second later, a series of flashes bloom along the street.

The bomb set off almost twenty improvised explosive devices just on that one road alone. We watch in silence. Soon, the entire street is obscured by smoke. It is a sobering sight. Had a dismounted platoon been in the middle of something like that, there'd be nothing left to identify.

"I am not going to rattle off what the acceptable attrition is according to command, gentlemen. We will seize Highway 10 and push into the industrial district. Expect some of the heaviest fighting in this area. Foreign jihadists will use hit-and-run tactics, but there are enough fighters in the city for them to have a mobile reserve. We could face counterattacks during the first day. The enemy has the forces to mass against us."

"Just like in Muqdadiyah, there will be no calling in a medevac chopper once you're in the city. It'll be too hot for the Blackhawks. We'll ground-evac our casualties to this cloverleaf east of the city."

The bad news continues as Captain Sims closes the laptop and turns to us. "We expect the insurgents have stockpiled drugs. We'll be facing fighters hopped up on dope again."

I look over at Fitts, and I know what he's thinking. If this is true, these guys are going to be hard to kill. In Muqdadiyah, my squad watched a drug-crazed Mahdi militiaman charge Cory Brown's Bradley. He climbed up the front glacis plate, screaming like a lunatic. The gunner blasted him with coax machine-gun fire, shredding his legs. He tumbled off the Bradley and flopped faceup onto the street. As we approached him, he started to laugh. The laughter grew into a hysteria-tinged cackle, then ended with a bone-chilling keen. That froze us cold. Watching us with wild eyes, he then pulled a bottle of pills out of a blood-soaked pocket and drained its contents into his mouth. Then he went for something under his jacket. Thinking he was about to detonate a bomb vest, three of us opened fire and riddled him with bullets. We shot and shot until he finally stopped moving.

Leaving my men behind, I went to investigate the corpse. His right arm was torn off. His legs were nothing but punctured meat. Most of his face was gone, and only a bloody lump remained of his nose. Both eyes had been shot out. I put a boot on his chest. The Mahdi militiaman didn't move. I kicked him. No movement. Given how many times he had been shot, I didn't expect anything else, but just to be sure, I shot him twice in the stomach. Then I marked him with a chem light so the body disposal teams could find him later that night.

A few minutes later, a Blackhawk landed and we started loading wounded insurgents into it. While we worked, two men carried the shattered husk of that Mahdi militiaman to the helicopter. To our astonishment, he was still alive. Blood bubbles burbled up through his mangled nose and mouth. Blind, in agony, he still managed to scream through broken teeth and punctured lungs. We loaded him on the helicopter and never saw him again.

We later discovered the Mahdi militia had gained access to American epinephrine—pure adrenaline that will keep a heart pumping even after its owner has been exposed to nerve gas or chemical weapons. A dude with that in his system is almost superhuman. Short of being blown to pieces with our biggest guns, he'll keep fighting until his limbs are severed or he bleeds out.

At the end of the briefing, Captain Sims brings in visitors:

reporters who are going with us into Fallujah. The battalion has already determined who goes with what unit. Lieutenant Colonel Newell and the battalion staff have cornered the network TV types, leaving us with the apparently less desirable print and cable journalists. A *New York Times* reporter is slotted to go in with First Platoon, Alpha. Third Platoon receives Michael Ware and his Russian photographer.

We have to decide which squad gets to babysit these two. I don't want them. Fitts doesn't either. We already have a pair of outsiders to take care of. Two Air Force forward air controllers, Senior Airman Michael Smyre and Staff Sergeant Greg Overbay, have joined us for the operation. They know nothing about infantry combat, and I suspect they'll be a liability once the shooting starts.

Earlier in the week, one of the Air Force guys had asked me to give him some room-clearing lessons. It was far too late in the game for that, so I told him, "Don't worry about that. Worry about calling in the bombs. I swear nothing will happen to you. The only thing that will bleed will be your hemorrhoids from sitting too long on a Bradley's bench."

Fitts elects to take Ware and Yuri. I get the Air Force types. My squad's got the better deal, but Fitts seems to think he's come out ahead. I guess we'll see who is right soon enough.

As the briefing winds down, Iwan speaks up. Grinning, he says, "If the worst happens, I have some videos of some mules in Tijuana on my laptop. If someone could just erase those. . . ."

I offer up a hollow smile, the best I can manage. Iwan has said this before and we've all cracked up. This time, things don't seem funny any more.

Fitts and I depart to brief the platoon. They've heard fragments of what we are to do, rumors of who we will face, but now is the time to give them the full story.

As we walk back to the platoon, Fitts is in a foul mood. "I'm bringing in Lawson to run weapons squad," he says for no particular reason.

"He's a fucking stud. Great move," I said.

"Cantrell is going to be pissed."

"Yeah, but Lawson is a good dude. And we need those machine guns in the fucking fight for once."

"Those boys need to know what is going on."

"About Iwan's laptop?"

We laugh. Then Fitts turns serious.

"This could be fucking horrible."

I nod. We finish the walk in silence.

When we reach the company area, I discover my Alpha Team leader, Sergeant Charles Knapp, has been very busy. He and the rest of my squad are surrounded by magazines and loose 5.56mm bullets. Knapp has decided to clean by hand every round of ammunition we will take to Fallujah with us. They've got four hundred magazines, which means they'll be cleaning twelve thousand bullets tonight. The effort will be worth it. Cleaning each one will minimize the chance of a critical jam in the middle of battle.

The sight sends a swell of pride through me. This is a shitty, boring job, but they're on it.

I call my squad away from their scrubbing and ask them to gather around. I start reading from my notes. The likelihood of casualties as we enter the city. The foreign fighters. The sheer number of enemy fighters. The IEDs. The drugs. The weapons. I feel the tension rising. Though nobody says it, they understand that there is no way we will all return home from this. Surreptitiously, as I continue with the briefing, I study each of my men.

Piotr Sucholas looks stricken. His mother is a Polish immigrant and she has written Captain Sims to ask him not to let Piotr do anything dangerous. To protect his mother, Sucholas has created a whole fantasy deployment for her. He's written long letters to her about life as a rear-echelon type, living the life of Riley inside the base compound. The truth is, he's blossoming into a first-rate team leader who never flinches from a fight, and he will face this battle with new responsibility. He's been my Bravo Team leader for only a few weeks. The burden of his new leadership role weighs heavily on him.

Despite how he looks right now, my intuition tells me he will be just fine. Outside of a firefight, he can be squirrelly as hell. When I made him my Bravo Team leader, Cantrell practically had kittens. "No way is that fucking meatball gonna be a team leader in my platoon. That kid is a fucking Martian." Cantrell was probably thinking about all the dumb-ass things we'd all seen Sucholas do. The morning after we flew to Kuwait from Germany, out in the desert, Sucholas limped up to me and asked for help. Drunk the night before, he had accidentally stabbed himself with a knife, leaving a four-inch gash on one leg. He tried to balm it with superglue. More than anything, it petrified him that Cantrell might find out.

Sucholas could be a meatball. But Cantrell had never seen him in a fight. I had. On April 8, I watched him shoot an insurgent in the neck. The man fell and began to bleed out. Rather than finishing him, Sucholas waited patiently for the wounded man's buddies to come to the rescue. Sure enough, three guys broke cover to get to their comrade, and Sucholas coolly dispatched all of them. He never panics, never recoils. He may look terrified now, but once we're in the shit, I know he'll be rock steady.

I don't have to worry about Knapp either. He has so much confidence that it borders on arrogance. In garrison back in Germany, that arrogant streak irritated the shit out of me. Here in Iraq, it is a comfort. He is unflappable in a fight, and I have long since learned to depend on him.

Tonight, his jaw is set as he listens to my brief. He looks resolute. No fear in his eyes. Instead, he's on top of everything and oozes professionalism. Frankly, he's a brilliant noncommissioned officer—aggressive, confident, and willing to execute any order. I will rely heavily on him in the days to come.

Ruiz sits through my brief and periodically rubs the letters he's written on his knuckles. He's composed as ever. He's ready. Ruiz can handle anything. I don't have to worry about him either.

Private Brett Pulley, Sucholas's rifleman and the squad's most junior man, stares at me with a look of bafflement. He's new and he's green. The rest of us have had to work extra hard to keep Pulley from getting himself killed. His lack of experience is a burden we will all shoulder together.

Homeschooled and highly sheltered as a kid, Pulley wasn't prepared to join the real world. Somehow, he fell into a job as a roadie for a rock band. When Pulley spoke of those days, his accounts were full of hard manual labor mixed with a steady diet of dope and booze. Squad leaders hear so many exaggerated stories of drugs and hardship from the lower enlisted ranks that rarely are they taken seriously. But Pulley's tales of woe were told with long satellite delays of sentences. I often wonder if this is all an act, or if his brain really had been stewed in a pharmacological soup for such a long time that he is beyond hope.

I search Pulley's face for any sign of comprehension. Does he understand the enormity of what we face? Where is the fear? A little fear is good; it will keep us on our toes.

"What the fuck you looking at, dick?" I try to rattle him.

"Nothing."

"Nothing . . . asshole? Nothing . . . motherfucker? Nothing . . . faggot?"

"Nothing, *Sergeant.*"

Knapp jumps up and gets two inches from Pulley's face.

"You better pull your fucking nuts out, Pulley, or you ain't coming home. You hear me, bitch?"

"Roger, Sergeant."

I see no fear in Pulley, but I'm hard-pressed to see signs of life at all. He's the one I will have to watch.

I wrap up the briefing. "We'll be leaving at oh dark, retard. Santos, how we doing on the C-4?"

"Sergeant, we got so many bombs, I can't count 'em."

Earlier in the week I gave Private First Class Victor Santos, my Alpha Team's grenadier, a pallet of at least a hundred pounds of plastic explosives. The engineers taught him just enough to get us all killed. He's spent the week packing Gatorade bottles with shrapnel, detonation cord, and C-4. Santos and I share a love for this shit. Knapp has taught young Santos everything he knows, and I can see his mind working overtime collecting each bomb he has made. Santos's scalp still bears the scars from an enemy rocket that slammed his guard tower back in June. He spent two weeks at the army hospital in Landstuhl, Germany before return-ing to us. Most recently, Santos waived his leave to make sure he didn't miss Fallujah. All he wants to do is kill bad guys.

"Go call your families," I say. "They'll be shutting the phones down as part of the OPSEC plan, so make sure you do that tonight."

After I dismiss my squad, Sucholas walks up to me.

"Sergeant Bell, I can't believe I'm going to die for this con-spiracy to reelect George fucking Bush."

I try to humor him as he continues. "I will die, you know. And it will be your fault. You'll go to hell for it, too."

He's said this a dozen times these past days, and I've usually laughed. Tonight, it isn't funny, not after my encounter with Chaplain Brown. The fact is, he may be right. Hell might be my ultimate destination. Sucholas departs, puzzled that I don't even fake amusement. He can sense my distraction.

I tend to my duties for the rest of the night, running around for more equipment, ammo, and gear my squad can use. I round up extra dressings, tourniquets, and batteries. I grab an extra five body bags from Staff Sergeant Diaz. Finally, I have to get some sleep, or I will be no good to anyone. The operational tempo has been brutal these past weeks. Train, patrol, train, patrol—it has worked us all to the bone. This might be the last chance for a decent night's sleep for several days.

I retire to my cot, but my mind refuses to shut down. I dwell on the skirmishes and firefights we fought over the summer. I refight April 8 and 9 in my head again, examining every decision I made and questioning every movement in order to glean more lessons, more ideas that might help us in Fallujah.

We'll be fighting house-to-house again. We'll be clearing rooms and fighting inside hallways at point-blank range. This will be my ultimate test. I have sought a fight like this ever since I joined the army.

Dominate the room.

Use controlled pairs.

Slow is smooth, smooth is fast.

Don't be in a hurry.

Recharge your ammunition at every pause.

It is the most brutal and costly form of modern warfare. The casualties will be appalling.

I am ready.

I close my eyes to start a prayer. Using the template Chaplain Brown provided, I decide to go with the theme of leadership and invincibility over evil. Cory Brown is watching a loud movie on a laptop computer two beds down from me.

The Exorcist.

I can't focus with all the noise in the foreground, not that communing with Him was going to be an easy exchange anyway.

I am ready. Dear Lord, I wanted to tell you. . . .

I think about my soldiers again. I see their faces and think about when I was their age. They are ten times the men I was. Not at that age.

I once was a meek boy with a coward's heart.

Not here. Not anymore.

Now I am a lost soul with hell on his shoulders.

And I am coming.

also seek his approval. In his twenty-six years in the army, he has seen the ass crack and armpit of every trouble spot from Korea to Kosovo. We fear his emasculating rants yet we stand in awe of him at the same time.

He's done almost everything you can do in the army, but he hasn't done this. Fallujah will be tougher than any fight since Vietnam, and the look on his face makes me realize he harbors no illusions.

"Ramrods, take a knee," he calls to us in his gravelly southern drawl. There are times I think he's speaking a foreign language, his southern accent is so indiscernible. It's like a cross between John Wayne and Ross Perot. Our task force is known as the Ramrods. Those of us in Alpha Company are the Terminators.

Alpha Company forms a horseshoe around Sergeant Major Faulkenburg. We get down on one knee and wait. At first, he says nothing. He spits a wad of Red Man chewing tobacco into the dirt as he eyeballs us with a squint. He takes the time to look each of us in the eyes.

I stare back at him. To me, he has always seemed big as a grizzly bear and twice as scary. But now as I study him, I realize he's wiry and short. It's the weight of his character that makes him seem so large.

"Men, I could not be more proud of you if you were my own kids."

We wait for him to continue. He hesitates. He's struggling with his emotions, and we see his eyes mist up. That sight sends a surge of emotion through me—part love, part despair, part blind loyalty.

"I couldn't be more proud looking at how far you all have come and what you are about to do."

He pauses again and lowers his head, his iron self-discipline fighting a losing battle with his heart.

"That's all. Go get 'em."

The mechanics and support guys start to cheer. Somebody shouts, "Give 'em hell!" Others shout as well.

For a moment, I can't move. Sergeant Major Faulkenburg is our father figure. He's the man I have most wanted to impress. I have wanted, and *needed*, to believe he was proud of me and what I've done with my squad. I never felt I did anything to be worthy of my own father's pride. My father was the first person in the history of the state of New York to go from junior college to dental school, starting with absolutely nothing and accomplishing so much on his own. I sought his affirmation, but always seemingly in vain. I always felt I never quite measured up in his eyes. To me, it was my fault for squandering so many chances.

Here, now, I want more than anything to stand with Sergeant Major Faulkenburg as we head into the fight and to measure up at last. This time, I am determined not to fail. His few words have had a more profound effect on me than any of the pep talks of the past week. A great speech is only partly about what is said. Often what matters more is who says it and how it is delivered. Our sergeant major's vulnerability and love for us spoke volumes.

As everyone else gets up to head for their Bradleys, I stay a heartbeat longer. Faulkenburg turns his steel blue eyes to me. No words are spoken, but in his eyes I can see something, a feeling coming my way. Respect.

A few months earlier, during a night firefight in Muqdadiyah, I was hugging a wall across the street from Sergeant Major Faulkenburg as he banged away with an M16 with iron sights. He could have taken a newer weapon and shortchanged one of his men. He'd sooner use a museum-piece rifle than shortchange one of his men. That is one of the reasons why everyone loves him: he never asked for anything more than what the worst-equipped man in the battalion had.

I remember working with the sergeant major that day. I had an M4 with all sorts of high-tech shit hanging off its rails. A hundred and fifty meters ahead of us, something piqued the sergeant major's interest. Faulkenburg took off and hobbled a ways, stopped, and fired a single shot. I was so intimidated by him, I didn't dare ask if he hit anything. He looked at me and scrunched his lip up in a pseudo smile. "Another day in paradise, son."

After that fight, Sergeant Major Faulkenburg gave me the same look he gives me now. I had stood with him as the bullets smacked around us, and he respected that. Now, twenty minutes before we roll into the fight of our lives, I can see he trusts me with his soldiers.

No words are said. I'd do anything for this man, and he knows it. I'd kill for him, and he knows that, too. I'd follow him anywhere because I trust him to always do the right thing. Few men are leaders. Even fewer are role models. Faulkenburg is both. We will fight like demons for him today.

And then the moment is gone, carried away by the surge of men flowing around us. I get to my feet and link up with Fitts. We lead our squads to our waiting Bradleys.

Our platoon sergeant, James Cantrell, rejoined us earlier in the morning. He had been on leave, and when he discovered that Fitts had reorganized the platoon, he demanded an explanation.

Fitts did the right thing. Our weapons squad leader had failed us in Muqdadiyah on April 9. Under withering fire, he took his squad across the road to link up with First Platoon instead of fighting his way to us. When we desperately needed his machine guns, they were nowhere to be found. After that, I couldn't really trust him again. Heading into Fallujah, we just can't have the machine guns sitting back away from our fight, supporting somebody else. They have to be up with us. Once Cantrell went home on leave, Fitts traded him to the

Bradleys and grabbed Staff Sergeant Scott Lawson out of Headquarters and Headquarters Company (HHC), where he'd been a supply clerk.

Lawson is a smart-ass. He sports Elvis-style sideburns that are way beyond regulation and refuses to shave them. His failure to give a shit about his appearance and his sarcastic personality have earned him a rebellious reputation in the battalion. Before he went to HHC, he served in Second Platoon, Alpha Company prior to our Kosovo deployment. Fitts and I had seen him then and had been impressed. Fitts rolled the dice and decided to give him a second chance with a line unit. It pissed off Cantrell, but we knew Lawson would be a fighter.

At the staging area just outside FOB Fallujah, we reach our Bradleys and begin to organize our gear. Our vehicles are lined up getting fuel, ready to convoy to the next stop.

We use the time to distribute our most important supplies: chew, dip, and cigarettes. We've been told we will be in the city for at least twenty days. We'll need tobacco to get through it. I make sure every man has a pouch with wet-dry matches and a lighter.

I had purchased a coffeemaker the day before, but Cantrell gave it to our chief mechanic, Staff Sergeant Jason Ward, because we had no converters for AC power in our Bradleys. Missing my morning cup of joe pissed me off. When I went to see Ward about it, he'd already brewed up a batch. The smell alone drives me crazy. I'm a coffee addict, and I've made a point of carrying around bags of Starbucks grinds. Ward at least offers me a cup.

When I return to my own Bradley with the coffee, I see Chaplain Brown nearby, going from track to track, talking with the soldiers. I avoid him. Today is not a day for another deep spiritual moment. It is a day to act.

I find my men busily loading the last pieces of gear into our vehicles. Third Platoon's Bradleys are crammed full of ammunition, rocket launchers, dozens of Claymore mines, grenades, meals ready-to-eat (MREs), Javelin missiles, and water. We will have to get cozy to fit everybody inside for the ride into the city.

Cantrell arrives to check on us. He sees one of my SAW gunners, Private First Class Alex Stuckert, reaching for a carton of smokes. Cantrell erupts, "Get your dick beaters off my cigarettes, meatball."

Cowed, Stuckert offers, "I thought they were mine, Sergeant."

Cantrell is a Missouri outdoorsman who learned to stalk and kill anything that shit outside since he could walk. While other platoon sergeants want to know how your children are adjusting to your deployment, Cantrell wants to know how long you are gonna waste his time with your "ball assing about your stupid family." He doesn't pretend to give a shit about your wife and kids. All he cares about are results and keeping his boys alive while they inflict mayhem on the enemy.

Cantrell's personality is uniquely suited to his position. He wouldn't last a week as an elementary school principal, but as a platoon sergeant he's tough and mean and leads only by example. If he told me to eat a shit sandwich, I'd do it without a second thought, or mustard. He makes mistakes, sure, but he never repeats them. In combat, his only weakness is his battle-fueled temper. He rages and screams at us in every fight. Call it tough love. He is the best in Third Brigade and he knows it.

"Sergeant Bell, did you buy premium smokes or are you settling for those cheap ones you get from back home?" Cantrell is busting my balls, as usual.

"I got the good shit, Sarge. If things get tough, I'll fall back on the Miami blend the Iraqis love so much."

"Miamis? You might as well wipe your ass with your hand, Sergeant Bell. Those are shitty cigarettes."

Not far from us are some troopers from an Iraqi Intervention

Force unit who look glum. They sit in their five-ton trucks staring south toward Fallujah with expressions on their faces that say: *I'm going to my own funeral.* They contrast sharply with us. We smoke and joke and keep it light. We are loose, ready, and even eager. Perhaps we're also in denial, but we know better than to explore that right now.

Cantrell observes the Iraqis for a long moment. He pulls out a Zippo lighter, flicks it, and lights a cigarette over the yellow-orange flame. He smokes in silence as he sizes them up. A minute passes. Cantrell takes another drag, exhales a cloud of smoke and shakes his head sadly.

"Look at those sorry bastards. They need a pick-me-up, Sergeant Bell. Go have a smoke with them."

I'm not sure why I have to be the one to give the Iraqi guys a morale boost, but orders are orders. I grab Stuckert, Santos, and Ruiz and motion our interpreter to come along. I call our 'terp "The Enigma"—nobody can figure out what gender he/she is. A debate has raged for months over this. Some have sworn they've seen him/her pissing standing up in the latrine. Others swear he/she is a woman. Money has been wagered, and that bet is still riding. I just wish somebody would go ask, "So, are you a dude?"

I call our androgynous interpreter "Pat." He/she follows us over to the Iraqi rigs. The first Iraqi I come to looks at me like somebody's just shot his dog. I give him a slap on the shoulder and a big smile. Santos and Ruiz do the same.

An Iraqi asks a question. Pat translates, "He wants to know why you are so happy."

"We're happy," I begin, "'cause we're gonna kill some fucking bad guys today."

Pat translates. I add, "This is it, dudes. Everyone in that bitch . . ." I pause and point to Fallujah, ". . . is bad. Bad dudes, man, and we're gonna fuckin' murder 'em."

Did the tone get lost in translation? I don't know, but suddenly the Iraqis crowd around us. One of them even cracks a smile. Guys jump off the truck to join us. They score more smokes from Santos and Stuckert. Ruiz is busy pantomiming a conversation with his own cluster of Iraqis.

Another Iraqi soldier asks me a question. Pat translates, "He asks if his unit is going into the city first."

I know we're supposed to be the lead. My platoon will be the first infantry element through the breach. But in the spirit of allied cooperation, I don't tell these Iraqis that.

I turn to Pat and say, "No. We go in together."

As soon as that is translated, the Iraqis break out in cheers over this news. They must have thought they'd be going in first as cannon fodder. Now they hug one another and start to sing. Some of them start dancing. Soon the whole group is leaping and gyrating.

"Oh shit," says Santos, "It's the fucking Iraqi gay dance again."

This is not a very soldierly dance. The moves are distinctly feminine. They throw a Shakira-like pelvic thrust into the mix every now and then. Sometimes they passively look away as they grind into each other. As I watch this, I have a flashback to my English mastiff's insemination a few years ago. It makes me a little uncomfortable.

"What is wrong with these guys, Sergeant?" Stuckert asks in total astonishment.

"It's like a Rock Hudson pool party over here. Let's get in on this before they tire out."

"That guy over there is eye-fucking me."

"Which one?" asks Santos.

"Pat." Our translator is in the middle of the Iraqi gaggle, dancing in between the three men as they bump him/her from side to side with their pelvic regions, like some homoerotic tetherball.

This is not a pretty sight.

We retreat back to our track, saying farewell as the Iraqis continue to make a spectacle of themselves. Pat reluctantly detaches him/herself and trails along behind us. The Iraqis are a happier bunch now. Driving through IEDs like the ones we saw on that film, in unarmored trucks, probably won't be a hell of a lot of fun. We'll pave the way for them.

Back at our Bradley, I discover the men are sharing their deepest secrets with one another. They're still smoking and joking, but the mood is more serious. Soldiers who ordinarily do not hang out huddle together, talking in rushed voices. I overhear snippets of a dozen ridiculous conversations at once.

"I look over and see the red on my knuckles. I lick it, right? It is fucking lipstick. Dude, I knocked the fuck out of a bitch. I thought she was a dude, but it was fucking lipstick. . . ."

"I had fifteen hours of plastic fucking surgery after that car accident. Man, my scalp was peeled all the way back. No shit. My mom about fucking had a heart attack. And we didn't have insurance either. This shit was serious."

"Hey, I want you to know man, that from the first day I met you, I thought you were a fucking good dude. . . ."

"You, too, man, let's get a picture."

Throughout Alpha Company, digital cameras appear, and soon the men are posing for one another. Nearby, our embedded reporters take this all in. They cluster together like the new kids in second grade, watching the scene as awkward outsiders.

These photos are crucially important, a form of insurance against our own mortality. A few months back, we lost a man and realized to our unending dismay that no one had a single photo of him to display at his memorial service. It was disgraceful. Surely this is in the back of everyone's mind now. This time we will have a record of every soul who goes through the breach.

Michael Ware breaks ranks from the cluster of journalists with Yuri in tow. They come over to Third Platoon and offer to take our picture. The platoon lines up and they go to work. The other embeds see this and promptly stream to their assigned units, taking cameras and snapping pictures of the men. As they click away, they are no longer awkward outsiders. Now that they've found a way to help us, they circulate among the soldiers and start to fit in. They've shown us they're human, and the company appreciates that.

After Michael and Yuri finish up, I light a smoke and stretch out on the ground next to the track. It is almost 0900. The morning is crisp, cold, and punctuated by distant artillery barrages. Every few minutes, an Apache thunders overhead. Fast-moving fighter jets crisscross the sky above them.

I turn to Ware, who is fiddling with a camera. "If this man should fall," I say dramatically, "who will carry his boom mic?" It is a parody of that great Matthew Broderick moment in *Glory* just before his regiment charges Battery Wagner. Ware laughs, but I don't think he gets it. Yuri looks stone-faced as usual. I conclude he's one hard son of a bitch.

I look over at the Iraqi Intervention Force guys. They're not dancing anymore. Instead, they're smoking and joking, just like us. A few have produced digital cameras, and they're snapping pictures in small groups. It is a comforting scene.

This is where I belong. It's the first time in my life that I have found my place. It's a reassuring thought that eases some of the butterflies fluttering around in my gut.

I wonder if this is what it was like for the soldiers of the Union Army during the Civil War. *Tenting Tonight on the Old Camp Ground* and *All Quiet on the Potomac* have been replaced by our percussion-heavy modern metal riffs from Mudvayne and Dope, but we're still basically the same. The details vary from war to war, but no matter the epoch, the camaraderie remains. It's a closeness that no civilian will ever really understand.

A Bradley swings out of the column and starts toward us.

Lieutenant Colonel Newell, riding shotgun in the turret, yells at the troops as he passes. He looks like Patton must have looked as he raced alongside one of his flying columns in a jeep, dressed like he was ready for a parade. Patton sometimes stood on the passenger seat to shout at his GIs. Newell can't do that in a modern-day Bradley Fighting Vehicle, but the similarities are striking nonetheless.

Our task force is a hundred vehicles strong. Newell's track runs the length of our column like a steel sheepdog shepherding us forward. As he passes by, I hear him bellow, "Let's go! Go! Go! Go! Go!"

CHAPTER FOUR

Land Rush

Lieutenant Colonel Newell swings around the front of the column and blitzes back down the other side. In his wake, Task Force 2–2's soldiers scramble to their feet. Cigarettes are stomped out. Last words are exchanged. We throw on our full battle rattle, which includes: ballistic-proof eye protection, smoke grenades for concealment, reinforced knee pads any skateboarder would envy, a five-quart CamelBak reservoir of water that can be accessed by a mouthpiece, thirty-five-pound Interceptor Ballistic Armor fully loaded, two-and-a-half-pound Kevlar helmet, night vision, grenades, weapon, and ammunition. It's about sixty-five pounds of gear, but we're so jacked up we scarcely notice the load. We saddle up for the ride to the attack position.

Just as I get to my Bradley's ramp, Lieutenant Iwan appears. He's making one last sweep through the company to make sure everyone's good to go. He is in an armored Humvee. That strikes me as odd, so I smile at him and bust his nuts a bit.

"Hey sir!" I call from the ramp, "where's the Brad?"

"It broke down. It's a piece of shit. Fucking 1988 relic."

I call from the ramp, "Whatever happens, we'll always have Paris."

He laughs, "Yes, Sergeant Bell, we'll always have Paris."

I notice that Joey Seyford is gunning for him. Joey's a close friend of mine. He's also the unluckiest human I've ever known. In basic training, he nearly died in a vehicular rollover. Later, on a training range, one of his own SAW gunners accidentally shot him in the ass at point-blank range. He recovered from that only to slip while trying to take a piss in the dark. That mishap severed two tendons in his wrist. There's bad luck and then there's Joey Seyford.

"Joey? Sir, what the fuck are you letting him gun for? He's cursed."

Our XO shrugs and smiles. Joey seems hurt. "I'm golden, man. That shit is in the past. Check it out: I can almost close my hand now." He balls his fist and pumps his arm. "I'm GOLDEN, Bell! Fucking GOLDEN!" He laughs and waves as the Humvee speeds off and leaves me standing on my Brad's ramp.

And then I'm inside the belly of our steel beast. The ramp closes, and I squash down next to Lawson. Normally, Brads carry five to six men. Today, we'll ride into the city with eight. I've got my Bravo Team, led by Sucholas, plus Lawson and Pratt from the weapons squad. Pratt had been one of my soldiers, but Lawson needed a team leader so I swapped him Pratt out of my squad. With all our gear stored and stacked around us, the ride will be cramped and uncomfortable as hell.

We start to roll. The tracks clank, the Brad bounces us around. Through the viewing ports, I can see column after column of vehicles—Marines and Army both—moving toward the staging area. The earth rumbles from within, as if a gigantic subterranean machine has just been activated.

A half hour later, we reach the attack position, which is nothing but a vast stretch of empty desert just over a mile northeast of Fallujah. The ramp drops and we spill out into the morning again. We're surrounded by vehicles. From horizon to horizon, they carpet the desert like long trails of ants. There are gun trucks and five-tons, armored personnel carriers, Humvees, Bradleys, and Abrams tanks. To the west I can see the Marines' Light Armored Vehicles (LAVs) and their boat-shaped amphibious vehicles. Beyond them, a new Stryker unit has taken its position on the western flank. Longbow Apache helicopters buzz protectively over them.

And then the Paladins—155mm self-propelled artillery tracks, essentially gigantic cannons on wheels—unleash their firepower. Huge shells pass overhead to burst inside the city. The ground quakes. The Air Force, Navy, and Marines send waves of F-16 and F-18 fighter jets. They whistle over the city to drop laser-guided bombs and satellite-guided Joint Direct Attack Munitions (JDAMs). The *whomp-whomp* of their detonations can be both heard and felt, even at this distance.

I take this all in, watching with awe as a fresh wave of Apaches and Cobra helos provide security to our flanks. So much power. So much strength. How can anyone stand against it? I try to notice everything, every detail, every explosion. I don't want to miss any of it. This is the moment we've trained for since we first joined the army as raw recruits. The Greatest Generation had Normandy. Generation X will have Fallujah.

Sergeant Charles Knapp settles down next to me in the powdery sand and opens a ready-to-eat meal. We share few words. He's intent on eating. I'm intent on watching.

If this is it, I've got to be able to tell my grandkids some day. I want to remember the feel of the sand, like hot cocoa mix. I want to remember the sizzle and swoosh of the rockets. I want to remember what those 155s sound like. I need to be able to tell them what this day meant to all of us.

Knapp polishes off one MRE and wades into another one. I can't eat. I'm too excited, too nervous, too everything. Yuri and Michael Ware appear. They settle down in the sand and start watching the show next to me. Knapp eats another MRE, and I start to wonder how many damn stomachs he has. He is ravenous.

Every weapon available in our arsenal short of nukes is turned on Fallujah. The pre-assault bombardment is unrelenting. Jet after jet drops its bombs and rockets. Warthogs—the big, bruising A-10 Thunderbolt II close-support aircraft—strafe the main avenues into the city with their 30mm antitank cannon. Fallujah is smothered in bombs, shrouded in smoke. Buildings collapse. Mines detonate. Artillery roar.

Meanwhile, Knapp continues his MRE-athon. I've never seen a man eat so many MREs. It borders on the obscene.

We're at the head of our task force's column. Just behind us are the engineer tracks, relics from the Vietnam era. Once we get to the pre-assault point, they'll pass through us and advance to the five-foot-high railroad embankment, called a berm, that runs along the northern outskirts of Fallujah. This is our breaching point. In order to get into the city, we must blow holes through this berm. Our engineers plan to use a Mine Clearing Line Charge (MICLIC) to get the job done. Essentially, a MICLIC is a 350-foot-long rope with bundles of C-4 explosive attached. They were designed during the run-up to Gulf War I to clear lanes through minefields. A hydraulic launcher throws the MICLIC several hundred meters. When detonated, anything surrounding the MICLIC gets vaporized. What the explosions don't destroy, the concussion waves finish off. Today, if there are mines or IEDs at the breach point, the MICLIC's devastating power should cause them to detonate harmlessly. Once the engineers have made the breach, we will drive through it in our Bradleys, supported by a pair of Abrams tanks. We Terminators, my Alpha Company, will be the first American infantrymen in the city.

Staff Sergeant Bryan Lockwald, one of the engineers, plops down in the sand next to me. He utters a greeting, then smiles devilishly. I've known Lockwald for over a year. I helped train his engineer platoon on room-clearing techniques back in Germany, and we instantly became friends. I can tell he's excited.

He looks out over the smoke on the horizon and remarks, "Imagine what our MICLICs can do inside that city."

"What?"

"Fire that thing down a street, and I'm talking everything three stories on down destroyed or dead from the concussion of this thing. If you wanna clear a neighborhood fast, this is the bad bear you want in the fight."

As an engineer, Lockwald loves the MICLIC because it is the most powerful arrow in his quiver. Yet Lockwald has spent the deployment trying to avoid killing anyone. He and his engineer mates have set off explosives plenty of times back at our base, but Lockwald was not like the others. He quit smoking in Iraq. He read literature and talked about God and nature. He wears wire-rim glasses and his passion for blowing stuff up stands in stark contrast to blowing *people* up. He always makes that distinction. I always had him pegged as a frustrated beatnik. He loves trees and plays folk music on his acoustic guitar. With his huge, handlebar mustache and his nostalgia for the natural world, he's long since become the spiritual leader of our engineer platoon.

Engineers usually get abused by the infantry, but the truth is they are the intellectuals of the combat arms branches. They have a million crafty solutions to problems that would make us knuckle-dragging infantry types scratch our heads and pause.

I pray he doesn't pull his guitar out. His impromptu folk-song sessions are unbearable. Fortunately, he just sits with me and looks on at the unfolding bombardment with the same awe I feel.

"Where did you get that coffee?" he asks me.

"Dude, don't even start."

Behind us, Lieutenant Joquin Meno gathers up the platoon. He spreads out a map on the sand and starts to talk. I get up and go over to the huddle. Fitts reaches it at the same time. We both notice that Michael Ware and Yuri are busily photographing and filming this spontaneous gathering. This turns me off completely. Is Meno's chalk talk going to turn into a posing session for the cameras? I stay in the back and avoid the discussion.

Meno wants to go over what we'll do once we're through the breach. Unlike what has happened in the past, he wants to make sure we fight as an integrated platoon, not as disparate squads. This sounds good to all of us.

Fitts says, "Alright, Bell, we're gonna take down the first building. You bring your boys into our foothold and we leapfrog. Don't get too far away. Then we'll bring Lawson's guns up and get them in the fight. We stick together, Hooah."

"Hooah."

"We'll pick out some good rooftops and set up those machine guns for overwatch," I add.

My squad is slated to make the first leapfrog after Fitts's boys secure a foothold, and the first leapfrog usually draws the first contact.

Just as we wrap up our chalk talk, Lieutenant Meno gets a call from Captain Sims, who orders him to take a Humvee forward and recon the breaching point. Meno grabs Sergeant Knapp and climbs into a Humvee carrying Chaplain Brown, Captain Fred Dente, and our forward observer, Sergeant Shaun Juhasz. The Humvee rushes past us, kicking up a plume of powdery sand behind it.

They find a small ridgeline and stop just shy of its crest. From this vantage point, they have an excellent view of the city. As they study the breach, Captain Dente spots a flash of sunlight reflecting on glass. It is an insurgent with a pair of binoculars. He's been watching them from the northeast corner of the city. Dente and

Juhasz call in a fire mission to take him out. Binos Man has the same idea. He calls his insurgent buddies, and suddenly Meno's Humvee vanishes behind a towering cloud of sand and smoke.

"What the fuck?" Somebody calls out.

The smoke clears. The Humvee is intact. Captain Dente and Chaplain Brown call in to say they are okay. It is a miracle—an 82mm mortar just missed their rig.

Juhasz finishes his call for fire. Seconds later, our own shells impact on a building. They're right on target, so now they fire for effect. It is over in seconds. All that is left of Binos Man is a pink splash and a mist of blood in the air.

Meno's rig scoots back to our formation, victors of this unusual artillery duel. I wonder what Chaplain Brown must be thinking after that brush with the hereafter.

The radio in our Bradley crackles. The marines from the battalion that will be advancing alongside us to the west want to know if we're ready to go. We are. They tell us to button up and wait for the signal to advance.

Lockwald shakes my hand good-bye and returns to his vehicle. I watch Ware and Yuri clamber aboard Fitts's overcrowded Bradley. The ramp goes up and shuts them inside like sardines in an armored tin. Then it's my turn. I settle down next to Lawson.

We're ready. Our synapses are firing; adrenaline is coursing through our systems; we grip our weapons and wait for the drive into the battle. If the Marines need us to go early, we'll go early.

Instead, we wait. The Brads idle and don't move. The air grows stale. It grows hot inside our metal boxes. We sweat and start to stink. Lawson mutters to himself. I grow anxious, wishing we'd just get on with it.

The Brad lurches forward a few inches, and I think we're on our way. Then we stop again. A few minutes pass, and then we're moving again. Is this it? Are we rolling now?

No. *Fuck*.

We jerk forward again and stop. Somebody grumbles, "God-damn, it's one dick tease after another."

The sun starts to fade in the west. The sky turns orange, then red. Still, we sit at the edge of the attack position. We must be waiting for nightfall after all.

Thanks for telling us.

As dusk darkens the desert around us, our engine revs and our driver throws our Bradley in gear. We're on the move.

The pre-assault area is our final stop just before the breach. Again, it is nothing more than a vast expanse of flat desertscape, perfect for organizing a massive armored assault. Every unit spreads out in a line and comes to a halt along the east-west line of departure laid out on our maps.

It is a dramatic moment, and I can see we've formed gigantic waves of vehicles that will soon pour forward and funnel into the breaches the engineers create for us. In the meantime, we've got all our fighting tracks on line. We can't dismount, so we're stuck inside. We face the waiting game again. It is interminable.

Off in the distance, a mortar round explodes. Another one soon follows. We're within indirect fire range, and the insurgents are throwing what they can at us. I peer out one viewport and see a mortar explode about two hundred meters away from our Bradley. That's not too close, but the enemy has been known to walk their fire, aiming steadily closer to a target until it gets hit on the third or fourth try.

More shells splash around us. Somebody says laconically over the radio, "I guess we're drawing fire out here."

"Fuck it," comes the response.

Not far from us, Lockwald and the engineers pile out of their vehicle and start to work on the MICLIC. The weapon is carried in a U-Haul sort of trailer that the engineers tow behind them.

Thommft! A 60mm mortar explodes right next to their

armored carrier. Somehow, Lockwald and his men escape injury. Amazed, I watch Specialist Michael Sievers adjust gear on the MICLIC as if nothing is happening around him.

More shells explode around us. Things are starting to get hot.

Over the radio we hear that two Marines have died when their bulldozer rolled over while moving for the breach. The news angers us. We want to just fucking go.

But still we wait, poised at the start line, engines revving. This must be what a NASCAR race is like seconds before the green flag is waved, only instead of a few seconds our wait lasts for hours.

Our asses grow sore. When we try to reposition ourselves, we squash our balls. I check my watch reflexively. The minute hand drags.

Bombs explode. More shells fall on the city. The pre-assault bombardment swells to a climax. Every three or four seconds a 155mm shell lands. Larger, deeper thumps shake the Brad. Those are the 500-pound precision-guided JDAMs. And we sit.

The air grows wretched. Every breath is unpleasant. I'm jammed between the ramp and Lawson, unable to move more than an inch or two in any direction. In Fitts's track, Michael Ware starts to lose it. He screams, "Drop ramp! Drop ramp!" The crew almost does it until Fitts drowns him out. When that doesn't work, Ware pounds on the ramp and screams some more. He's far from a coward, just claustrophobic.

We all feel the same way. Facing bullets is nothing compared to this. Another hour passes, and some of us have to piss. Our leg muscles start to spasm. Mine cramp up altogether. Still we don't move.

Another volley of 155mm artillery explodes much closer than usual. The Brad quivers from the concussion wave. I can hear a flight of jets surge onto the scene and I picture their strafing runs along the northern edge of the city. An AC-130 Spectre gunship rumbles overhead at ten thousand feet and spits out greetings to the insurgents with its whirling Gatling guns and 105mm howitzer. There is nothing more terrifying than the sight and sounds of that gunship. With its wings banked, it unloads an unbelievable barrage of bullets and shells into its targets. "*Grrrrrrrrr*— Boom—Boom—*Grrrrrrrrr*. . . ." The AC-130 is the closest man has come in imitation of the fist of God.

The driver shifts into gear. We surge forward. This is it. I say a quick prayer.

Ten feet later, we halt again.

Mother fuck.

The wait continues. We endure, but only barely. In Fitts's track, Ware is completely beside himself and hammers again on the ramp. Everyone's on edge.

And then it begins. Several of our tanks cross the line of departure and move to the berm. They volley-fire their 120mm cannon into the buildings closest to the breaching point. This is the cue for the engineers to come up. Led by Lieutenant Shawn Gniazdowski, they pass through our ranks and speed ahead.

We roll forward again. Is this it? Adrenaline surges into us. We stop. We're here to provide support fire for the engineers. Some of the company's Bradleys pick out targets. Their cannons bark.

We're still trapped in the depths of our metal boxes, unable to see more than a keyhole-sized sliver of the battle raging around us. Our bodies are totally confused. Should they be relaxed or pumped? The anticipation drives us all crazy.

Finally, we're off. Our driver floors it, and the Brad charges forward. All around us, every vehicle, tank, and track takes off in one pell-mell chase for the breach site. We have faith in our engineers. It is total chaos, a modern-day version of the land rushes of Wild West lore. As our Brad works up to its top speed, we're thrown around like bowling pins. My head cracks against the bulkhead, then I'm thrown against the ramp. Just as I recover,

Lawson's Kevlar slams into my chin. Gear starts flying around us. A machine-gun belt lands on top of us and uncoils like a snake. More belts fall, and soon we're tangled in our own ammunition.

Outside, the explosions grow in volume and intensity. I look out the periscope viewer in the back of the Bradley. Blurring, jarring images flash before me. I see tracers, and fire, and more lights on the horizon. I sweep my eyes left and catch sight of the Bradleys on either side of us, keeping abreast.

The engineers' vehicles come into sight. They're catching hell at the berm despite all the suppressing fire the task force can muster. Tracers form fiery webs over them. Bullets spark off the armored flanks of their trucks. An IED detonates. The engineers ignore it all. Sievers and Lockwald fire their MICLIC rocket carrying the long rope of explosives. An enormous series of blasts follows. The concussion waves slam into our Bradley and stir our guts. The embankment sports a gaping new hole.

The radio crackles, "Go! Go! Go!"

On the fly, we swing into a column. We close on the railroad embankment.

Wham! Our Brad rocks on its tracks. An IED has exploded close by. Another one detonates, then another. Soon, we're engulfed in a series of near-continuous explosions. Shrapnel whines off our thick metal hides. More of it clatters overhead or strikes our turret.

Don't break track. Don't break track.

Flares and flashes line the horizon. Off to the west, I see a steady series of IEDs going off. The Marines are getting hit as hard as we are.

We're in column now, my Brad in the lead. Ahead, we see the breach. We steer through it, careful to stay between the chemical lights and tape the engineers have used to mark the lane they've cleared. In seconds, we're out the other side and racing for the city. Ahead is an Abrams tank, battering its way forward. Another stands to one side, spewing flames from the tube of its 120mm gun.

Lieutenant Edward Iwan's Humvee, with eternally unlucky Specialist Joey Seyford, slams to a halt near the breach. The heavy armored vehicles have had no issues getting over the blown railroad tracks, but the light-wheeled Humvees and trucks are stymied.

"Get this fucking bitch over the berm," Iwan says to his driver.

As Staff Sergeant Lockwald and the engineers rig up another charge to blow the gap wider, a mortar round whistles in and lands right next to Seyford and Iwan's Humvee.

SHHH-FROMMM!

Shrapnel blisters every inch of the rig's windshield and side windows.

"What are the odds it hits us," Seyford shouts down in amazement from atop the cupola of the Humvee.

"Pretty good with you around, Seyford. When this calms down I want you as far away from me as possible. You are fucking cursed."

"Cursed? We're fucking lucky. That should've taken my head off," Seyford replies with a laugh.

Boom! An RPG. *Boom! Boom!* Two more strike nearby. More IEDs explode. Mines, more explosions, dirt, smoke, and flames erupt all around us. We're surrounded by detonations, and our Brads plough through squalls of shrapnel, which sound like hail on a tin roof.

A Humvee driven by the Air Force controllers pulls between two First Platoon Bradleys and Lieutenant Iwan's borrowed rig. The sight of the Humvees unable to cross the breech encourages the enemy. They direct their fire at these vulnerable vehicles. Two RPGs scorch the night. One scores a hit on the Air

Force Humvee, seriously wounding Senior Airman Michael Smyre in the foot.

Joey Seyford, standing in Iwan's turret, takes a piece of shrapnel and his hands fly to his face.

"Fuck! My eye!" he screams. Seyford clutches his open wound with both hands. Blood pours down his face.

"You're right, dude, you are lucky. You get to go home, Joey. You lucky bastard," shouts Iwan over the battle's din.

"I'm not going anywhere, sir. Fuck that shit." Seyford wipes the blood from his face, racks the bolt on his 50-cal M2, and starts hammering the enemy with it.

Another rocket sizzles into Staff Sergeant McDaniel's Bradley to our right. It explodes below the turret. Behind us, Sergeant First Class Cantrell's Brad takes a direct hit and bursts into flames. Fire scorches its flanks as the vehicle lurches forward. Seconds later, it runs across an IED, which explodes with such force that the entire back end of the Bradley leaves the desert floor. It plummets back down, causing the rig to rock backward and lift the nose up.

Shit.

Our own Brad suddenly stops. We tumble against one another and curse. Our driver, Luis Gonzalez, has hit something. He backs up and floors it. We spring forward, jump clear of the obstacle and crash back down on the wrong side of the engineer tape.

Voices boom over the radio. "Oh shit! You're out of the lane! Get right! Get right."

We start to swing back to the lane. A shattering blast engulfs us. The back end of our Bradley is thrown upward. Dust and smoke spiral around us. I choke and gag and try to scream for my guys. All that comes out is a hoarse rasp. I can't hear anyone respond. Lawson, just inches away, doesn't answer me either. I wonder if I've been deafened by the blast. Or maybe everyone but me is dead.

CHAPTER FIVE

Machines of Loving Grace

Smoke. Eyes burning. I suck air, which sears my throat. I paw my eyes, smearing grime across both cheeks. I blink. The Brad's interior comes into view. Through the smoke I see the red lights on our gunner's panel. Gossard is firing the 25mm cannon, but I can't hear it. All I hear is a steady, high-pitched buzz.

Lungs full of smoke, I try to shout again. All that comes out is a hoarse, "Smack my knees. Smack my knees if you're okay!"

Lawson turns and puts his lips close to my ear. He must be okay. He's alive, anyway. He's shouting something, but I can't hear any of it.

Dim shapes take form around me. I see my men, darkened silhouettes inside our titanium box. I can't tell if anyone else is alive or dead.

The Bradley churns upward, then thumps back down. My head rebounds off the bulkhead behind me. At least we're still moving.

The buzzing grows louder and louder. Then it starts to morph into something else. I realize I'm hearing the 600-horsepower engine that drives our thirty-ton monster screaming and whining in protest. Throttle open, our driver pushes it beyond all sensible limits to get us out of this kill zone.

As if down a long corridor, I begin to hear Lawson's voice, still muted and hard to comprehend. For the moment, I ignore it. I yell again, "Smack my knee if you're okay!"

A hand snakes out of the darkness and whacks my knee. Another follows. Then three more.

Lawson takes a deep breath and bellows right into my ear. This time I hear him. "We're all okay, Sergeant Bell! You're screaming like you're on fire!"

How the hell did we survive that blast?

Another sound swells in my ear. Explosions. They thump through the Bradley's hull, *boom-boom-boom*. Our gunner keeps up a steady rate of fire, and now I can feel the vibrations of the 25mm through the seat of my pants.

I lean forward and try to lay eyes on the Bradleys behind us. I catch sight of Sergeant First Class Cantrell's track. Fitts and Ware are in it, too. Last I saw of it, the insurgents were pounding it with everything they had. Somehow, it has weathered the storm. Flanks scorched by numerous hits, it grinds through the Fallujah sand, keeping up with us while the turret traverses in search of targets. Judging by their radio silence at least, Ware is calm. Then a rocket sears the darkness and slams into the side of the Bradley.

"That was an IED," Ware announces.

"No, that was a rocket," Fitts replies tersely.

A few seconds later, another explosion engulfs them. Their Bradley vanishes in the smoke and flying sand, only to emerge a second later, seemingly unscathed.

"*That* was an IED," says Fitts.

The radio is full of competing voices. I can't make out much of it over the din of battle. Then Cantrell's voice breaks through. "Shut the fuck up!" he screams through the airwaves.

Staff Sergeant Brown echoes him, "Shut the fuck up, goddamnit!"

More voices. They step all over each other. Lieutenant Iwan's voice breaks in, "Clear the net! All Terminator elements, clear the net!"

It dawns on me that somebody else's broadcasts are leaking onto our company and platoon nets. This is not good, especially since we're within minutes of dropping ramp and assaulting the city on foot.

Lieutenant Meno and Captain Sims try to wade into the chatter with final instructions. Their voices are garbled, their orders lost. I listen to other voices interloping on our frequency, and it becomes clear they're a bunch of Marines.

What the fuck are Marines doing on our net?

"Get the fuck off our net!" Cantrell shrieks. Sims tries to speak, only to be drowned out.

"Fire base Thunder, this is Alpha 2 Bravo. . . ."

Okay: the Marines on our net are a relay team, passing instructions from their forward observers to the gun line to our rear. They tell us to go to hell, and keep right on talking. "Fire base Thunder, Fire Base Thunder . . . !"

Our track suddenly slams to a stop. The ramp drops. My heart jumps into my throat. Adrenaline blasts through my veins. This is it. This is our Normandy beachhead.

I turn to jump out into the fight and see Ruiz staring at me. *What the hell?*

He looks sheepish, which is bizarre amid the chaos around us.

"What the fuck are you doing?" I demand, now half in, half out of the track. Behind me, the rest of the men have frozen in mid-dismount.

"I gotta . . . uh, fill your radio, Sergeant. We gotta change our coms."

"You've gotta do *what*?"

"I'm supposed to refill your radio, Sergeant. Somebody's on our net."

"You've gotta be fucking kidding me, Ruiz."

"No, Sergeant Bell. I guess battalion just worked out a new company net for us."

I step off the ramp into the powdery sand. Ruiz steps behind me and pulls my radio out of a sleeve on the back of my body armor. He starts fumbling with it, while I take a knee.

The platoon is strung out in a column, perhaps a hundred meters from the city. I can see the Fallujah skyline silhouetted by artillery strikes to our south. We're on the verge of our entry point to the city, but our charge has come to a crashing halt.

"We're doing a COMSEC changeover a hundred meters from the city," I scream to no one in particular. "After all this? You're shitting me. You're shitting me, right?"

Ruiz fiddles with the radio. I fume. The Brads train their turrets left and right, looking for targets.

"Dude, just fucking keep it. You are my new RTO." My new radio telephone operator.

"Awesome, this is the demotion I've been waiting for."

"Your call sign is Cannabis 2. You got that?"

"Roger, Sergeant. Cannabis 2." Ruiz takes the radio and begins to reload different frequencies. It's a joke of course—I need that radio, and he has a job to do.

"You're still gonna kill more people than smallpox, Ruiz. You just get to tell everyone about it now."

"Thanks." He pauses, then deadpans, "This makes me complete now."

Inside our track, the radio crackles. It is the young lieutenant who is the leader of the tank platoon that has been attached to us. He tells Staff Sergeant Biden Jim that he cannot use any of the streets in our entry point. "You'll have to make your own path through the city," he says.

Jim is a native of Saipan, an NCO with no tolerance for bullshit. The choices of driving his tank through buildings, or blazing a trail over land mines, seem more than a tad west of reckless.

"How am I supposed to know where I am, sir? I don't have a map. Remember you lost yours and took mine."

"You won't need a map. I'll tell you where to go."

Trusting this young lieutenant is the last thing Jim wants to do.

"Goddamnit, Lieutenant, bullshit. You follow me. I am the fucking lead track."

"Just settle down there, Sergeant."

"Fuck you, LT."

Sergeant Brown comes out of his hatch. He looks at me and points to his helmet/radio headset, a big smile on his face.

"You hear this guy talking to his cherry LT?"

"Sergeant Jim and Sergeant [Matthew] Phelps are my fucking heroes. Fuck that LT, Sarge. Fuck him."

Ruiz finishes up. "Okay, Sergeant Bell, we're good to go." He dashes off to Meno's track.

I climb back into our Brad. The ramp goes up and I'm sardined next to Lawson again.

I swear I can't take much more of this bullshit. Let's just get into the city.

We roll forward, churning sand in our wake. The rest of the platoon follows behind us. The city looms ahead. At last we hit asphalt, the road that runs east-west along the northern edge of Fallujah. We're almost there. The treads grind across the broken pavement, crunching debris and throwing us around in back.

We swing left, pivot right, swing again, and suddenly the ramp drops. I look left into total darkness.

"Dismount left," Brown screams over the intercom.

"Let's go, let's go! This is it!" I shout.

We pile out of the track. The other Brads are clustered around us so that we can all dismount and use them as cover. We spread out and take up positions alongside our Bradleys.

All around us, the darkness is broken by fires of all sizes and shapes. Buildings blaze. Rubble smolders. Debris burns in the streets. Reddish embers of fires not quite burned out dot and dash the otherwise black cityscape. As I scan for targets, I see white phosphorus everywhere around us. We're surrounded by the stuff. It's manna from hell. It reminds me of the burning liquid metal of *Terminator 2*. Entire rivers of flame cut through the night, dancing with little peaks of sharp red-white flames. This stuff is death to all it touches. It can't be doused with water. Water just makes it burn hotter and higher. Fire extinguishers can't touch the stuff either. Smothering it with sand is about the only way to put it out. Our 155mm artillery pieces have been firing it into the city well in advance of the assault, alternating between white phosphorus (WP) and high explosives (HE). The artillerists use the WP to drive the enemy out of their positions, then lob HE on them while they are out in the open. It is a tactic called "Shake and Bake" and it is deadly.

Using our Brads as cover, we watch as our gunners prep our first objective area. Tracers streak from their barrels and disappear into the buildings ahead of us. I flip my night-vision goggles down over my left eye and study the buildings. Nothing looks familiar. In fact, the entire area bears no resemblance to the dismount point we've studied for the past several days. We've practically memorized our aerial recon photos, satellite imagery, and road maps. We know every building we need to assault, every corner we need to cover down on, and every street we must lay eyes on in our assigned area.

Yet none of this looks familiar. The pre-assault bombardment has turned this part of the city into a holocaust of twisted wreckage, mangled buildings, and broken vehicles. Houses have been cleaved in two, as if some sadistic giant has performed architectural vivisection on the entire neighborhood. Floors and rooms have been laid bare, exposed to the ravages of the night's shelling. Furniture is thrown haphazardly about. Smashed desks, burned-out sofas, faceless TVs lay in heaps within these demolished homes.

The Brads cease fire. Sergeant Jim's Abrams tank lets loose with one more 120mm main gun round, which blows an enormous chunk off a building down the street. Then his Abrams falls silent, too.

Not a shot comes our way. The scene is eerie, suddenly quiet. It sends a chill up my spine.

Where's the counterfire? Where are the waves of foreign muj ready to counterattack?

We wait, not quite sure what to think.

Lieutenant Meno decides to consolidate the platoon to the left of the Brads. We move over against a ruined building and take up positions. Now Meno discovers that we've dismounted about fifty meters from our specified point. We're a block short of where we're supposed to be. Not that it matters; our original plan is irrelevant. The buildings we planned to seize are little more than heaps of brick and splintered concrete.

Meno sketches a new plan, which boils down to "take any building still standing." Using his night vision, Fitts picks out a three-story house that looks relatively intact. At least it still has walls. Fitts declares it will be our first objective.

Behind us to the north, the sound of engines grows to a steady rumble. I look back and see a glow of lights on the horizon. I can detect Bradley engines and five-ton trucks. But there are other motors, too, and I don't recognize them. I assume they're Marines.

A couple of five-tons roll into view. They stop right on the edge of the city. Dozens of Iraqi soldiers spill out onto the sand. Instead of pulling security, they gather in clumps and plop their gear down and collapse next to it. The next thing we know, they're smoking and joking again, just like we'd seen earlier in the day.

Unbefuckinglievable.

"Sir," I say to Lieutenant Meno, who is on the radio, "What the fuck is going on?"

Meno steps up toward my squad. As he does, his boot splashes into a puddle of white phosphorus and catches fire. I stare at it without reacting.

"Listen," he says, "Something's happened at the breach. Captain Sims is getting briefed by Ramrod 6." Lieutenant Colonel Newell. "As soon as he knows what's going on, he'll disseminate to us. In the meantime, here's what we're gonna do. . . ."

His pant leg catches fire. A sheet of flame races up his calf.

"Sir, you're on fire," somebody points out.

Meno looks down and sees the flames. He stomps his boot, but that just causes the flames to grow.

Somebody should put up a sign: DO NOT TAUNT THE WHITE PHOSPHORUS.

The fire eats away at his pant leg. He's in danger of getting cooked. Several men grab him and throw him to the ground, where they roll him back and forth until the blaze is finally smothered.

Thankfully, Meno is unhurt. He is a Guamian who grew up in Inarajan, a town the size of a Photomat. He's not a native of the infantry; he transferred from the Adjutant General branch. Nevertheless, he's turned into a first-rate infantry platoon leader. His NCOs are hard on him, and when he makes a mistake we let him know. But there is mutual respect between us. He's a good man, and I know that even if half his calf had been burned off, he'd still stay with us. No way would he leave his men at a moment like this. Fortunately, it didn't come to that.

As we check him out, Staff Sergeant Jim's voice comes over the radio, "I got a white van inbound!"

We're under orders to destroy every vehicle we encounter. Even if it is tucked away in a garage, we're supposed to treat it as a VBIED—Vehicle-Borne IED. A van moving through the carnage and destruction to get at us is clearly a threat.

Jim's gunner, Sergeant Denny Taijeron, is Meno's cousin from Guam. They went to high school together and later attended Guam Community College, where they evidently both majored in wanton urban destruction. They joined the army at the same time and came to Germany together. Taijeron doesn't hesitate a bit. The 120mm gun fires, bathing the street in a hellish light. The shell blows the van apart. Pieces spin off into the darkness. When the smoke clears, not even a tire remains.

A second later, an AK-47 barks and an insurgent heaves into view.

Over the radio, we hear Jim say, "Check this guy out."

The lone gunman stitches the tank with his bullets. He might as well have been an ant throwing grass seeds at a lawn mower.

"Are you fucking serious? Look at this fool."

Another tanker's voice replies, "Awww man, that guy is cute."

Jim's turret turns, the gun's elevation changes. Suddenly, the entire street lights up again. The insurgent is vaporized.

Jim's and Taijeron's stock is rising by the second. They're using main gun rounds to kill individual insurgents.

A rocket-propelled grenade sizzles from an alleyway to the south and explodes against the thick, sloped hide of the tank. The turret swings again, the 120mm tube flames.

"RPG team destroyed."

As we listen to this, somebody remarks, "Those fucking tankers are studs."

The radio chatter helps us pass the time. The wait is interminable, and we cannot figure out why we're not allowed to move forward. After an hour, we learn there's been a big snafu behind us. For whatever reason, Marine units are using our breach, and a traffic jam has swollen up around it. If the insurgents knew what was going on and could counterattack in force, we'd be in serious trouble.

Rifles ready, SAWs leveled to the south, we wait for that counterattack. We've been given so many worst-case-scenario briefings that the general tranquility seems more a trap than a comfort. But the waves of enemy do not come.

I fuss and fidget and grow anxious. This is not how I imagined our first hour in Fallujah. I expected to be charging ahead and laying into the swarming enemy with every weapon at our disposal. Instead, the advance has come to a complete halt before we make contact, and we've even dismounted. I'm frustrated by this ridiculous sitzkrieg. But at the same time I'm hyperalert and constantly running every possible scenario through my head.

That window up there . . . that would be a great sniper position . . . keep an eye on it . . . there's an alleyway up ahead—it'd be an excellent spot to place an RPG team. . . .

A combat infantryman's job is like playing infield in baseball. You are always thinking, *What am I going to do if the ball's hit to me?* You must constantly evaluate threats.

Let me snap off that first round. Get these kids focused on the task.

I look at my guys. They are scanning everything in front of them. Tristan Maxfield, my SAW gunner from Denver, is sweating profusely. He's also totally focused.

I lean over to whisper in his ear, "Your first day on mission with this squad, you cut a dude in half who tried to run over LT, remember that?"

"Roger, Sergeant."

"Not everyone has the nuts to stand in front of a speeding car and unload a hundred-fifty rounds. Right now there is a muj shithead shaving his head. Cleansing himself. Praying. And

I'm not scared, 'cause I got you. And dude, you are gonna bend that motherfucker's ribs inside out, right?"

Maxfield starts nodding his head, careful not to look away from his scan of empty windows and doors.

"Maybe we shoulda shaved our heads, too. The whole squad," he whispers back.

"Dude, if I wanted to run around with a bunch of bald pussies, I would've coached my daughter's soccer team. Scan your fucking sector and don't let me down, dick."

Finally, I can't stand the wait anymore. "Hey, sir," I call to Meno, "We're like sitting ducks out here. Let's take a fucking building down."

Before he can answer, a star cluster flare explodes to the west. Our entire area is backlit. Another one follows. It explodes right where the Marines are supposed to be grabbing their foothold, so they must be the ones firing the shells. The light from the star cluster washes out our night-vision goggles.

"Jesus," somebody mutters, "I hope that doesn't fucking continue."

"Yeah, how the hell are we supposed to use our NODs"—night observation devices—"if that shit keeps up?"

Meno gets on the radio. Seconds later, he shouts, "Okay, First Squad: Go! Go! Go!"

Fitts and his squad spring forward into the night. Fitts runs with an obvious limp, but he's still more agile than me on my best day. I watch several of the men stumble over debris and wreckage, but nobody completely loses his footing. They get to the doorway of the target house and flow inside. Each man carries a SureFire flashlight on his rifle, and as the squad enters the house, Fitts tells his men to turn them on. Through the windows, we see the white light beams dancing across the interior walls as they clear each room. The squad is at its most vulnerable point now.

Oh my God. Something horrific is about to happen. The building's wired to blow. It's an ambush point. We're being funneled into a trap.

My mind plays havoc with me. The wait seems to last forever. And then it is our turn. "Second Squad! Let's go!"

We race forward with Lawson and the machine guns in tow. Piles of debris litter our way. Some of the rubble is chest high, including torn bits of concrete with metal struts sticking out. As we run, the struts tear at our pant legs like miniature Freddy Krueger claws. I slip, catch myself, and keep going.

We reach Fitts's house. There is no front door anymore, just a huge, inviting hole made by an exploding tank shell. We stream inside. Fitts shouts to me, "How do I get on the roof?"

Using our SureFire flashlights, we search for the stairs. I turn a corner, boots crunching on layers of broken glass, and find a doorway. My SureFire explores it, and I discover the entrance has been bricked up. In the next room, the men find another bricked-up doorway.

The enemy has prepared this house for our arrival. They know our tactics in an urban environment. They know that after we secure a house, we'll set up watch on the rooftops. That's where we like to fight. Roofs are the high ground with the best fields of fire.

The mortar on these bricks looks fresh, like the walls have been built in the last few days. In fact, as we study the house we've taken, we discover that there is only one exterior door not bricked up. Every way up is blocked. Every way out is sealed except our entry point and this back door. The insurgents are trying to funnel us into an ambush.

I peer out the back door. It opens onto a huge open field carpeted with debris and rubble. Each side of the field is flanked by darkened, skeletal buildings. Dozens of dark windows present vantage points over the field. This is what infantrymen call a danger area. In combat, open spaces like this one can be lethal. There are only three ways to deal with a danger area: avoid it altogether; set up near and far rally points with security before crossing it; or use a box tactic by moving along the outside edges and avoiding the open space.

This is where Fitts and I had decided to begin our leapfrog into the city. It now appears to be a perfect place for insurgents to attack us while we maneuver. The insurgents *want* us to go through that door, and if we want to push on to the south, we will have to do what they want.

"Knapp! Knapp, get up here."

"Yeah, Sergeant Bell?" Knapp appears next me. He's sweaty and already dirty, but good to go. I put my infrared light on a building about thirty long meters behind ours.

"Every swinging dick is gonna cover your movement. You got that building across that danger area. Box it." I want him to work around the edge of the field in order to take the building facing us.

"I can go wide and just hook it into the door," Knapp says after evaluating the area.

"Alright, that sounds good. Let me set up security. You get far side and strobe us for B Team and Sucholas." Once he and his men are in that building, they can signal us with a flash of light for the next team to follow them.

"Got it."

When security is set, Knapp runs through the doorway with Ruiz, Santos, and Doc Abernathy behind him. They sprint along the outline of the danger zone, hugging the buildings, drawing no fire. At the far edge, they turn and keep following the flanks. They reach the far corner across from us and dogleg left until they reach the doorway of our next target house. Knapp enters first, like all combat leaders in our battalion. He stays visible long enough to send an infrared strobe.

"Sucholas, your turn! Let's go."

My Bravo Team sprints into the night. This time, instead of using the box tactic, they go straight across the danger zone while Knapp and Fitts cover them from either side. Halfway across, I see Stuckert trip and fall. He rolls on the ground like an overturned turtle. Sucholas doesn't look back. He keeps running and the rest of his team pull ahead of where Stuckert's gone down.

"Stuckert! Get up! And get over there!" I scream at him.

I yell, "Sucholas! Look behind you!" He doesn't hear my hoarse, raspy voice. He doesn't slow down, and he doesn't look back. Stuckert's in trouble.

Knapp sees this and shouts for Santos. He rushes to the doorway, spots Stuckert, and charges out into the danger area, passing the rest of my Bravo Team as he runs. Sucholas hits the door and leads his men inside. They push through into the house to help clear it just as Santos gets to Stuckert.

Stuckert's been caught after stepping in a tangle of heavy-duty electrical wire. The wires have closed around him like the leaves of a Venus flytrap. The more he struggles, the tighter the wires grip him. Fortunately, Santos has clippers, and he goes to work. But his legs soon get tangled in the stuff, and he's trapped as well.

This is it. This is my worst case. Helpless. In the open. This is where it is going to happen.

My heart starts to pound into my throat. I can't feel my legs. I've got two men in a danger area, totally exposed. They work frantically to free themselves, but I don't see much progress.

A block to the west, just on the other side of our field, I hear an AK report. Then another. An M4 replies. A machine gun chatters.

They're going to kill Stuckert and Santos.

I can't lose men this way. I can't.

I leave Fitts's doorway and run to their aid, pulling my Gerber knife from my pants pocket. As I get to them, I see coil after coil of wire wound around both men. They're hopelessly snarled. Santos is snapping furiously, but it doesn't seem to be doing any good.

I curl the knife under one coil and yank. The blade cuts through the rubberized coating, but doesn't sever the copper cable inside. I start to saw back and forth. It is maddeningly slow work.

A 7.62mm bullet pings into the debris not ten meters to our left.

Oh shit. Not this way. Not like this. Please God. . . .

Another one follows. This time, the bullet whines overhead and smacks the ground hardly a stone's throw from us. To the west, another rash of gunfire erupts.

If we have to die, let us die in a stand-up fight. Not trapped like this.

I rage at the wires, hacking at them with my Gerber. Santos grunts, cuts, and swears. Stuckert pulls and prods. We're bathed in sweat now, and as we struggle, concrete dust boils up from the ground to stick to every exposed part of our bodies. Our faces get covered in the stuff. We look like ghosts.

A block away, machine guns echo through the night. AK-47s bark. M4s beat a response. The firefight grows.

CHAPTER SIX

The First Angel

Meanwhile, to the west, total chaos. The troopers from the Iraqi Intervention Force have hit a bottleneck right at their entry point into the city. Their five-ton trucks jam together in one tangled mess as Marine units try to skirt around them and loop farther west.

It starts with a few shots. AK-47s crack. Bullets spring off the five-tons. The IIF guys have little in the way of leadership. Some dismount to mill in the street, unsure what they should do. Others stay put in their trucks. The traffic doesn't move. The vehicles are vulnerable. The men are vulnerable. A disaster is about to happen.

From the west, a squad-sized element of jihadists strikes. They move into alleyways and rooftops and bring their weapons to bear. They have easy targets. The Coalition traffic jam offers little in the way of cover. The Iraqis, not quite in the city, but not able to pull back, are trapped.

Command Sergeant Major Steven Faulkenburg steps from an armored Humvee. Just before the assault, he volunteered to go with the IIF unit as their American liaison to the rest of our task force. He realized the Iraqis needed a steady, veteran leader, and he elected to fill that role himself.

His relentless personality helped drive the Iraqis through the railroad breach and to the threshold of the city. When they stopped and just dropped into the sand next to their rigs as we entered Fallujah, it was Faulkenburg who got them moving again.

Now bullets fly. The insurgents lace the convoy with long bursts from their AKs. Another force takes up position on the east side of the street. The jihadists have the IIF in a cross fire. Men fall. It is a nightmare.

Faulkenburg realizes he must act swiftly. He shouts up to his gunner, Staff Sergeant Raymond Wray, and gives him a fire command. Wray swings his machine gun out even as Faulkenburg barks orders to the Iraqi soldiers in the street around him. His face, wrinkled and hard, exudes strength and confidence. He moves through the confused and unsteady Iraqis, his very presence electrifying them. A few quick gestures, a few quick words, and the Iraqis form up with him. Though separated by culture and language, the IIF soldiers see not an American, but a combat leader. They're ready to stand with him and fight. Faulkenburg intuits this; the decisive moment has come.

Faulkenburg levels his rifle. He knows the only way his force can extract itself from this predicament is with a vigorous assault straight down the street. The enemy must be driven from their vantage points and pushed back away from the traffic snarl before they can start using mortars or rockets.

Faulkenburg calls to his Iraqi force, then half-limps, half-runs forward. The Iraqis behind him follow without question. Rifles blazing, they pour into the street.

The insurgents catch them cold. Buildings on both sides erupt with muzzle flashes. The battle is joined. It is the first major firefight of the battle.

A bullet strikes Faulkenburg just above his right eyebrow, a millimeter below the rim of his Kevlar helmet. He falls. The fight rages. Inspired by his example, the Iraqis charge on and drive the enemy back. Others risk their lives as they dash to Faulkenburg's aid. Our sergeant major lies unmoving in the street. The Iraqis lift him from the street and carry him to the rear. He's placed on a stretcher, where one of our medics, Doc William Smith, sees him. Faulkenburg looks so small and vulnerable, so unlike his indomitable persona. Smith notes that his feet don't even reach to the edge of the stretcher.

The fighting continues. The IIF takes more casualties, but the insurgents are driven back. The breach is ours.

CHAPTER SEVEN

Battle Madness

Knife in hand, I hack away at the wires trapping Stuckert and Santos as the staccato beat of AK fire fills the night. Santos swabs his face and eyes with his sleeve, then gets back to work with the wire cutters. I'm still frantic, but part of me realizes that the gunfire we hear is not directed at us. Whoever was supposed to watch this ambush point is either dead or has more urgent business elsewhere.

Stuckert finally breaks free from the wires. Santos yanks and rips his feet clear. We're good to go. Panting, we sprint across the rest of the danger area and careen into the house. To the west crescendos a furious spasm of machine-gun fire. Peering out a window, we can see tracers zipping in all directions through the blackness.

It is Fitts's turn to leapfrog. We cover the danger area, and I call him over. He takes his squad and breaks through a wall, which gives him a much shorter area to traverse to get to us. It's a creative solution to our tactical dilemma. A few seconds pass, and he runs into our new foothold and joins up with me. Knapp and Sucholas have already cleared the house—what parts of it they could, anyway. They discover that the stairwells are again barricaded with fresh walls.

Fitts and I open the back door. It faces south and opens into a small courtyard. Flannery, one of Fitts's SAW gunners, is already out here standing next to three or four fifty-five-gallon drums.

"There's hardly any lume"—light—"for the NODs" I say to Fitts as we study the courtyard. Aside from the tracers tearing up the night a block over to our right, this is among the darkest places I've ever seen. Our night vision requires a little bit of light in order to function, sort of like a cat's eye. In zero light, it is useless.

Flannery leans against one of the barrels. It tips, and a wave of fluid pours out. "Oh shit!" he exclaims, "I'm sorry, Sergeant."

The smell of gasoline assails my nose. I walk over to the barrels. "Hey Fitts, check this out."

In one of our pre-assault briefs, we'd been told the enemy would try to counter our thermals (infrared optics) and night vision by setting fires. Gasoline, for instance, would do the job just fine. All four drums in the courtyard are almost full—that's nearly two hundred gallons of gas. Inside, the rest of the men find more drums. They're tied together by wax-covered rope. Fuses. The entire house is one big incendiary device.

Next door to our house is another one with four stories and a walled roof. This one looks more promising. The platoon climbs over a cinder-block wall in the courtyard to gain access to it. From an outside stairwell, we climb onto the rooftop. It looks purpose-built for combat. The wall running along the edge of the roof is thick and high. It will definitely stop an AK round. Cut into the wall at intervals are decorative openings that can double as firing slits. Best of all, the view is spectacular. We can see the whole neighborhood from here. We have our first position.

I stand on the rooftop and watch the firefight to our west. I can't see much between the buildings in that direction, just flashes of light and an occasional tracer. The fighting seems to be dying down.

I look back behind us toward our entry point into the city. There are some five-tons back there with Iraqi allies moving around on the ground. I see a body in the street. Then another, and another. All three are being attended to by the Iraqis, who have put blankets over two of them. Other soldiers work to put the third one in a body bag.

Despite the intensity of combat just a short distance away, all is quiet for us. Urban warfare is not like fighting out in the countryside where each platoon or company can support one another. In a city, the close confines fragment the battlefield. Each platoon must fight in isolation, supported only by the assets attached to it.

We need to stir something up. The entire time I'm on the roof, the skin on the back of my neck crawls with that feeling of being watched. The enemy is out there someplace. I know it. And I know they're studying us and waiting for the right moment to strike. We got lucky in the danger area. We may not get lucky again.

I climb down off the roof and return to the courtyard with the gas. Just as I reach it, the firefight to the northwest suddenly picks up. Furious bursts of automatic fire echo through the empty streets. A second later, not a shot rings out. The silence is unearthly. Seconds ago we'd been yelling at each other just to be heard; now we start to whisper, unwilling to break the sudden stillness.

Lieutenant Meno appears. "Captain Sims is coming in."

Fitts is not pleased. He hisses, "Goddamnit, this is not a dog and pony show!"

Meno shakes his head, "No," he whispers. "You've got a good house. We're going to overwatch the neighborhood with it."

Fitts looks pissed, but I'm okay with it. Sims learned from Muqdadiyah. He's not going to stay in his track. Nevertheless, Fitts and Meno continue to argue the merits of captains on the frontline while I walk over to the back gate at the far end of the courtyard. Opening it up, I discover our access to Fallujah proper. The street behind us runs south through a residential neighborhood. The houses are so close together, we could probably move from rooftop to rooftop for at least the rest of our block. About a hundred meters away sits a municipal building of some sort, perhaps a school. A propane tank the size of a tractor-trailer is attached to the left side of that building.

This gives me an idea. I grab Ruiz, our rocket man. He's fired more AT4s than any three others in our battalion. These 84mm rockets aren't terribly accurate, but they can do a lot of damage. Ever since Muqdadiyah, we've made a point of carrying them and using them. Ruiz is our expert.

Together, we start to prep an AT4 rocket. Meno ends his hushed conversation with Fitts and heads for the roof. Fitts, no longer distracted, sees what we're doing and comes over.

"What the fuck are you about to do now?"

"I'm gonna shoot this propane tank with a rocket," I reply.

"Why?"

"So it will explode."

"Ok? Why?"

"Well, we have to instigate something. You know there are fucking dudes watching us out there," I wave my hands to the south. "We've got no Brads or tanks—they're still back at the entry point. If we blow this thing up, I guarantee the motherfuckers will start shooting at us. Then we can kill them."

"Dude, that is a big fucking tank. What do you think the blast radius will be on that bitch?"

I do my best to counter with a no-bullshit assessment. "Fittsy,

I'm thinking like five . . . ten . . . maybe fifty-nine . . . meters. I have no idea, bro. But it is going to be really fucking loud."

Fitts nods. "It's worth a try. Just make sure Ruiz hits it."

As we finish prepping the rocket, Captain Sims and his command group arrive and climb onto the next-door rooftop. Most of the platoon remains up there, but Knapp's team comes down to me.

"Okay, listen Knapp," I begin as he reaches me, "you're gonna be the first one out. We're gonna go through this fucking door at the back of the courtyard. You're gonna run across the street—five meters at most—and take down that big mother-fucking house over there." I point to a house that looks relatively intact. Knapp nods his head.

"Ruiz, you got that AT4 ready?"

"Yeah, Sarge."

I move to the doorway. Fitts follows me. I pop my head out into the street and lase the propane tank. Eighty-five meters. I turn and whisper to Ruiz, "Dude, aim high. If you don't hit the tank, you'll hit a building and somebody will shoot us. The whole point of this is to get someone to instigate a fight. We need to start killing these fuckers. Got it?"

Ruiz nods his head.

Just then, I hear glass crunching. *Swoosh-swoosh-swoosh*. It sounds like somebody's out there, walking through the rubble in flip-flops. I snap my night vision down and scan the street. From around a corner just short of the propane tank comes a single man. He's got an AK slung over his shoulder, which makes a small metallic *ting* as it hits his leg with every other step. His hands are full. He's carrying something. As he rounds the corner and starts walking straight for our position, I can see it is a car battery. Insurgents use them to detonate large IEDs.

The sight of our enemy sends a bolt of terror straight through my system. I've seen Mahdi militiamen up close before. I've seen the face of our enemy. But here, in Fallujah, this is different. These fighters are supposed to be the most committed jihadists in the world. They are the enemy's first team.

And one of them is walking straight for us, his weapon on his shoulder.

He does not see me. That realization dissipates the momentary spasm of terror. Now I'm in control. I am not the hunted. The enemy is right here, before me. And I have the upper hand.

My heart had been fluttering faster than a hummingbird's only a split second ago. Now, I'm suffused with calm and my heart rate drops to normal. I edge my head back into the courtyard and whisper to Fitts, "Oh my God. Oh my God. Check this out!"

Fitts moves to me, his Mossberg 500 pump-action shotgun at the ready. "Whatcha got, bro? Whatcha got?"

Fitts and I peer around into the street again, and I point out the insurgent. He's taken another dozen steps toward us now, and is probably about fifty meters from us. He's got a big bushy, mountain-man beard and is covered with filth. His clothes are smeared with gunk. His face is splotched with grime. He looks like a street person.

Fitts and I observe him. I shoulder my M4. I'll take the first shot, as Fitts's shotgun has no night optics.

Swish . . . swish . . . swish . . . footfalls in a hellish night. This man is about to die.

It is unusual for me to be the hunter. Usually, we react to ambushes set by others. Usually, we use our skill and firepower to avoid being the prey.

Sergeant First Class Cantrell loves to hunt. His mother back in Missouri has sent him a steady stream of hunting videos and magazines. Months ago, out of complete boredom, I started watching some DVDs with him. I've never hunted before, but these videos contain nuggets of useful information, some of which proved helpful during our counter-IED missions. Now I recall one video showing how the best hunters will make a little noise just before they shoot a buck. They do it because the deer will turn and present them a better target picture to shoot.

I wonder if that will work now?

The insurgent takes another half-dozen steps.

"Hey," I say in an almost casual tone.

He stops and looks up, just like the buck in the hunting video. It gives me a magnificent feeling.

I squeeze my trigger.

A tracer streaks out of my barrel and disappears into his chest. A small puff of smoke, like exhaust from a cigarette, plumes from the hit.

Did I get him in the lung?

I squeeze the trigger again. The tracer hits him in the shoulder. His eyes bulge. It is his turn to be gripped by terror.

I squeeze again.

He keens in agony.

One more. He howls, a long, mewling, pain-wracked scream.

Yet he is still standing. The battery's still in his hands. He's too surprised to drop it and reach for his weapon.

Fitts swings around the gate and rests his shotgun right atop my Kevlar helmet. His forearms jam down on my shoulders. He uses me as a damned tripod.

The shotgun roars. A spurt of flame jets two feet out of the barrel, bathing the street in a red-orange glow. The fin-stabilized slug tears a chunk of the insurgent's arm clean off.

He racks another slug, levels the shotgun on my head again and fires. The slug blows a hole through the insurgent's hip. He fires again and hits him in the other hip.

Total silence. The jihadist drops the battery and sags into the street. He lays unmoving for several seconds. Suddenly, a SAW on our rooftop unleashes a burst into him. It is overkill. The bullets pockmark the street and pepper the corpse, which doesn't flinch. Fitts and I have done enough damage.

My grandmother always taught me to fight fair and never hit a guy when he's not looking.

Wrong, Grandma. That's the best time to hit him. If you get a free shot, knock the corn out of his shit.

"You see that?" Fitts asks, a big grin on his face. He feels the same way I do. He flicks his night vision up as I smile back.

"I can't fucking hear. Did you have to use me as your fucking tripod?" I ask.

Fitts slaps me on the shoulder and just keeps grinning. "That *was* unnecessary, wasn't it?"

Ruiz appears and looks out over the street. "Whoa, awesome," he reports.

Sims calls down from the roof. "Nice shot."

"You saw him, sir?"

"Yeah, I saw him."

"Why didn't you shoot him, sir?"

"I wanted to see where he went. Besides, he was no danger to us . . . at least not until he hooked that battery up."

I take another look down the street.

Never hit a man when he's down? Bullshit. Show me a better time.

Combat distilled to its purest human form is a test of manhood. Who is the better soldier? Who is the better man? Which warrior will emerge triumphant and which will lie in a heap in the street? In modern warfare, that man-to-man challenge is often hidden by modern technology—the splash of artillery fire can be random, a rocket or bomb or IED can be anonymous. Those things make combat a roll of the dice. Either you die, or you don't; your own skill doesn't have a lot to do with it. But on this street and in these houses, it can be man-to-man. My skills against his. I caught him napping and he died. That is how the game is played. Tomorrow I might be the corpse in a heap on the street. But tonight I am alive, and I rejoice in that fact.

I scream at the top of my lungs. It is a victory cry. I am euphoric. I have killed the enemy and survived. Infantrymen live on the edge. We are hyperalert, hyperaware of our own mortality. It makes us feel more alive, more powerful. Death is ever-present, our constant companion. We can use it or be victimized by it. We either let the violence swallow us whole or it will drive us insane. There is no room for Chaplain Brown out here.

As infantrymen, our entire existence is a series of tests: Are you man enough? Are you tough enough? Do you have the nuts for this? Can you pull the trigger? Can you kill? Can you survive?

Yes.

I feel loose inside, like my vital organs have been rearranged by the euphoria that consumes me. I scream again. Battle madness grips me. Combat is a descent into the darkest parts of the human soul. A place where the most exalted nobility and the most wretched baseness reside naturally together. What a man finds there defines how he measures himself for the rest of his life. Do we release our grip on our basic humanity to be better soldiers? Do we surrender to the insanity around us and ride its wave wherever it may take us?

Yes.

I embrace the battle. I welcome it into my soul. Damn the consequences later, I am committed, and there's no road back.

I cup my hands to my mouth and take a long breath. "You can't kill me!" I rage into the night, "You hear me, fuckers? You can't kill me! You will never kill me!"

"Bell, chill the fuck out." Fitts is crouched next to me, working a wad of dip in his cheek.

Too late.

I am the madness.

CHAPTER EIGHT

Doorways

"Dude, you sound like a retard. Stop screaming already."

Fitts brings me back to reality. I quit howling. This is not the time to be a philosopher. Silence fills the street as I calm down.

Fitts and I confer. We discard the idea of firing the rocket into the propane tank. The enemy knows we're here; we no longer need to instigate anything.

Footfalls down the street signal the enemy is on the move. We peer down toward the municipal building but see nothing. More footfalls. Glass crunches. It sounds like several people.

"Are they coming at us, or running away?"

"*Shhh.*"

We listen. The footfalls grow distant.

"Dude. You scared 'em off with your rant," says Fitts.

"Yeah. And the shotgun rounds you put into Johnny Taliban were what, supposed to lure them in?"

Fitts glares at me, and I realize he's pissed off by my display. "I'm just saying . . . nah, fuck it. Go ahead, scream like an idiot."

Ruiz comes up to us. Fitts's shotgun work has rocked his eardrums as badly as mine. "WHAT? DO YOU NEED ME, SERGEANT BELL?"

We shake our head no as Fitts spits a wad of dip on the wall.

"Fitts, you're filled with negativity. We need to have an intervention here. This shit motivates me. This is my joy. Remember the old days. It used to be your joy. Where's that guy? Can he come out and kill terrorists with his pal?"

"Sorry I don't ooze with optimism. Getting shot repeatedly kinda took the fun out of it for me."

We're no longer joking with each other, and I realize just how deeply April 9 has affected my friend. A moment ago, we'd both been smiling over our kill. I took it too far, and now we're both uncomfortable. It has highlighted the two directions we've gone since that day in Muqdadiyah. I love this job. Fitts doesn't anymore, but he'll do it because he believes in it.

"Fitts, you're different," I stammer.

He looks down at Ruiz, who is still scanning the street.

"Let's not have this conversation in front of Ruiz."

"Dude, he's completely deaf. Seriously. Check it out. RUIZ. RUIZ."

Ruiz doesn't respond.

Lieutenant Meno shouts down from the roof, "What are you guys screaming about?"

"Nothing, sir. We got it."

We grow silent. There's a breach between Fitts and me now that didn't used to exist. It is out in the open, and we've both acknowledged it. It leaves me puzzled and dejected.

Our street is quiet. We return to business and decide to move south down the street and take over a house with a better view of the municipal building. Our tanks and Brads are still to our north, apparently unable to get through on any of the main roads. We'll have to continue our advance without them. This makes both Fitts and I very nervous.

A mech infantry company is only half-complete with just the dismounts. We fight as an integrated team with our tracks. We complement each other. They are our heavy support. We are their eyes and ears. It is a perfect balance, and to be most effective, we have to work together.

Still, we must press ahead. We cannot let the insurgents fall back and regroup. We've grabbed a foothold in the city. Now we must exploit it and drive as deep as we can.

I call for my Alpha Team leader. Knapp dashes up to me. Six foot one and about 205, he's tough and rangy, with a cannon for an arm, the product of his years as a high-school quarterback. He joined the army in 2001 and made E-5, buck sergeant, in only two years, a phenomenal rate of advance. He'd been Brigade Soldier of the Quarter before we'd left Germany for Iraq.

"Knappy, I want you to take down that house across the street. The big bitch."

"Roger, Sarge."

Knapp turns to his guys, gives a few quick orders, and moves to the back gate. Sergeant Hugh Hall, Fitts's B Team leader, throws a grenade toward the municipal building. When it explodes, smoke and dirt swirl around the street. We fire a few 40mm M203 rounds for good measure. They blow up and add to the makeshift smoke screen. Misa steps through the gate and bowls another frag down the street. If anyone's left down there, they're either suppressed or blinded.

Knapp slips through our door into the street, winds up, and slings a grenade clear over the front wall of our target house. A muffled *thump* follows. Overhead, Pratt and Lawson cover us with their heavy guns.

Knapp now launches himself fully into the middle of the street. The man is all steel and guts. During a firefight in Muqdadiyah last August, he stood atop a building and poured hot slugs into a group of about twenty insurgents. Bullets and RPGs flew all around, but he never even flinched. He stood and took it, and dealt out much worse.

He reaches the far side of the street. As he does, I urge the next group forward. Slapping helmets, I hiss, "Go! Go! Go!"

Fitts's squad follows us out of the courtyard. We dash across the street and into the compound of our target house. As I get close, I see Knapp frozen in the doorway.

What the fuck, Knapp? Get inside the fucking house!

The rest of the squad stacks up behind him, and though I try to stop, I career into the men. We've got one big gaggle fuck right in the front yard, and we're vulnerable as hell.

"Get the fuck in!" I order.

Knapp immediately counters with, "No! No! Get the fuck out! Get out now!"

"Whaddya got?" I demand, still trying to get untangled from the rest of the squad now backing off from the entrance.

He swings around and grabs my body armor. As the rest of the men back up indecisively, he drags me into the doorway.

"Knapp, what the fuck . . . ."

"*LOOK!*" he roars.

The first thing I notice are the wires. Wires are common all over the ruins we've traversed so far, but they are always dirty, torn, and dull in color. The wires I see inside this house are crisp and clean and bundled neatly with zip ties.

That is not good.

"GO! GO! GO! Get the fuck outta here," I scream to my squad.

A cluster of wires funnel through one wall, then fan out all over the inside of one room just inside the door like green and orange ivy vines. I follow a few with my eyes and see they end in undersized bricks. This puzzles me for a split second, then I realize the bricks are chunks of C-4 plastic explosive.

Another group of wires runs to a pair of go-cart–sized propane tanks stacked along the nearest wall. More explosives are scattered around them.

But the pièce de résistance, the stroke of insurgent genius here, is the centerline aerial drop tank sitting in the middle of the room. Designed to give MiG fighter jets extended range, it's a fuel tank that looks like a misshapen teardrop. The insurgents have slipped garbage bags onto its tail fins. The nose has been removed. The wires disappear inside from there. Using jet fuel as a bomb is what caused the fireballs at the World Trade Center on 9/11. This tank makes one hell of a weapon.

We could lose the entire squad—we could lose most of the platoon—right here, right now.

I turn to Knapp. "Get back to the other house, now!"

He grabs the other men and everyone careens back across the street. I'm left alone in the doorway, staring at this enormous booby trap. I'm horrified by the thought of what almost happened to my platoon.

Fitts jogs to me. "What's going on?"

I'm so stunned, I can only point.

He peers inside the house and flips out. "What the fuck is this? Holy shit!"

"This is a BCIED, man." Building-contained IED. "Fucking . . . building bomb." I can't even talk in complete sentences.

"This whole block would go," Fitts adds.

We can't let the shock overwhelm us. I struggle to regroup.

"What the fuck is this, Bell? Who drags a fucking drop tank into a house?"

This is as close as I have come to seeing Fitts flip out. It's unlike him. In fact, it is usually Fitts who stays calm in a crisis while I flip out. In October, just before we learned of our Fallujah mission, the platoon was on a routine patrol. Specialist Michael Gross tripped on a branch and fell face-first into the dirt. When he pulled his head out of the turf, he saw a trip wire only a few inches from his eyeballs. It was connected to a land mine. Gross yelled at the tops of his lungs. The squad stopped as I shouted, "Freeze! Everyone freeze and turn off your equipment!" We discovered several more mines strewn around us. Immediately, I tried to go through the doctrine on what to do in a minefield.

Fitts and his squad were directly behind our wedge. Fitts saw he needed to keep all of us calm, starting with me. "Listen, Bell," he said in a controlled, mellow voice. "I understand what you're doing. That's fucking Hooah. But you don't need to turn off all that shit. What exactly is going on?"

"Dude," I said getting even more excited, "this is a fucking minefield."

Fitts barked out, "Listen up. I need two SAW gunners pulling security at 9 and 3. A 203 looking 12. Light up anything outside our area. Everyone get probing back to the path. Look around you."

"Gross, don't move yet. I am looking behind you." I was starting to think straight again. Fitts had cleared my head in a stressful situation, as usual.

"Fitts, we are being overwatched. You don't put up an obstacle unless you are watching it."

"I know, that's why I set up security. "

I crawled behind Gross. He was able to get up and move out. After a while I started digging a small hole with my knife near the base of the mine.

"Bell, we are clear to move back here. What the fuck are you doing?"

"I am going blow this bitch up." I pulled a block of C-4 from my butt pack and placed it inside my little trench.

"Let me get these guys outta here before you get us all killed," Fitts replied.

"I got this, man. You gotta trust me."

"You don't know what the fuck you're doing, Bell. Stop poking that danm thing with your fucking knife."

"We may very well all blow up, okay? That is a very real possibility. But I need to focus and you are not helping me to fucking focus," I shouted in frustration.

"What the fuck. You doing this from what? Reading books with Lockwald and the engineers?"

"No, this is from their PowerPoint presentation. Remember? The one you said was a fucking waste of time. Well check it out, dude, this is an Italian toe popper."

"Just let me get these boys outta here," Fitts protested again.

Our soldiers crawled out of the minefield one by one. I looked around and realized that I was left alone. I began poking another small trench on the side of the second mine and planted another brick of the C-4. The next thing I knew, Fitts is laying on his stomach next to me, his shotgun at the ready.

He locked eyes with me and casually asked, "You got a dip for me?"

It was typical of the roles Fitts and I played with each other. When I flip out, he stays calm and cools me down. He keeps me in control when I'm on the verge of losing it. Similarly, when I push the envelope and take risks, he's always there to stop me from going too far. Whatever my state of mind, whatever situation I get us into, Fitts is always there for me. But he never has a dip. The bastard.

Fitts is very uneasy. I realize that I've got to be the calm one this time, at least to pay him back for what he did for us in the minefield. This role-reversal is not easy for me.

I suck air and work at staying calm. I must think this through. *What did we learn from the minefield?*

A minefield is an obstacle. The enemy places obstacles to slow infantry down and funnel them into kill zones. Kill zones mean they are overwatching the obstacle.

Somebody must have eyes on this place.

At the corner of the house, I examine the hole dug in the wall through which the wires sprout into the room we almost entered. This makes me wonder where they go and what they're attached to, if anything.

Fitts and I walk into the courtyard and do a little exploring. The wires run through a tunnel burrowed under the outer south wall of the compound.

"They burrowed under that bitch?" I say in incredulity. That looks like a hell of a lot of work. Why didn't they just run the wires over the wall?

Because they'd be easily visible from the outside and vulnerable to shrapnel from artillery or bombs.

This shows me a level of sophistication that sends a chill over me. Whoever built this trap is good.

We swing out into the street and move along the compound wall to the next house. The insurgents burrowed through this yard as well. They weren't booby-trapping the house. Their tunnel runs under another courtyard wall. This must have taken hours of digging, and there's no loose dirt anywhere in sight. They concealed their work carefully.

We follow the tunnel to yet another house, where it ends in a well-camouflaged hole. Right next to the hole is the shredded remains of the Battery Man.

Well, Captain Sims has his answer. Now we know where he was going.

It is easy to see now what he was doing when we shot him. His mission was to sit in the hole and wait until we took down the booby-trapped house. Then he would have touched the wires to the battery and blown us all up. Had we been five minutes slower, we'd all be mist adrift on the desert winds. The bulk of an infantry platoon shredded to pieces.

Earlier in the spring, a Special Forces unit got a tip and hit a warehouse in Baghdad. After they stormed it, the insurgents detonated a BCIED. The better part of that highly trained team was blown to fragments. Such traps are almost undetectable until it is too late.

I tell Fitts, "You realize by stealing my kill and waxing this piece of shit you saved our entire platoon, right?"

Fitts shines a confident smile, "I stole *your* kill, huh?"

"Fittsy, if you were a field grade officer, I think this would result in a valor award. This fucker was going to blow us all up. Instead he's in hell blowing Hitler."

He laughs at that, and for an instant, I catch a glimmer of the old Fitts.

We report in. I pass along what we've found to Cantrell. He passes to Meno, who reports to Captain Sims. Our commander wants clarification. He bumps his radio down to our platoon net and talks directly to us.

"What is it that you've got?"

"It's a BCIED," I reply, "a big one, sir."

"Are you sure?"

The question annoyed me. Who was Sims to doubt my judgment? Then I realize that I did the same thing to Knapp. Knapp must have felt the same annoyance with me.

"Yes, I'm sure, sir."

Fitts gets on the radio. "Hey sir, this is a fucking BCIED."

"Okay, come on back."

We return to our courtyard. Sims has been thinking about this new threat. When we give him the grid location of the BCIED house, he writes it down and calls it up. Then he orders us to mark it. We toss an infrared strobe onto the roof. This way, the tanks or air overhead will recognize it as a threat.

"Okay, change of plans," Sims tells us, "We are no longer going to walk separate from the vehicles. We'll keep our support by fire base."

Fitts and I are greatly relieved to hear this. It means we won't be kicking in any more doors without the Brads and tanks backing us up.

Sims gets on the radio. I hear him tell the tracks, "I don't give a fuck what happens if we have to go down phase line Abe, or go down phase line Cain." Those are the two most heavily barricaded and IED-strewn roads in our sector. "We're not leaving our dismounts alone anymore."

Sims tells us to move out. His plan is to push south to an intersection and link up with our armor.

The platoon files into the street, the BCIED weighing on all our minds. What door will bring us to another one? Can we get this lucky again, or will we run into one lone insurgent with a battery, squirreled away in some hole waiting for his big chance?

If we face it again we'll need to handle things differently.

For starters, I should have trusted Knapp. I undercut him in front of his men. I can't do that again. I've got to be their leader and not micromanage, not second-guess.

One night a few weeks back, Fitts cut me to the bone. "Bell," he said, "You've got to quit being a soldier and be a squad leader." At the time, the comment hurt. Now I understand what he meant. Part of being a leader means you must trust your subordinates to do their jobs, and that requires trusting their judgment.

I can't be a cock-strong asshole. Knapp needs to know I trust him. If he tells me to turn around, I'll do it. His judgment is sound. The kid is on the ball.

We reach the big intersection, our rendezvous point with the armor. It is early morning now, and the night's chill soaks through our uniforms, leaving us shivering. Minutes pass. Sergeant Jim's tank rumbles around a corner and links up with us. Cantrell in his Bradley is not far behind. Soon, the entire platoon is reunited.

Our tracks had a hell of a fight to get to us. They've shot their way south through the city, killing every insurgent in their path. Sergeant Jim's tank has been busy blowing up booby-trapped IEDs and Texas barriers with its big 120mm gun. Now we mount up and continue the advance.

We come to a new block of houses. We're in the heart of the Soldier's District, the upscale neighborhood of Saddam loyalists, Ba'athists, and retired military. The Brads stop. The ramp drops. We pour into the street and break into a house. Just before we burst through the door, my mind races. What will the house contain? Will we die and never know what hit us as a BCIED vaporizes us? Will there be bad guys waiting for us? What other booby traps might they have devised for us?

The first house is cleared without incident. The stairs have been ripped out so there's no access to the roof. We find food rotting in the kitchen and a layer of dust a half-inch thick on all the tabletops. This one's been long abandoned. We move on to the next building and find children's toys scattered all over the floor. Clothes are strewn about; the place looks like the family fled in great haste, or somebody has looted it. The house is rank with human stenches. Somebody's been living here. We are extra vigilant, but we find nothing.

At the next house, a bricked-up stairwell leading to the roof is, for a change, a welcome sight. The insurgent who built it was obviously a greenhorn mason. The wall looks weak. We give it a solid series of shoves and it collapses into a heap of bricks and broken mortar. The way to the roof is open.

The platoon assembles on top of the building, and Lawson sets up our heavy guns. Now we can clear the neighborhood by jumping from house to house. Instead of going in through the front doors, we can drop into them. Coming in from above surely will surprise anyone inside. It has its difficulties, as we encounter bricked-up stairwells or other obstacles on our way down. In some houses, the windows are sealed and the insurgents have built serpentine pathways out of barriers and bricks. They're designed to funnel us into a trap, but in every case, they lead to empty fighting positions. The bad guys have melted away from us. It leaves us puzzled.

Toward the end of the block, we reach a house that is separated from the others in the neighborhood. It looks like about a four-foot jump across to the roof's parapet. I go first and fling myself at the far side.

Instead of just a foot or two, I fall about ten. I slam down into the second floor of the house. For a moment, I think I've broken my back. I can't move. Everything aches. Ruiz and Santos suddenly crash down next to me.

I look up. The roof is gone. We've jumped into the house itself. That we didn't break a bone is flat-out miraculous.

"Look! This is from artillery," somebody says.

"Bullshit," I reply, "This was done with sledgehammers." I point to the scrapes and scuffs along the wall where the roof had been. There are no shrapnel marks on the walls. The muj knocked this roof out themselves, which only means one thing: they expected us to move atop the buildings. This was another of their booby traps. And we thought we were outsmarting them.

They seem to be one step ahead of us. But where the fuck are they?

We pick ourselves up and get the rest of the platoon down into the house. After we clear it we work our way up to the next rooftop. We cross to another house. This one has a pillbox-shaped room with thick walls sitting in the center of the roof. It is our entryway to the building below.

Knapp gets his squad to the door of the pillbox. Sucholas and my B Team are ready behind him. Fitts's guys wait nearby. They're just about to go inside when something causes me to rush at a window to the left of the door. The men stop and stare at me. I don't know why I'm doing this, but something's spurring me forward. I jump through the window.

As I jump, Knapp finds a wire partially concealed under the door.

Inside the house, I start to move to the door. Before I can take a full step, I see a trip wire. It runs across the door and up along the doorjamb. Dangling from the wire is an orange-red pineapple grenade the size of a Nerf football. The pin is missing and the spoon is held on by the wire. If we open the door, the spoon will fly off and detonate the grenade in our faces.

"Knapp!" I shout.

He comes over and peers through the window.

"Check this shit out," I tell him.

He fingers the trip wire and sighs. "You know what? I've told my guys not to check for booby traps. This is high-intensity MOUT." Military Operations in Urban Terrain. "We're looking for bad guys. We don't have time for precision MOUT."

"No, you're right we don't. We could have dudes in the house ready to kill us. We've got to be ready for them, not heads-down searching for trip wires."

Knapp nods. We've got a serious tactical dilemma on our hands. If we're to treat each house as if it is booby trapped, we'll go in cautiously. In house-clearing, confidence and quickness are absolutely vital. If we hesitate, if we methodically search for booby traps, we hand the initiative to any insurgents who may be in the house. We'll get lit the fuck up. Moving swiftly and decisively from room to room is the only way to surprise the enemy and minimize our exposure to their fire.

So far, we haven't seen anyone inside these houses. Yet if we continue to move this quickly, we're likely to trip a booby trap. Right now, I can't see how we're going to get through this without anyone getting hurt. Either we move fast and hit a trip wire, or we move slowly and get shot at.

"Okay, Knapp, let's keep this to ourselves."

"Yeah, alright. We don't wanna fucking freak the guys out even more than they already are. I don't want them going into houses with this shit at the back of their heads."

Knapp pulls out a pair of wire cutters and snips the grenade off. The spoon flies and the thing begins to hiss. I grab it and shout, "Frag out!"

On the roof, everyone ducks. I throw the grenade over the nearest wall. A second later, it explodes with a muffled *Phoompt!*

Fitts comes up to me, "Hey, Bell, you coulda given me some warning that you were gonna do that."

"Work with me here, Sarge. It wasn't planned."

We finish clearing the house, then move into the street. This block is done. We load into the Brads and head south. Sergeant Jim's tank moves first. He rumbles up the street, swings west, and gives us flank security.

As Jim swings a block or so over from our route, a lone gunman slips into the street and unleashes a volley from his AK.

Jim's main gun fires. A few seconds later, the speaker in the back of our Bradley crackles. "Oh my God. That was fucking horrible, man."

Jim replies, "Hey! That guy had an AK. He was shooting at me. He shouldn't do that."

Suddenly, our Bradley commander, Staff Sergeant Cory Brown, cuts into the chatter. "VAN! We've got a van!"

Sure enough, the enemy has sent a van loaded with explosives. Specialist Shane Gossard, Brown's gunner, swings his turret and spots the van as it closes on us. Gossard is generally considered the best Bradley gunner in the brigade. Outside the turret, he's a gentle soul who plays guitar and sings. In the turret, he's a true killer.

He takes careful aim and triggers a steady stream of cannon

rounds directly into the vehicle. It explodes with fiery intensity. Another threat eliminated.

Minutes later, we run into IED-laced Hesco sandbags. Gossard lights three of them up. The secondary explosions rock our tracks.

"Hey, I got a hot spot on the thermal," Gossard whispers over the intercom. We can barely hear him through the speaker, but he's clearly excited.

"And he's got a buddy."

The 25mm bucks twice. The Brad vibrates from the recoil.

"Nice shot!" somebody calls.

Two more bad guys down.

We fight our way south through another block. At the other end, we hook up with Jim's tank. Together, we convoy through the next neighborhood.

Someone yells, "RPG!" A rocket sears the darkness and strikes Jim's tank. A splash of flame streaks across its flank.

Jim's gunner, Sergeant Denny Taijeron, swings the big Abrams turret left. A split-second later, the 120mm booms. The entire front of a nearby building collapses. Just after he hits the building with the 120mm shell, a number of insurgents break cover. Taijeron switches to his .50-caliber gun. We can hear it barking even over the din of our engine. A second later it falls silent. The muj do not escape. We keep rolling.

"I got T-barriers," Taijeron calls out next. Jim tells him to fire. *BOOM!*

"Barriers clear."

Alpha Company grinds south to our next major objective, the Imam al Shafi Mosque. It is the command and control center, and supply base, for the majority of the insurgents in the Soldier's District. It is the heart of their defenses here, and we're going to tear it out.

CHAPTER NINE

Dorothy's Oz Gate

The night is surreal and confusing. Overhead, AC-130 gunships circle like vultures, picking targets and flaying them with their fearsome armament. The surround-sound echoes of gunfire, mortars, and artillery play tricks on our ears. In the empty city, every sound is magnified, every noise bounces from building to building to create a cacophony of battle with no point of origin. It is combat in a vacuum, a gigantic mishmash of sound and fire that leaves us unable to distinguish who is shooting or from where.

The cityscape suits a Godzilla movie. Heaps of bricks block the streets. Downed power lines drape the rubble. Houses are ripped and crushed. Storefronts are smashed and broken. Inside these shops, little remains but splintered shelves and furniture. The darkness is relieved only by dozens of small fires smoldering in the ruins. The horizon glows reddish-orange. Fallujah is in its death agony.

The night's work leaves us bathed in sweat, which the predawn breeze quickly chills. Our uniforms are slick. We ache and shiver. Clearing houses, we stumble across a cache of Vietnam-era Starlight scopes, off-the-shelf night-vision gear, and American uniforms and medical supplies. By now, we've all got nicks and cuts on our hands, arms and faces; our pant legs are torn or burned. The urban environment is a constant physical challenge for us. Every step brings the danger of a fall among rubble. Broken glass coats each ruin like ice crumbles on new fallen snow. Our boots crunch it underfoot, but when we slip, our hands break our fall and end up studded with shards of glass. We pick them out as best we can and keep going.

We find a rhythm. We're not supposed to clear every house and pull out every weapon or cache of supplies we find. That would take us days. This is a hunt. We look for bad guys and move on. Sergeant Jim and his Abrams tank prove vital to our speedy advance. He uses his main gun to blow holes in buildings, which we use as entry points. This is much safer than constantly rolling the dice and kicking doors down. The 120mm gun is so powerful that it blows holes in three or sometimes four houses at once. The firepower of this svelte sixty-eight-ton monster allows us to move through each block on a fresh path, avoiding the funnels and kill zones the insurgents have so meticulously laid out for us.

Two hours before sunup, we reach the mosque. It sits square in the middle of a block of residential homes. This is the nexus of the Askari or Soldier's District. The neighborhood is imposing. Every house has a huge, thick outer wall and metal gates. Balconies built like square castle turrets overhang the interior courtyards, providing excellent spots from which to cover the outer walls. It looks like the entire neighborhood was designed by siege architects.

Yet we encounter no enemy fighters. Reaching our first major objective inside the city proves anticlimactic.

The platoon moves to the mosque's front gate. The walls around it are at least ten feet high. Broken glass is embedded on the parapet—a very effective alternative to barbed wire. The gate itself is thick solid steel and stands over ten feet tall. We've got to get through it in order to clear the mosque.

Overhead, an A-10 thunders past us with its unique "*brrrrrbbr-rrrrrrrrbbb*" sounding 30mm cannons. It strafes a target to the south and pulls up.

Hall is our door-crushing expert. Part of Fitts's squad, Hall is not very tall, but he's built like a human battering ram with thick, muscular shoulders and a low center of gravity. I call him over. He takes one look at the gate and says, "I ain't fucking breaking that thing, Sarge. No way."

I turn to Fitts, "I'm gonna blow this bitch with C-4."

Fitts nods his head and pulls the platoon back out of the blast range. I take a block of C-4 and stick it into the gate. A few seconds later, I finish wiring it. It blows up, but when the smoke clears, the gate looks virtually undamaged.

What next?

"Let's use a Bangalore torpedo," Santos suggests. These are World War II–era engineer tools designed to blow barricades and obstacles. Essentially, the Bangalore is an explosive charge mounted on a pipe, or in this case a fence picket. We wedge one against the gate, set the fuse, and move away.

Boom! The gate withstands this assault as well.

"Unfuckingbelievable," I mutter.

Fitts tells Knapp and Misa to lob some grenades over the wall, just in case there's anyone waiting for us on the other side. The two go to work, pitching frags into the mosque's inner courtyard.

I have a better idea. I tell Ruiz, "Prep an AT4." I turn to Fitts, "Hey, bro, keep everyone back."

"What? What are you doing, Bell?" he asks.

"We're going to shoot the gate with an AT4."

Everyone backs up. "Ruiz," I say, "can you hit the locking mechanism?"

"I can try, Sarge."

"Do it."

Ruiz takes aim from almost point-blank range. He triggers the AT4. With an enormous flash and roar, the rocket arrows forward into the gate.

The smoke clears. The gate still stands.

"Ruiz, you stupid motherfucker, how the hell did you miss the goddamned door? It's five fucking feet away, dude!"

"I swear I thought I hit it, Sergeant Bell."

I turn around and walk to the gate. Sure enough, Ruiz scored a direct hit on the locking mechanism. In fact, his 84mm rocket went straight through the keyhole. A scorched, perfectly symmetrical hole has been blown right through it. Yet the gate refuses to give.

Stymied by a fucking hajji gate. Are you kidding me?

Santos sticks a Claymore mine on the hinge. It blows, but again the gate withstands the blast.

"Santos: get the Javelin."

"Fuck this, man," Fitts says. He wants no part of the big FGM-148 antitank missile. Those suckers are more than five inches in diameter.

Jim's voice comes over the radio. He's been listening to updates on our conundrum. "Hey, Sergeant Bell, you need to peel that wall back."

"Well," I reply, "that would be the best solution."

We normally don't use our Brads as battering rams. It is too easy to damage them, and if they go down, we lose a key casualty producer. But this time we're going to need a Brad.

The nearest one is Lieutenant Meno's. Meno has dismounted to join up with us, leaving the track in the hands of Sergeant Chad Ellis, a five foot seven, bulldog-framed gunner. Ellis has been in Third Platoon since 2001 and has personified the face and attitude of our family, known affectionately as the Third Herd.

He's a solid NCO and excellent Bradley gunner, but he's not used to commanding a track. His driver, Specialist Gregory Marcoot, is relatively new as well. Not an optimum situation, but we call him forward anyway.

Jim's tank rumbles up to us and edges over to one side of the street to let Ellis pass him. Acting as Marcoot's eyes and pulling security is tough to do simultaneously in a Bradley. As the Brad edges forward, Ellis traverses his turret away from Jim's tank. The barrel of his gun collides with the side of the mosque with a dull thud. Ellis reacts to the impact and Marcoot slams the Bradley into the back deck of Staff Sergeant Jim's tank.

"What the fuck?" somebody hollers.

The Brad stops, but Ellis continues to rotate the turret. Like Paul Bunyan's ax, the barrel hacks into a nearby telephone pole. *Thwack!* The pole snaps in half, dropping wires like serpents all over the street.

"Dude, what the fuck are you doing?" Fitts shouts.

Ellis finally gets the turret realigned with his line of march. The track jerks forward to the gate. Ellis takes aim and opens fire with his gun. The 25mm barks out a few rounds, which do little more than blow holes in the gate. Then his weapon jams. That's hardly surprising, given what it has just been through. Ellis switches to the coax machine gun and rips off a short burst into the lock before this gun also jams.

The Brad has only one weapon left, its TOW antitank missiles. Ellis tries to raise the box that serves as the weapon's base, but it refuses to lift up into the firing position. His track is effectively neutralized. Not a single weapon functions.

At least it can still act as a giant battering ram. Marcoot inches forward and puts his left fender on the gate. He hits the gas, but the Brad stands at an odd angle and he can't get traction. The gate withstands even this assault.

Jim watches all of this and finally says, "Come over here

behind me, and I'll give it a try." The Abrams rolls forward and Jim jams his left front fender right into the corner of the mosque's concrete wall. Then he pivots to the left. The power of the tank's 1,500-horsepower turbines is simply staggering. The pressure this maneuver creates fractures the wall. From the gate to the corner, it buckles and then collapses inward. I've never seen anything like this.

"Wow," I say over the radio. "Thanks for that, man."

The platoon enters the compound to find a stockpile of weapons, equipment, and ammunition. As we move through the courtyard, we're surrounded by heaps of mortar shells, piles of rocket-propelled grenades, crates of ammunition, and other explosives. If we get in a firefight now, this is the only cover we'd have.

We secure the courtyard and find even more stuff, including radio gear and more American supplies. Due to the rules of engagement, we are not allowed to enter the interior of the mosque itself. This would offend Iraqi sensibilities since we are unwashed infidel Christians. We certainly wouldn't want to do that *and* destroy their fucking city at the same time.

Meanwhile, our enemy uses his holy sites as supply bases.

The Iraqi Intervention Force battalion that followed us through the breach now rolls up and dismounts. This time, the soldiers are committed. They look pretty high-speed to us as they line up at the entrance. They kick in the front door and swing inside, weapons blazing. We stand outside, listening to the shooting and wondering if we're missing out on a firefight.

A few minutes later, the IIF leader bounds back through the front door. He looks at Meno, smiles, and gives a thumbs-up. "Okay!" he proclaims in broken English, "You're good!"

Key objective secured. Huge ammo cache discovered. No bad guys in sight. It's a weird start to the Götterdämmerung of Iraq.

•   •   •

With about a half hour of darkness left, Meno tells us to grab a house, set up security, and get some rest. Fitts leads his squad across the street and takes up position inside an intact house due north of the mosque. Second Squad and I go to the end of the block and clear a two-story house just to the northeast of the mosque and across the street.

I set up security on the rooftop. The rest of the squad flops down to catch a quick nap on the second floor of the house, just inside the entrance to the enormous roof. I linger a few more minutes to give instructions to my soldiers. Lawson agrees to keep an eye on things for the next twenty minutes or so. That done, I head down the stairs to guard the front door.

In the room above me, Michael Ware and Yuri Kozyrev are sprawled out on the floor. Doc Abernathy is next to them. A few of the other guys are smoking or cleaning their weapons. We'll give these guys an hour to sleep, then rotate some of the men off the roof so they can get some rest.

I sit down, light a cigarette, and take a deep drag. My nerves are taut, but I feel like I could sleep for a week. Yet I know this is only the beginning.

The squad has performed very well so far, and I am proud of my men. We're working together, and the men clearly trust one another.

It didn't used to be like that. At the beginning of our rotation months ago, I caught one of my soldiers huffing compressed air, trying to get a high from the whippetlike chemicals inside. I was furious. I lined them up and demanded to know who else was involved.

Fitts, Staff Sergeant Omar Hardaway, Brown, and I grilled each member of my squad. I turned the clock back to 1965 when NCOs were still allowed to give "wall-to-wall" counseling. Feelings were hurt, ribs were smashed, faces were thwacked, but no tears were shed. More importantly, not one soldier turned on his comrades. Instead, two guys who had nothing to do with the incident took full responsibility.

That was the day my squad came together. They had stayed loyal to one another, and I respected that. They learned they could trust one another. It was also the day I learned how much I truly cared about these men.

Now I take another drag on my cigarette and dump my gear out. I'm busily rearranging my ammo pouches when Lawson appears at the top of the stairs.

"Hey, Sergeant Bell," he calls, his voice hushed and low.

"Yeah?" Lawson's as white as a sheet.

"Stuckert thinks he saw something."

I grab my gear and head for the roof.

CHAPTER TEN

Shadows and Wraiths

"Whaddya got?" I ask Stuckert when I reach the roof.

"Sarge," he whispers, his SAW pointed at a barred window not five feet away on the roof of the house next door. Our rooftop shares a common wall with the next house. The two are connected west-to-east.

"What are you doing?" I say with a full voice. I can't know for sure, but I suspect Fitts and his boys are in that building.

"Sarge," Stuckert whispers, "There's a guy in there. I saw a hand move the curtain."

Stuckert's eyes are saucers, and the hair on the back of his neck is standing at attention. Something has given him a *Nightmare on Elm Street* spooking.

I edge up to the wall and peer over at the window. I see no hand. I see the curtains, torn and filthy, fluttering gently in the breeze.

"Dude." He's got me whispering now. "Dude, come on Stuckert, the wind is blowing the curtains. You're cold. I'm cold. You're exhausted. I'm exhausted."

I pause. He looks crushed.

"Stuckert, are you positive you saw this?"

"Sergeant Bell, I'm positive."

Start trusting these guys.

Stuckert is a Californian who came to the army as a troubled boy from a wealthy family. His uncle is the mayor of his town back home, and his father is very successful. Since he's been with Second Squad, he's been on the ball. He's a good soldier, a good kid who has made great strides toward becoming a *man*. He's not prone to hysterics, and his bravery cannot be questioned.

Be a leader. Trust your men.

I've got to be sure. "Hey, Maxfield, Sergeant Lawson, did you guys see anything?"

"No, Sergeant Bell."

I don't know where Fitts is right now. He's somewhere to the west of me on the same side of the street. Could he have moved next door without us knowing? Before we start hosing the window, I've got to make sure we won't kill our own.

Stuckert's still behind his SAW. Even if Fitts isn't in the house next door, we run the risk of hitting him incidentally if we pour machine-gun fire in his direction.

"Okay, Lawson, get your nine out. Stuckert, get one, too." Lawson unholsters his pistol and grips it, never taking his eyes off the window. Stuckert grabs one from the 240 Bravo machine gunners. He slides back into his spot along the wall and points the stubby barrel at the window.

"Okay, pull security with the nine mils. If you see something, don't fucking hesitate. Use your judgment. Use your judgment, Stuck. I trust you."

"Roger, Sarge," says Stuckert.

I grab my radio and key the mike, "Hey, Fittsy, where are you at? My guys see a dude in a building and I wanna make sure I'm not shooting you."

"I'm two houses down. I don't see shit out here."

Doc Abernathy appears in the doorway to the pillbox room. He moves over to us, bent low to keep his body below the level of the wall.

He lines up next to Lawson and gets his eyes on the window.

Could we really have bad guys right next door to us? Why didn't they shoot us when we were in the street trying to get the mosque gate open?

Lawson jerks back. The sudden movement makes me jump and I look over at my guys. Doc Abernathy ducks and turns to me, "Sergeant Bell, Sergeant Lawson sees something."

Lawson's eyes are riveted on the window.

"What the fuck is going on here?"

"Hey man, a fucking hand just moved the goddamned curtain." Lawson glances at me, and he's got the same chamber-of-horrors look Stuckert had.

"Stuckert, put your fucking nine mil on the edge of that hole. You're gonna shoot at a forty-five to the left, got it?"

"Roger, Sergeant Bell."

"Lawson, you're gonna shoot forty-five to the fucking right. When you run low on ammo, I'll stick a shotgun in there."

"Roger," they say in tandem.

Lawson draws a bead. Stuckert does the same. They squeeze their triggers, the nine mils crack.

"*BAAAAAAAAAAGGGH!*"

Somebody is screaming behind the curtain. It is so sudden and so loud it scares the shit out of us. I'm so surprised that for a moment, I'm rooted in place. Reflexively, the boys pour more fire into the window.

"*Aaaaaaaaagh!*"

Lawson drains his clip and slams another home. Back in a shooter's stance, he peppers the window. Blood spatters across the curtain. Between shots we hear a thump, as if somebody has fallen off a chair or tabletop onto the floor.

"*Yaaaaaaaaaaaeeeeeee*," the voice behind the window is pain-wracked and terrified. We've caught him completely by surprise, and he's severely wounded.

We try to finish him off with a grenade through the window, but the bars are so close together we can't get a frag through it. Instead, Stuckert and Lawson keep firing.

Above the din, the screams continue. The man cries and bellows and babbles in Arabic. We can't see him, and this makes it eerie. Some of the other men add their weapons into the mix. We're filling the room behind the window with a hornet's nest of bullets.

How is this guy still alive?

"Cease fire! Cease fire!" I call. The men ease up on their triggers. I lean out over the wall and stick my head against the window bars. It is too dark to see inside the room, but I hear him moving around. His footsteps are slow and shuffling, and it sounds like he's staggering downstairs.

"Oooooooooohhh."

That sounded like it came from outside.

"*Aaaaagh*."

"He's in the courtyard!"

I swing over and look down to the north. The two houses share a common courtyard, complete with ornate pillars. I notice that most of the northern compound wall has been totally destroyed by artillery fire, making our house a much less defensible position than I had originally thought.

"There! There he is!"

The Screamer half runs, half staggers to one of the decorative pillars. He slips behind it and disappears before we can get weapons on him.

Fitts comes over the radio, "What the fuck is that?"

"Hey," I reply, "we just shot a guy. I think he's on your level now."

"He's really close to me, but I'm not sending my boys out until I know exactly where he is."

"Okay. We're gonna fucking move him with 40mm grenade fire. We'll shake him outta there. If he moves, you guys get the shot. If not, we'll take it."

"Sounds good."

I turn and shout, "Santos! Give me a fucking 40mm. Lay some 203 down on that pillar!"

Santos slides along the wall until he has a clear shot of the courtyard. He pumps off two rounds. Shrapnel tears through the insurgent, who keens like a car-struck cat.

"Knapp!"

Knapp comes up and lays fire down on the pillar. We fire a few more 40mm rounds. Lawson preps a grenade and pitches it into the courtyard. To our surprise, it doesn't explode. Santos takes aim with his 203 launcher and lets fly. The 40mm grenade explodes and knocks Lawson's frag into the street. Another shot causes it to detonate.

All the while, the Screamer wails. It sounds like all the pain and misery of this place wrapped into one dying voice.

"Cease fire! Cease fire!" I shout. We've done enough damage. Now let's see if he'll come out in the open so we can finish him off.

No luck. He stays put and continues to fray our nerves with his agony.

By now, the sun has just started to crest the horizon to our east. The sky has morphed from black to golden orange, and long shadows crease the street around us. Fog and smoke hang low over the city, limiting our view and adding to the creepiness of the moment.

The Screamer goes quiet. Off to the west, we hear distant gunfire. First Platoon must be engaged around their first objective, a school.

We look at one another, wondering if the Screamer has bled out. We hold fire, but wait, fingers tense on triggers.

The Screamer bellows something in Arabic at the top of his lungs. I don't understand what he says, but others do. To the north, somebody answers him. Seconds later, another yells a response. Three, four more sound off. To the south, behind us, a fifth call comes up from the ruined city.

All around us, voices haunt the fog and smoke. Stark terror has me in its grip.

What have we just unleashed?

Fitts calls over the radio, "Bell? Bro? Do year hear this shit?"

"Dude, what do you think? Fifteen to twenty?"

"I'm thinking forty to fifty."

"Fuckin' A, bro."

"Fuckin' A."

A whistle blast stops us all cold. It sounds sharp but rich and powerful. I can't tell where it came from.

Another whistle blows. Another one answers. Two more reply.

Oh my God. They're all around us. Our Brads are to the west between us and First Platoon. Ellis is in the intersection to the south and east, but he has no functioning weapons. We've got an eagle's span across this part of Fallujah. It is a solid position, but we have no depth.

I spin around, listening to the chorus, reminded of the legendary bugle calls the Chinese used before their human-wave assaults in Korea.

"Prepare to defend yourselves!" I quote Sam Elliott playing Sergeant Major Basil Plumley in *We Were Soldiers*. It is not as funny as I thought it would be. The men look stricken but resolute. Michael Ware and Yuri are on the roof now with us.

"Check this out, man," I say to Ware, "This is the fucking story. Right here. Right now."

Ware stares at me. I turn to my squad. "This is the fucking

story you're gonna tell your kids. Look, we've got perfect cover. These fucking dudes are about to charge us, and we're gonna shoot fish in a motherfucking barrel. Got it?"

Nods all around. I continue, "We're not gonna bring any Brads up, 'kay? We're gonna make them think they've trapped dismounts in the open without support. They're gonna rush us, and we'll fucking take them out. Hooah?"

"Hooah!"

"Okay, get your ammo out. SAW ammo at your knees. Line your mags up where you can get to 'em quick. We're not leaving this roof. We're not moving. We'll stand and fight right the fuck here."

The men reach into their pouches and spread their mags out at the base of the wall. Knapp, Sucholas, and I split the squad up and assign sectors of fire. We're thin, but we have fire-power. Lawson's M240 Bravos are the heart of our strength. We put the two 7.62mm medium machine guns to the north, where the gunners, Specialist Joe Swanson and Private First Class Jamison McDaniel, can scan an open expanse of the city for targets. Sergeant Alan Pratt settles between them, ready to assist on either gun. I put two men on the south wall with M4s. If we're rushed hard from that direction, we'll be in trouble, but I'll be able to pull men off the north and west sides if necessary.

We have excellent cover. We have a central fighting position. My boys trust one another. I trust them. We will win.

Get pumped. Use the fear. Don't let it own you. Own it. This is the fight you've always wanted. This is the fight you were born to win.

I want to be on the wall with the men, weapon trained and ready, but that is not my job. I must be a leader, not a soldier. I walk my firing line, checking on my men. They're ready, and I can't be more proud of them.

The whistles fall silent. Now comes the sound of feet, like galloping horses, echoing through the empty streets and alleys around us.

They're coming. They're coming for *us*.

The Screamer keens and wails. His salvation is at hand.

CHAPTER ELEVEN

Rooftop Alamo

The first charge comes from the northwest, toward Fitts's squad. We hear the beat of footsteps on rubble and we brace ourselves. Santos turns and points in the direction of the Screamer and mouths something, but his words cannot compete with the explosion of gunfire coming from First Squad's sector. SAWs rake the street. M4s snap. A grenade explodes. It swells into a chorus of combined arms. For fifteen seconds, the street to our west is a kill zone, thanks to Fitts and his boys.

The last bullet ricochets off the asphalt. Cheers erupt in its wake.

"Weeehaww!" shouts Fitts over the radio, "Game over, man! We just took out a fire team plus. Linear ambush!"

The first wave ran right in front of Fitts. His men were waiting in the windows and doorways of the house he had taken. The insurgents had no idea he was there. They charged headlong into his skirmish line and seven or eight died before they ever knew what had hit them. It is a great way to start this fight.

"Great job, bro!" I call back.

"Hey, Bell. That's about all I've got in this house. I'm outta here. We're comin' to you."

"Roger that."

I turn to my guys, "Hey, hold your fire! Terminators comin' in!"

To Fitts I say, "Do you know where I'm at?"

"Yeah. Comin' to you now. We've got to consolidate."

He's right about that. We're going to need every rifle and every SAW on our rooftop to withstand what's coming.

From below, I hear Fitts yell, "Terminators coming in!" First Squad rushes into our house. The men stream upstairs and onto the roof. Third Platoon is one again. Fitts and I reset our squads and reassign fields of fire. Stuckert gets moved to the far side of the roof, with an alleyway to cover. It is the least likely avenue of approach, and Stuckert isn't happy. After all, he helped pick this fight in the first place.

The sun is still below the horizon, but we can feel the predawn glow of another golden Mesopotamian morning. I move over to the north wall. Somehow during the night the enemy evaded us. They've infiltrated our rear and flanks. Now they are poised to strike.

I scan the rooftops, at first only seeing the big water reservoirs the Iraqis have built for their gravity-fed plumbing systems. Next to one reservoir, I see some sandbags, a fighting position. It is one of many. Every roof is studded with defensive emplacements. Some have overhead cover. Some rooftops even have brick and wood bunkers. We're right in the middle of an entire network of insurgent defenses.

A stillness descends around us. No more footfalls in the streets, no more rattle of gear or the *swish-swish-swish* of pant legs brushing against each other as our enemies rush forward.

A sudden noise catches our attention. It came from a rooftop to the northwest. We look over, but see nothing. The tension on the roof ratchets up another notch. Next comes motion to the northeast. I jerk my neck around, just in time to see a brick fall from a bunker. It clatters to the rooftop. Still not a soul in sight.

Stay calm. They probably don't even know where we are yet.

I move to Joe Swanson, one of our 240 gunners. "Remember, Swanny, aim low, adjust up. Got it?"

"Got it, Sarge."

"Allah! Allah!"

What was. . . .

"*Argggghh!*"

I move along the roof to look over toward the northwest. A solitary figure stands in the street. He's cloaked in shadows, but I can see his outline, rigid and tall.

He begins to chant.

A surge of terror streaks up my spine. His voice is determined and full of passion. This one's a believer.

I wonder if you're ready to die.

He steps out of the shadows and into the orange dawn's light. His stride is measured and proud. He repeats his chant. His right arm holds a belt-fed machine gun. The ammunition is wound around his left arm, Rambo-style. He curls his fingers and beckons to us to bring it on.

We stare at him, stunned. He takes no cover. He seeks no protection. He strides through the middle of the street, his machine gun ready. He acts as if it weighs nothing.

What is this man doing? He is begging to be shot. What sort of man throws his life away like this? Up until now, I've had little but contempt for our enemy. Now as I watch this man, I have to respect him. He is a warrior, a man who believes that his cause has value and is worth his life. We have that much in common.

But he still must die.

He is less than a hundred meters away now. His voice lowers, but there's not a tremor of fear in it.

When we don't know where our enemy is, we shoot downrange and wait to see what happens. This is called reconnaissance by fire. The only explanation I have for this suicidal behavior is that the muj are probing us. This lone fighter is a sacrificial lamb, baiting us to open fire and reveal our positions. It is a chilling way to employ a comrade.

We are not fighting amateurs.

The man growls and repeats his chant. I wish I knew what he was saying. Though I understand quite a bit of Arabic, I can't pick the words out.

Okay, that's enough.

"Swanson: Give this guy what he wants. End him."

The 240 roars to life, the sound like a giant zipper being ripped open. Swanson's aim is low. His first burst tears apart the asphalt right in front of the insurgent. The man turns to us and screams with rage. The raw hatred in his voice sends another chill up my spine.

The insurgent's machine gun spews fire. He's standing in the street shooting it out with Swanson, machine gun to machine gun. Swanson adjusts upward and his bullets swarm and dance around the insurgent's feet. Swanny makes another minute correction. His next burst saws the man's legs clean off. White bone exposed, the insurgent collapses onto his severed legs, finger still on his trigger. He screams in agony, but refuses to give up the fight. Blood pools around him in the street. He lays on the trigger again. Bullets spring off our house and buzz overhead.

Swanson fires again. Bullets rip into the insurgent's chest, but he refuses to die. Now Jamison McDaniel opens fire with his own 240. The scene in the street goes from grim to a carnival of gore. Steven Mathieu adds his SAW. The insurgent's PKC machine gun falls to the asphalt, the insurgent is ripped apart. Chunks of flesh spray across the road. Still, our men linger on their triggers.

"Cease fire! Cease fucking fire!"

Everyone's a little freaked, but the guns fall silent.

Hardly had our last bullet gone down-range when the world

explodes. Bullets rake the rim of our wall. An RPG sizzles across the rooftop. Everywhere I look, muzzle flashes wink from doorways, windows, and corners of buildings.

The enemy now knows where we are and what we've got. The fight is on.

I look over and see Stuckert. He has left his position to fire into the insurgent with the others.

"Stuckert," I shout, "you're not in your sector. You've got to stay in your fucking sector of fire, you hear me?"

He nods and returns to guarding the alley. It takes a lot of courage to trust your buddies and stay in your own sector, especially when the heaviest fire is coming toward the back of your neck.

The enemy is hitting us with everything he has. AK-47s bark. Machine guns rip off long bursts. Our wall becomes torn and pitted along the west and north sides. Figures dart between buildings and race across the street below. The M240s rock and roll, and their incredible firepower makes all the difference. This is standoff combat, a machine gunner's fight. The enemy is trying to pin us down so they can rush us again. We must stay up and on our guns or we will be overwhelmed.

Swanson chews through his belt of ammunition. He drops under the wall and begins to reload. The guy's a pro, very methodical, but sometimes he seems to be working in slow motion.

"Swanny, load that bitch faster! We need that gun in the fight!"

Swanson looks up at me, then something clicks. He's a great kid, a stalwart soldier, but sometimes he needs a well-placed boot up his ass to get him in gear. His hands fly over the receiver. He locks it down and is about to stand up when somebody shouts, "Rocket!"

Everyone ducks.

Fsssssssttttt—BOOM! The RPG slams into the front of the wall that protects us and explodes. Jagged chunks of concrete, masonry, and shrapnel shower us. We ignore them and come back over the rim of the wall, weapons blazing.

Misa suddenly pirouettes and falls to the roof, clutching his face. I rush to his side.

"My face got hit!" he mumbles.

A fragment of a white phosphorus tracer bullet is embedded in his cheek, hissing. His skin is boiling, and black blood is oozing from the wound. I reach up and pluck the chunk of shrapnel out with my gloved fingers. A second later, my hand feels like it's melting.

"You're good bro, okay? You're just burned. I saw that shit. You scared me, dude."

Misa, dazed, nods. His cheek looks terrible. Any open wound in a sewer like Fallujah is a magnet for infection. Misa doesn't care. He gets back to his feet and returns to the fight.

To the west, a vicious firefight breaks out around First Platoon, which is pinned on a rooftop without proper cover. Our two Bradleys shift over to help them out and are soon working their Bushmasters to the bone. Virtually our entire task force is getting rocked by this counterassault.

Michael Ware and Yuri move among us, photographing and filming the fight. Neither hesitates to expose himself to get a shot, and my respect for both of them grows. Twice, bullets ping off the rim of the wall right next to Yuri. Ware is nearly hit by an RPG. Still, they stand right behind our guys and film the return fire.

We're holding our own, but the volume of insurgent fire is growing. The enemy screams and yells around us. It is unnerving, but we shout and swear back at them. At one point, an insurgent spotter appears on a roof directly above the suicidal machine gunner. I see him point us out to his buddies.

Fuck him.

I stand up on a chair, point back, and roar, " 'I am become Death, the destroyer of worlds' . . . you fuckers!" Ware thinks this is hilarious. He knows I'm quoting Robert Oppenheimer quoting Vishnu. The insurgent doesn't get it.

Steven Mathieu, one of our SAW gunners, burns through an entire box of ammo. He takes a knee, grabs another box, and jumps back up. His gun chatters as he fires in disciplined bursts. He's one of Fitts's men and is the oldest soldier in the platoon at thirty-seven. He's hanging in there alongside the younger kids.

I catch Stuckert sneaking out of his sector again, dying to get into the fight. I kick his ass back to his spot covering the alley. He curses in frustration.

I move over to talk to Fitts, but he's nervous about the two of us being so close together. He has a point. As we're talking, a bullet hits the wall right next to his neck. He winces, ducks, and gives me a look. I know he's thinking about the three bullets he took on April 9. I try to distract him.

"Fitts, how far can you shoot those shotgun slugs?"

"I don't know."

He stands back up and pumps out six shots with his Mossberg 500, tearing up a wall 150 meters away.

"Did you see that shit?" he asks proudly. He sits back in a chair right behind his men and returns to directing the fight. Then he's up and moving around, shooting his Mossberg.

"Hey, we got a guy behind that wall!" shouts Hugh Hall as he points to a courtyard to the northwest.

Ohle and Metcalf rake the wall with their SAWs. As soon as they pause, the insurgent rushes through a gate, sending a long burst of fire our way.

Sergeant Hall preps an antitank rocket launcher.

"Fire in the hole!"

Everyone moves clear of the back blast.

Phooooossh! The rocket lances the gate. Ohle and Metcalf come up firing and catch the insurgent in the open. He dies, screaming epithets in Arabic.

Lieutenant Meno is on the radio, coordinating with Captain Sims at the command post and passing along information. But things are getting too hot. We run a very real risk of losing fire superiority. If that happens the insurgents can either swarm around us or break contact and fight another day. Either way, we lose.

Meno calls for a Brad. The only one available is Staff Sergeant Brown's. He's been in the intersection to the south covering Sergeant Ellis, whose track has no working weapons.

Brown rumbles up the street. Gossard, his gunner, unleashes the Bushmaster. The 25mm rounds blast chunks out of buildings on both sides of the street. Gossard swings his turret left and right, annihilating any insurgent foolish enough to expose himself.

Meanwhile, an insurgent force to the south starts bounding toward Ellis's Brad. He's sitting in an intersection behind the main fight, unable to defend himself. Ellis has been trying to fix his coax machine gun but is seized by stomach cramps. He searches for an MRE bag to use as a toilet, pulling his pants down while RPGs start skipping off the road around him. One explodes against the Brad's reactive armor just as his bowels unleash. He blows diarrhea all over Meno's console. Another spasm sends more all over the inside of the Brad. It reeks like a Baghdad sewage trench, and Ellis is coated in his own filth.

He continues to fight. Three insurgents appear on a nearby rooftop. Ellis swings open his hatch, draws a bead with an M16 rifle, and starts suppressing them. That rifle is now his track's main weapon.

Accurate machine-gun fire laces our wall. For a moment, we're pinned down as everyone takes cover. Then Ruiz exposes himself and screams, "Fire in the hole!" We get out of his way just as he sends an AT4 down-range. Flannery fires another one. We're using everything we've got, but the enemy is slowly gaining the upper hand.

Fitts hammers away with his shotgun. Lawson pops targets with his Vietnam-era M14 rifle and scope. We start taking more fire from the east, and as I look over there, I see several buildings taller than ours. My stomach drops. If this latest push allows the enemy to reach those platforms, they'll be able to pour fire down on us.

"Knapp!"

"Yeah, Sergeant Bell?"

I point to the nearest building to the east that is taller than ours. "Can you make that throw?"

"Sure."

I gather every frag grenade I can find and tell Knapp to go to work. Meno sees the danger and tells Brown in his Brad to pound the building Knapp is grenading. Together, they light it up and keep anyone from getting above us.

Hall spots a vehicle. "Hey! I got a white truck tucked in this dude's garage."

Misa shouts, "Can you hit it with an AT4?"

"Yeah, I got it," responds Ruiz. "Fire in the hole!"

"Get ready, go!" Misa shouts.

"Shoot that bitch!" I yell.

He shoulders an AT4. Once again, we get out of the way. The rocket sizzles down and scores a hit but doesn't explode. Brown moves up the street to allow Gossard to rip into it with his Bushmaster.

An RPG slams into our wall. The entire roof shakes from the concussion. More enemy machine guns and AKs join the fight. I can just feel it: we're right on the edge of losing fire superiority. We've got to do something quick.

"Fitts?"

"Yeah?"

"Do you think Brown would do a strafing run?"

"What are you talking about?"

"Drive all the way down to the middle of that danger area to the west, shooting everything that moves, then back up really slow. They might think he's all fucked up? Then as he passes us, we come over the rim and shoot 'em up. Do you think they'd fall for that?"

"I don't know, but it'll take a fucking stud to go down there and draw all that fire."

We get on the horn and talk to Third Platoon's beast, Staff Sergeant Cory Brown. He fights with all the tenacity of a grizzly bear. He listens to the plan and likes it. "Grizzly" needs no coaxing to get knee-deep into a brawl. The Bradley rolls forward down the street and straight into the insurgents. At first, they're astonished the Brad is counterattacking by itself. But they quickly swarm the Brad with tracers. RPGs strike the road around it. In return, Gossard uses his Bushmaster like a deadeye shot. His chattering 25mm gun swings back and forth, spewing fire. He pounds buildings, strafes rooftops, sweeps the street ahead. At times the targets are so close that he can't lower the barrel enough to get a shot at them.

Brown reaches the edge of the danger area, a big open field to our northwest. Suddenly, the track disappears in a swirling brown-gray cloud of dust and smoke. Something big just exploded.

Gonzales, Brown's driver, shifts into reverse. Slowly, the track reappears out of the dirt and smoke. He backs up toward us just as Meno gets on the radio and tells Brown to go help Ellis out. Ellis is in danger at the intersection behind us. If he gets taken out, our whole southern flank will be in trouble.

The Brad creeps in reverse, still taking fire. From out of the dust at the edge of the danger area, Fitts and I see insurgents running through the street. They think they've got a crippled Brad, and they're pushing their luck trying to bag it.

Fitts tells everyone: "Hold fire! Don't fucking shoot! Forty millimeter, then everyone else, got it?"

Santos nods. He's our best grenadier.

As Brown's Bradley continues its reverse crawl toward us, Fitts shouts, "Now!"

Santos launches a grenade. It arcs dangerously close over Brown's track and lands harmlessly over a group of seven insurgents. Slinking up the street, they spread out in an effort to surround Brown's Bradley. As the dust settles, the rest of the platoon rips into them with everything we've got. They die in the street or flee for cover.

As Brown pulls back, we see an insurgent team break cover on a roof down the street. They set up an RPG launcher beside a gigantic metal cistern and pull the trigger. The rocket streaks into the street and explodes near the Brad. They've made a terrible mistake. Not only did they miss, but Gossard and Brown have seen them.

Brown raises his TOW missile box. If there's one weapon the insurgents don't want to face in this fight, it is this antitank missile launcher. Accurate, powerful, and deadly, it is the biggest weapon in our platoon's arsenal. Some say the big wire-guided missiles went out of fashion after we stopped confronting enemies equipped with heavy mechanized armor. I say otherwise: when it comes to urban fighting, a TOW is a gift from the Pentagon gods.

The missile rushes out of the launcher like a flaming comet. The insurgents have a couple of seconds to appreciate its monstrous size hurtling down the street. A few break cover and try to get away, but it's too late. The missile explodes, blowing the cistern to fragments.

Seconds later, the few survivors make a run for it. Our guns cut down seven of them. I see Ruiz drop another with his M4. The insurgent runs out of his sandals before Ruiz shoots him in the belly. Our men cheer wildly and shout taunts.

Yet even as we celebrate, a new danger arises behind us.

From out of the industrial district on the other side of Highway 10, insurgent reinforcements rush north. Sensing they've got a cripple, they race for Ellis's Bradley. At four hundred meters, they hunker down behind some reinforced concrete barriers and start lobbing RPGs at Ellis. The rockets run to the end of their range and burst in the air around the track. Other insurgents start moving up the street in buddy teams, under the cover of the RPG barrage.

We've got to help Ellis out. Our north is quieting down. The two massacres we just accomplished seem to have driven most of our attackers off. We can afford to pull guys off the wall and move them to the other side of the roof. But we don't have a very good field of fire on the insurgents to the south. The taller house next to us to the east does, however. We need to grab that rooftop, but it isn't connected to our house. There's a body-length gap between the two buildings with a fifteen-foot drop to the concrete walk.

We've gotta get to Ellis.

I shout to Fitts, "If you have a scoped weapon, I need you on this other rooftop now. Give me a 240 and a SAW. We gotta get those dicks shooting at Ellis."

Fitts guffaws, "Whoaaaa, Bell. That is a dangerous jump—it's over five feet across, dude. Get some furniture to get across that first."

There isn't anything that will work. Then I remember the breach ladder strapped to Brown's Bradley. Before we left for Fallujah, I insisted that we bring it along. The damn thing is built out of titanium alloy and weighs sixty-five pounds. The rest of the platoon thought I was nuts for bringing it, but now we've actually got a use for it.

"Sucholas . . . Ruiz . . . go down and get the breach ladder!"

The two men scamper down the stairs. A second later, they appear in the street behind Brown's track. Just as they reach it, insurgents hiding in the compound that houses the white truck suddenly hose the street with automatic weapons. Bullets ricochet off the Bradley. Tracers zip past both my men. Ellis forgotten, Brown reacts to the fire by charging forward into it. The Brad speeds north as Gossard's Bushmaster spouts flame.

Ruiz and Sucholas are left behind, standing in the open in the middle of the street. Their cover has abandoned them.

We lay down suppressing fire. Gossard's gun tears up the truck again. He flays the compound and buildings around it. Ruiz and Sucholas start running after the Brad. It is a morbid Keystone Kops moment. The white truck finally explodes, and a greasy coil of smoke rises up from its garage. Gonzales eases off the gas and the track crawls to a halt.

Sucholas and Ruiz reach the Brad. Ruiz takes a knee and puts down fire as Sucholas jumps onto the Brad's back deck. He quickly cuts the ladder free. Together, they haul ass back to us, carrying the ladder as AK rounds snap around them and gouge the asphalt at their feet. They reach our house and throw themselves inside. A moment later, they come through the pillbox door and deliver the ladder to me.

"This is the wrong ladder, assholes. I wanted the BREACH ladder!" Pause. I start laughing at the absurdity of my own joke. They glare up at me, panting for air. To make them feel better, I toss them a couple of cigarettes. Ruiz and Sucholas deserve a short smoke break after what they just did.

We throw the breach ladder across the gulf between rooftops. It serves as a bridge to our new fighting position. McDaniel, Santos, Ruiz, Lawson, and Knapp move over to the new roof while somebody fires an RPG from a window a few doors down from the mosque. It sails past and explodes on the other side of the house. Some of the other guys reposition to the south of our first rooftop. Soon, we've got Hall, Pulley, Pratt, Meno, and me covering from our old building. Michael Ware looks on and films the action.

The insurgents continue their rocket barrage on Ellis. They're at least four hundred meters away from us, a stretch for our M4s with laser-dot sights. Our scoped weapons should handle the range better. The SAWs go to work. Ruiz sets up next to Knapp. He's got his M68 laser sight and he does an aggressive scan of the road in front of Ellis's Brad. An insurgent breaks cover next to a Texas barrier. He charges laterally across the street and fires an RPG. Ruiz bangs away at him. The insurgent ducks back behind the barrier, reloads, and comes back for more. It's a tough deflection shot, but Ruiz almost gets him this time, putting rounds on either side of his hip. The insurgent stumbles, but keeps going. He launches another RPG, then dives behind the Texas barrier again.

RPG on his shoulder, the insurgent breaks cover again. This guy has brass balls, I'll give him that. The M4 snaps, rounds crease the air inches from the guy. It looks like Ruiz has him cold now.

Clank! He runs out of ammunition.

"Goddamnit! I had that asshole!"

Just to see what would happen, Santos tries to launch a 40mm grenade to the Texas barrier. It doesn't cover the distance. Lawson and our M240 guns are our only hope of hitting these guys.

Meanwhile, to the east, an insurgent sharpshooter steps into the street. He takes aim at Private Brett Pulley, who is standing on the first rooftop, seemingly oblivious to everything going on around him. The sharpshooter's AK cracks. The bullet whines past Pulley, who doesn't react. He fires again and just misses. Pulley is a statue.

Lieutenant Meno happens to be nearby. He hears the incoming rounds, looks over to the east, and sees Pulley still unresponsive. Meno reaches over and pulls him down to the rooftop just as bullets skip off the rim of the wall right where Pulley had been standing.

Hugh Hall sees the sharpshooter, "He's right behind there!"

Before anyone else can shoot, the big sergeant drills the shooter in the sternum. The sharpshooter dies, but his buddies open fire from nearby windows and doorways. More bullets sing overhead.

Meno swings back up and unloads his rifle to the east. He hammers every window, doorway, and corner he can see. More rounds strike around him, all coming from this new direction. Our lieutenant is giving them hell. He drops his mag out, reloads, and goes back to work.

"Pulley! Launch a grenade at 'em," Meno orders.

Pulley stands back up, braces his left elbow on the wall, and lets fly with a pair of 40mm rounds. The grenades explode in quick succession. There is no more incoming from the east. Pulley's lucky to be alive. Now he's pulled his A game out of his ass.

Ellis is still in trouble. We're not having much luck reaching the insurgent rocket teams to the south behind those Texas barriers. Our guns work them over, but their RPGs continue to airburst around our Brad. Brown and his crew are still engaged on the other side of us and are unable to get to Ellis.

Finally, Sergeant First Class Cantrell arrives in his Bradley. Our platoon sergeant has been busy elsewhere, throwing his ferocity and his weight into the fight to save First Platoon. We're glad to have him back. He rolls around the corner, passes Ellis, and lets fly with a TOW. A small corner window in a building halfway down the road vanishes in smoke. The explosion of the missile and then a big secondary explosion rock the street. Cantrell and his gunner, Sergeant Brad Unterseher, have just killed an insurgent who must have had a stockpile of RPG reloads. Close behind Cantrell comes Staff Sergeant Jim, driving that glorious Abrams. First Platoon has no doubt benefited from their service. That battle's under control. Now they've come to bail us out.

Jim's gunner blows the Texas barriers apart with HEAT (high-explosive antitank) rounds. Cantrell's 25 mike-mike stitches the street where a scattered squad or two of insurgent fighters are rallying. Their attack broken, they fall back across Highway 10 and disappear into the industrial district.

All morning long, Stuckert has been babysitting his alleyway as the other guys pinch his ammo. He has yet to take a shot. Frustrated, he stayed in his sector of fire while the firefight raged around him.

Suddenly a man pops into Stuckert's alleyway. He's wearing an American Kevlar helmet and body armor. Stuckert doesn't hesitate. He trains his gun on the man and rips off a long burst. He stays on the trigger and whipsaws the barrel back and forth, raking his target. Any human being, armored or not, simply cannot take the absurd volume of lead spewing from Stuckert's SAW. The man disappears in the fusillade.

Stuckert is finally in the game. He turns to the other guys, smiles and nods, then reloads. He looks at Flannery and laughs.

"Hey Flan-tastic. You like that shit? You like that, huh?"

Stuckert is calmly pleased with things now. Not me. Stuckert's victim was wearing our gear. While we did get intel that this would be happening, I fear we've killed one of our own. I do a quick head count. Fitts notices it and says, "Hey, Sarge, he did good. Stuckert did good. We're all here."

I nod. Fitts addresses the platoon, "Hey, this fucking enemy of ours is wearing our shit, men."

Well, at least we know two hundred rounds from a SAW will negate Kevlar helmets and body armor.

We've stopped the enemy cold. His counterattack failed, thanks to the timely arrival of the Brads. Had it not been for our tracks and Sergeant Jim's tank, we would have been in real trouble.

As it is, I'm concerned that the first thrust came from our rear to the north. How'd they get behind us? We had cleared that entire neighborhood and didn't see a soul while dismounted. Yet they managed to work their way behind us in force.

We know we face a crafty, skilled enemy. We've seen them bound in two-man buddy teams. They move with fire elements covering their advance. These guys aren't the raw Mahdi militiamen we killed in Muqdadiyah. They are a military force.

Yet we've scored a significant victory this morning. We suffered only one slight wound and killed many, many bad guys. More importantly, we withstood a multidirectional attack for over three and a half hours. I'm proud of my men, and my confidence in them is cemented by their actions today.

My own confidence grows. This morning, I was a leader. I walked the firing line, encouraging and directing the men. When we needed to expand our fields of fire, we were flexible and figured out a way onto the other rooftop. I never triggered my own weapon; I was too busy managing my boys. Fallujah is turning me into a real squad leader. I take pride in that.

The last AK fire drains away. Our guns fall silent, their barrels smoking in the cold morning air. Bucket loads of 5.56mm brass click and tinkle underfoot.

It is time for us to continue the advance. Although there is more mopping up to do, securing Highway 10 is crucial to cutting Fallujah's resistance in half.

CHAPTER TWELVE

The Stay Puft Marshmallow Cock

They're following us.

Not five minutes after we leave the house to mount up in our Brads, the muj flow around into the alleys and side streets. From a safe standoff distance, they watch our convoy, they pace our southern advance on parallel roads, they nip at our coattails just out of our reach. Sergeant Jim's tank leads the way while the rest of us follow inside our Brads. My track, Staff Sergeant Brown's, is a mess. The strafing runs Brown executed in the fight left our Brad severely bullet-scarred. Two of the dismount viewports are destroyed, and all the gear on the exterior has been punctured. Nevertheless, he has ample fuel and plenty of ammo for the Bushmaster. Brown and his crew are more than ready for another fight.

In column formation, we drive down the southern road past the ruins of the Texas barriers Jim destroyed with his 120mm. We've moved four hundred meters from our rooftop redoubt. Around us, insurgents dart from corner to corner, always just out of our vision and range. It is an *Escape from New York* scene that leaves us tense and adrenaline-filled.

We reach a three-way intersection with a frontage road that

stretches out east-west parallel to Highway 10. Highway 10 has been designated "Phase Line Fran." It is our main objective in Fallujah. We've reached it less than twelve hours after breaching the city's northern berm.

Gossard and the other Bradley gunners rake the buildings around us, prepping the area with high-explosive rounds fired into windows and doors.

We dismount into the silent street and enter a beautiful house right on the edge of the highway. It is three stories tall, and the second floor opens onto a rooftop balcony that covers at least a thousand square feet. An exterior stairwell gives us access to the roof over the third floor, providing an excellent view of the area around us.

We get word that First Platoon has reached Highway 10 as well. They set up in a building about five hundred meters to our west. Captain Sims establishes his command post between us. Again, we form a solid front, but our position lacks depth. And this time we know the enemy is swarming around our rear and flanks. We can't stop them. Where the Marine battalion on our western flank is, we have no idea. Fortunately, the muj stay at arm's length and refuse to expose themselves. They seem content to be shadows.

Lieutenant Meno sets up on the roof of the second floor. Pratt takes McDaniel and a 240 Bravo machine gun up to the third-floor roof. Part of my squad heads up there with them. Fitts and I set up 360-degree security as Michael Ware pulls out his satellite phone and tries to hook up to CNN for a live broadcast. Fitts and I have no interest in CNN, so we duck into the house and plop into a couple of plastic chairs. We might as well take advantage of the stillness of the moment. I pull out a precious cigarette and light it. Fitts pulls out a Black & Mild cigar Sergeant Hall gave him. For the moment, we sit and inhale in relative tranquility.

The walls around us are ripped from shrapnel strikes. Aside from these two chairs, not a piece of furniture is intact. Cabinets look like Swiss cheese. Glass litters the floor, and every dish and decoration is in pieces.

These are the telltale signs of Gossard's work on the Bushmaster. He prepped this house before we dismounted and did a superb job, placing each high-explosive round in the corners of the rooms he targeted. By hitting the corners, he maximized the blast effect. He made every shot count and saved ammo.

Outside on the second-floor roof, Michael Ware makes contact with CNN. He starts his first on-the-scene report for the network. Yuri sits beside him. The quiet around us enhances the clarity of Ware's transmission.

That is, until a lone gunman appears on the frontage road. He walks into the open, weapon at the ready. The insurgents are reconning by sacrifice again. The platoon doesn't hesitate. The rooftops explode with machine-gun fire and the sharp crack of our rifles. The muj runs for it, bullets chasing him all the way. A hundred and fifty rounds later, he's facedown on the asphalt, his body peppered and torn.

Tracers zing into us from a position to the northeast. Our men on the third floor return fire. More fire opens up from the northwest, near the mosque we've just cleared. As we moved south, the insurgents must have moved back into that area. This is not a good sign. We didn't have the time to destroy all the supplies and equipment we found there.

An insurgent dashes from an alleyway toward the mosque. He's got an M16 slung over one shoulder, a Kevlar helmet on his head, and an olive drab chest protector. He even has neck and groin protectors attached to his body armor.

The men hesitate, unsure if he's an Iraqi soldier or an insurgent. Nobody has seen an enemy fighter with an M16 before. He sprints for a building across the road and to our north. As he runs, our men see he's wearing U.S. Army–issued boots and an American desert camouflage shirt under his body armor.

He's also carrying a car battery.

The platoon opens fire, but it's too late. He ducks inside the building and disappears.

Michael Ware has just been handed the opportunity of a lifetime. He's live with CNN, and our current firefight lends drama and excitement to his report. He's on the satellite phone, talking in rushes between bursts of gunfire.

A deafening thunderclap engulfs our house. Then another. And another. My chair snaps, and I tumble to the floor. Fitts crashes down next to me as a massive concussion wave blasts through the room. The floor quakes. Shrapnel scythes the walls and ceiling. Smoke billows out through the windows. I try to sit up, but another explosion rocks the building, casting shards of metal into the room.

I lie flat and just try to stay alive amid the debris. One more gigantic detonation slams our building and shakes it violently. I wonder if the walls will collapse. I'm dimly aware that the men outside are firing furiously. I have to get out there.

The smoke begins to clear. The walls are scored with new scars. The windows had briefly been funnels of death. Had Fitts or I been behind them, it would have been lights out. We are lucky to be alive. The collapsing chair probably saved me from harm.

We scramble to the second-floor roof, where I find Ohle behind his SAW. He sends a long, angry burst up the road to the north. I am relieved to see every soldier safe behind the sturdy cover of the roof's parapet. I can't make out what is happening on the roof above, but their weapons are barking enough for me to think that everyone must be okay.

"What are we shooting at?" I ask Ohle.

"There's a fucking dude. He went into that house over there."
Ohle pauses, points, then gets back behind his SAW.

The entire block is shrouded in smoke. Telephone poles
have snapped like toothpicks. The road we came down is pockmarked with holes. Chunks of asphalt lie scattered around. To
the west, an entire building is little more than a burning heap of
rubble. Bullets that were inside the building periodically cook
off from the heat of the blast, sending lead in random directions.

The M16-armed muj has devastated this neighborhood. He
had wired up his battery and detonated more than ten massive
explosive devices all at once. Half of them were strapped to the
telephone poles at our Bradley commanders' eye-level. Others
were embedded in the road or hidden alongside. The multilevel
explosive ambush created a typhoon of steel in the street.
There's not one building in sight left intact; all are riddled with
shrapnel holes and most have big gouges torn out of their walls.

But the topper was the final explosion. The house that is now
burning was one big improvised explosive device. Had we chosen it as our next foothold, we would all be dead. Once again, a
single insurgent could have killed our entire platoon.

A heavy machine gun opens up on us. It rakes the street
beside our house. It seems like small potatoes now. We try to suppress the gunner, but we can't see him. We're not even sure
which building he's using for cover. Our weapons rattle. The firefight is on.

Fortunately, a Bradley is close at hand. Here comes Brown,
rolling up the shattered street. The turret spins. The Bushmaster
booms. The insurgents respond with RPG fire. A rocket whips
right over Brown's head and blows up in a house across the
street. Brown is unfazed. He stays put while Gossard pours
rounds into enemy positions.

At the same time, our company's forward observer, Sergeant

Shaun Juhasz, sees movement across Highway 10. Insurgents are creeping up to firing positions to the south of us. Juhasz calls in an artillery fire mission. Seconds later, the air is full of the *whoosh . . . booom!* of 155mm shells. It is the first time since we entered the city that we've had our own indirect support, and Captain James Cobb, our task force fire support officer, lays it on thick. Soon, the buildings in the industrial districts of the south side of Highway 10 are smothered in smoke and flames.

On the roof, we unload grenades onto the enemy to the north. Knapp adds a few frags to the mix, just to liven things up a bit. This fire and the presence of Brown's Brad finally convince the muj to break contact again. As the 155 shells fall behind us, the incoming from the north ceases.

The artillery barrage peters out. The fight is over.

"Was that guy the enemy or was someone from your media pool running batteries to you," I jokingly ask Michael Ware.

"That was crazy, mate. Just blew up out of nowhere."

I hear a shuffling noise and turn to see Sergeant Alan Pratt coming toward me.

He is walking with an exaggerated bowlegged sidle that looks ridiculous. I crack up and give him a big smile, glad that he can go for a laugh even in the midst of all this.

"Sergeant Bell," Pratt says in a weak voice, "I'm hit. I been shot."

"What?"

He limps toward me, leaving boot prints in blood in his wake. The levity we'd felt just a second before evaporates. Pratt really is hit.

We all rush to him. He's in tremendous pain. Blood covers his pants and both hands.

"What the fuck is going on?" I shout up to the third-floor roof.

"Sergeant Pratt's been hit," Sucholas calls back.

Thanks for fucking telling us.

Medic Lucas "Doc" Abernathy eases Pratt into the house. We lay him down and the Oklahoman goes to work on him. I cradle Pratt's head. The worst thing possible for a wounded soldier is to see his own wounds. I hold his head so he can't look down.

Doc cuts away Pratt's pants.

Pratt writhes in pain. "It's my dick!"

He tries to look down. I fight him and keep his head up.

But I look down.

"Oh my God! Pratt, you're hung like a Lincoln conspirator."

He smiles a little through the pain. "Yeah. . . ."

Doc is focused on his patient and Pratt is in no mood to laugh. *So much for keeping everyone loose.*

Then I see why Doc is so engrossed. Embedded in the side of Pratt's penis is part of a dead-bolt lock from an exterior gate. When the building exploded, he was standing on the third-floor roof. Bits of the house, gate, and wall from across the street acted like shrapnel and blew across to us. Pratt was in the way.

Doc Abernathy eases the chunk of lock out of Pratt's flesh. Sergeant Pratt takes my hand and squeezes it. It is slick with blood and slips out of my grasp.

"Sergeant Bell, I know it's my dick!"

"Pratt, It's fine. You got hit in the leg."

"Don't lie to me, Sergeant Bell. My dick hurts!"

He grabs my hand again, but we're both slippery with blood now, and again I can't hold on to him. I wipe my hand, reach for his, and try to keep him calm as Doc Abernathy continues to work.

Doc really impresses me. He works methodically, but fast and professionally. He locates another wound. Pratt took some shrapnel in the scrotum, and the tear it left is bleeding pretty seriously. Doc fights to staunch it.

Pratt closes his eyes and grimaces in agony. He is terrified that he might have lost his equipment, but he doesn't moan. He endures. He's a man.

Ware and Yuri come inside and snap photos. Pratt opens his eyes, and I see he's in despair.

"My God, it hurts so fucking bad. . . ."

I look up at Ware. "Hey dude, what the fuck? You're not gonna take pictures of him."

Ware promises, "I won't put this in the magazine . . . you won't see his face."

"Come on. Now is not the fucking time, dude."

"We want to show what you guys are sacrificing."

"You could publish these."

Ware shakes his head. "I'd never do that, mate. This is about the sacrifice. . . ."

He clicks a few more photos. Pratt tries to retain his dignity by conquering his pain with remarkable self-discipline. He doesn't complain. He doesn't scream. He takes it.

This kid is a fucking stud.

Doc Abernathy pours Betadine over both wounds. I cannot even imagine how much that would hurt.

Doc reaches for some gauze and starts to bandage the shrapnel wound on his scrotum. Meno gets on the radio to Cantrell, who is nearby in a Bradley. Meno's outside on the roof, but I overhear him say, "Pratt's shot."

Cantrell's voice booms back, "Who's hit? Who's fucking hit?"

I stand up and move to the roof, then key my mike, "Sergeant Cantrell, Blue Three Alpha is hit."

"Fuck the feeder card. Fuck his battle roster number! Just tell me who the fuck it is!" roars Cantrell. He's beside himself with fury.

"It's Pratt," I say.

"Pratt?"

"Yes, Pratt."

Cantrell's great weakness is his temper. It is directly tied to his feelings for his platoon. He loves us. When he hears one of us has been hit, it is like a knife to his gut.

He starts calling in a medevac dustoff to get Pratt out of here.

"Blue Seven, this is Blue Two. He's got shrapnel wounds to . . . near . . . the groin, genitals. Negative gunshot, shrapnel wounds in the dick zip code."

Pratt looks up. "What'dja say, Sergeant Bell?"

Fitts looks down. "You're good, Pratt."

I reaffirm, "Seven, let me get more info."

Cantrell demands answers. "Where is he injured? How serious?"

"Priority, possibly urgent—" I pause, and then add, "depending on what you call a limb."

I am trying to be serious. The rule for calling in an air medevac is "life, limb, or eyesight." I'm not sure what category Pratt's wound falls under, but I do know we need to get him to the battalion aid station fast.

Cantrell is now confused and enraged. He shouts into the radio, "Bellavia, what the fuck are you talking about?"

I walk away from Pratt and look over the roof at Sergeant Cantrell standing chest high out of his turret. His screams are hitting me a nanosecond after his mouth moves.I whisper to him, "His cock. He's got wounds to his cock, Sarge."

"What are you whispering? What the fuck is wrong with you? We're going to ground-evac Pratt. Get him down here," Cantrell says.

I walk back inside. Doc Abernathy is furiously wrapping Pratt's penis in gauze.

"Hey, Sergeant Cantrell wants to load up and take him to the cloverleaf. Let's get him on the litter and out of here," I tell Doc.

As I say that, Pratt becomes desperate. "No! NO! I'm good! I'm good to go!"

Unfortunately, Cantrell hears Pratt over Lieutenant Meno's radio and loses his mind. "WHAT THE FUCK DO YOU MEAN HE'S GOOD?"

I try to calm Cantrell down. "He's trying to be a hero, Sarge. He's not good. The kid is outta this fight. He's outta this fight, okay?"

Pratt refuses to accept this. "I can still fight! I CAN STILL FIGHT!"

Fitts remarks, "Pratt, you have no fucking pants on. How're you gonna be in this fight? Did you bring an extra pair of pants?"

"I did, Sergeant Fitts. I did! They're in the Bradley. I'm good."

Sucholas shows up. He's been on the third-floor rooftop this entire time. "Hey, Sergeant Fitts, Pratt was hit during the explosions. There's a shitload of blood up here. I've been pouring dirt on it."

Pratt looks waxy and wan.

"Pratt, you've lost a lot of blood. We're gonna get you outta here. We're not gonna fuck around with this one, okay?"

Lawson comes in, looks Pratt over, and agrees. "We need to get him out of here."

Pratt resigns himself to his fate. Doc Abernathy finishes bandaging his penis. It looks like a cast, and there's so much gauze and weight to it that when we get Pratt on his feet, it bends so far down he begins bleeding again. We ease him back onto the floor. Doc needs to immobilize the wound.

He slings Pratt's penis to his stomach. Everyone marvels at this. It looks like he's got a third arm wrapped in a cast.

"Dude, you should be a porn star."

Pratt offers a sickly grin.

Fitts says, "Okay, gut his shit. We need the ammo."

We take Pratt's ammo, night vision, and body-armor insert plates. He also has an M4 with a telescopic sight. I've got no scope on my rifle, so I grab it.

Cantrell hollers, "Retards! I'm waiting. Get his ass down here, meatballs!"

I move to the roof and peer over into the street. The platoon sergeant's got his Bradley parked right next to our front door. He's waiting impatiently, rage boiling. He makes eye contact from the commander's hatch and keys his mike. A half second later, his voice blasts through my radio, "Get your shit together, Sergeant Bell, and tell me what the fuck is happening!"

"He's coming down now, Sarge."

A moment later, Pratt walks outside to the Bradley. Cantrell looks down at him as the men load him aboard the track. His eyes flick back up to me on the roof. He scowls, tosses his cigarette over the side, and looks like he's about to chew my head off.

Instead, he howls with laughter. The absurdity of a stomach-slung penis is too much even for our platoon sergeant. I relax a little as Fitts comes up along side me.

"He looks like the Stay Puft Marshmallow Cock." I say, laughing.

"Frosty the Snow Dick."

Getting hit in the crotch is every soldier's worst nightmare. We can either dwell on it and drive ourselves crazy, or make fun of it. Laughter is our only defense.

Our battalion surgeon is a major named Lisa DeWitt. We all regard her as a maternal figure in our infantry battalion. The thought of her being confronted with Pratt's injury leaves Fitts and me in stitches. I say to him, "When Major DeWitt sees him on the operating table . . . they don't teach you to wrap a dick in any field manual I've read."

The Brad lumbers down the street, bound for our battalion aid station at the cloverleaf east of Fallujah. It is also where most of the reporters are hanging out. Pratt is sure to attract attention when he arrives. A lot of attention.

Poor bastard.

Fitts and I climb to the third-floor roof, and the sight there stops our laughter cold. Sucholas wasn't kidding. There's blood all over the roof and parapet. Spatters of it are everywhere. Pratt was wounded right at the beginning of the engagement. He stood with his brothers, ignored his wounds, and stayed in the fight. He fired his M4 until the enemy melted away. For fifteen minutes, Pratt bled through his crotch without thought of the consequences to himself.

I'd had my problems with Pratt in the past. He'd been in my squad at the start of the deployment. I thought he got a little complacent. Then he became a team leader in our weapons squad, and he did a good job. But now, as I look over the evidence of his selflessness, I realize Pratt had something in him beyond common courage. He loved this platoon. This last act with us was the ultimate display of that love. He refused to leave his brothers. He could have bled out and died on the roof. Yet he didn't say a word until after the fight was over.

Sergeant Alan Pratt of Philadelphia became my hero that day.

CHAPTER THIRTEEN

Where Feral Dogs Feed

As dusk begins to snuff out our first full day in the city, Michael Ware decides to make his presence felt. I don't know what prompts this. Perhaps it was the sight of Pratt bleeding. Perhaps he feels a connection to the men he has spent so much time with while covering the war in Iraq. Or maybe he's just trying to make sure he and Yuri survive.

It starts while Ware is still talking on his satellite phone. Lieutenant Meno gathers up the platoon's leaders to give us a chalk talk. Team leaders and officers hover around him. Meno tells us we've been given a warning order to move into a new area late tonight. We study the area on our maps. We know it already— we've got to countermarch north and re-clear the areas we had passed through earlier. We've got to eliminate the threat to our rear.

At one point, I glance up over my map and see Ware shutting off his phone. "Hey, whaddya say? Did the Marines catch up?" I ask.

"Mate, they are way the fuck up there. Some units are stymied and barely in the city. Just on the outer edge."

"Marines. Twenty years from now the Army will have never

been in Fallujah. You watch. Just like Guadalcanal, Saipan, and Okinawa. The Army was never there. Whole Pacific campaign was Marine led, Marine fought. General MacArthur? He wasn't Army either. All bullshit."

Fitts loves to talk about Marine conspiracy just as much as he enjoys sharing his hatred of the officer corps. He doesn't miss a beat to sink his teeth into my bait.

"My granddad got gut shot at Okinawa. He was Army infantry. Sat on that beachhead for two days until they found him. Wasn't ever the same fucking man after that. Let me hear someone tell me the Army wasn't at Okinawa."

"He wasn't there. You are a fucking liar. That never fucking happened. The Army never fought in the Pacific. And furthermore, we are not fighting here in Fallujah. This is a simulator at Fort Benning, you're all part of a *Jacob's Ladder*–type experiment, Dr. Bigsby," I cup my hands and scream off into the wall. "Run that firefight over again, this time let Pulley actually fucking do something of significance for his nation." Our platoon, Pulley included, are now all openly laughing at the absurdity of this entire bit. Fitts and I have once again taken stress off the minds of young soldiers.

"Where are the Marines, again? Hall asks Ware after we all settle down.

"All the way north," Ware tells him.

Meno hears Ware and stops what he's doing. "Sir, did you say that the Marines are barely in the city?"

"Call me Mick. And yes, I just got off the phone with reporters over there by them, and they tell me they are barely in the city. And some other units are stymied near the outer edge of the city."

Meno goes downstairs and grabs the radio. If what he says is true, then Mick has just given us better intelligence than Captain Sims is getting from battalion.

At that moment, everyone present realizes the importance of

Staff Sergeant Colin Fitts (right) and me during a routine patrol.
(Photo from author's collection)

My Second Squad. From left to right, Raymond Cullins (covered by weeds), John Ruiz (face concealed), Sergeant Allan Pratt, Michael Gross, Doc Lucas Abernathy. Staff Sergeant Fitts and I are in the back pulling security. *(Photo from author's collection)*

Command Sergeant Major Steven Faulkenburg.
(Photo from author's collection)

Third Platoon barber and Bradley gunner, Sergeant Chad Ellis, gives Staff Sergeant Cory "Grizzly" Brown a haircut. *(Photo from author's collection)*

Sergeant First Class James Cantrell in a less than jovial mood.
(Photo from author's collection)

Corporal Piotr Sucholas (left) and Specialist John Ruiz relax before another mission, May 2004 at FOB Normandy, Muqdadiyah, Iraq. *(Photo from author's collection)*

First Lieutenant Joaquin Meno. *(Photo courtesy of John Reynolds, LTC, USA)*

Captain Sean Sims (right) gives a thumb's up after a skirmish in sector, with A Company First Sergeant Peter Smith, March 2004 at FOB Normandy, Muqdadiyah, Iraq. *(Photo from author's collection)*

Lieutenant Colonel Peter Newell addresses his Task Force 2-2 Infantry the morning of the assault on Fallujah. *(Photo courtesy of John Reynolds, LTC, USA)*

Sergeant First Class John Ryan, Captain Jeff Jager, First Sergeant Peter Smith, Captain Sean Sims. *(Photo courtesy of John Reynolds, LTC, USA)*

Sergeant Garth Sizemore (glasses, in front) leads a squad from First Platoon, A Company, into battle in the industrial district of Fallujah. Sizemore would lose his life to enemy fire in October, 2006, on his second tour in Iraq.
(Photo courtesy of Stefan Zaklin EPA / Corbis)

Specialists John Bandy (top right), Pedro Contreras (middle), and another soldier secure a massive structure in Fallujah. *(Photo courtesy of Stefan Zaklin EPA / Corbis)*

Staff Sergeant Scott Lawson pulls security from a Fallujah rooftop with his Vietnam-era M14 rifle with scope. To his left is Sergeant Warren Misa. *(Photo from author's collection)*

Sawgunners from left to right: Jim Metcalf, Steven Mathieu, Matthew Woodberry, Brett Pulley, and Manimal Sergeant Hugh Hall. *(Photo courtesy of John Reynolds, LTC, USA)*

Sergeant Warren Misa and Specialist Lance Ohle (right) over watch from an insurgent's makeshift window barricade in Fallujah. *(Photo from author's collection)*

First Lieutenant Meno, Sergeant Jose Rodriguez, Specialist John Ruiz, Sergeant Chuck Knapp. *(Photo courtesy of John Reynolds, LTC, USA)*

Highway 10 overlooking Fallujah's bloody industrial district, November 11, 2004. *(Photo from author's collection)*

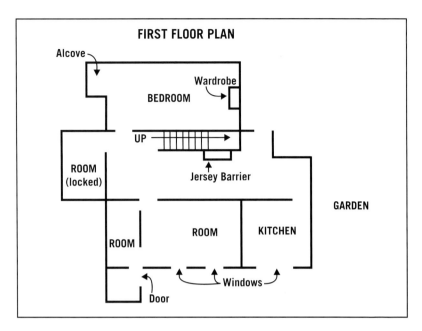

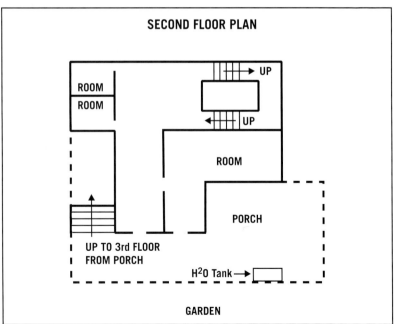

Floor plan of the house contested on November 11, 2004.

Michael Ware. He may be a media type, but he has intelligence that is vital to us. More importantly, he has no problem sharing it with us.

My interest in Ware grows. I offer him and Yuri a cigarette. "So you guys have been around the block. Was today in the top ten best fights you've ever seen?"

Yuri is so quiet, I don't think I've ever heard him say anything before. Another member of the media pool mentioned Yuri was actually captured by mujahideen forces in Afghanistan during the Soviet invasion in the 1980s. He nods in response to my question. "Good fight."

Ware adds, "In Samarra, things got pretty hairy. At one point we were crawling through body parts. It was pretty terrible, mate."

"That fucking sucks," says Misa. His cheek wound looks raw and ugly. It leaches black ooze. White phosphorus is just terrible stuff. My guess is that it's already infected.

Ware continues, "But as far as volume of fire, there was a lot today. But sheer danger factor, I don't know. You seemed to be handling it. Samarra seemed more dangerous."

Yuri nods his head.

I'm thinking about what he's just said when Ware offers," I will tell you this: this enemy is not done. Not by a long stretch. These men out there, they are here to kill you or die trying."

"You were here in April. What's different now?" Fitts asks.

Ware considers his response. Yuri stares at nothing.

We've got 360 security set up, and all is quiet for the moment. I sit down and light another cigarette. I've always considered the reporters and journalists to be little more than whores. They'll whore us out for whatever story they can get out of us. And they never care. Maybe Ware is different.

Ware finally tells Fitts, "Look. These are brazen, calculated, and organized fighters. They're not the boys who were here in April. These are foreigners, or battle-tested Sunnis from around the country. But they are certainly not the boys you have over in Diyala."

"Yeah, I hear that," Knapp replies. Ware's right. There is a level of professionalism in these guys we have not seen before.

Ware looks into my eyes and says, "They're here for one reason: to die in jihad. That's it."

We're silent. Ware continues. "They know they can't win. Look at all the firepower they face. But they'll take out as many of you as they can before they die. That's their whole reason for being."

The more Ware talks, the more surprised I become by his confidence in his assessment. Ware is giving us a lecture. And the more he speaks, the more we all realize he knows what he is talking about.

Ware launches into a story about the insurgents he's met. Early on, in 2003, he would sit and drink beer with them and smoke. They talked about money, girls, soccer, and Pan-Arabism. A year after the invasion, though, things have changed. Those who have survived have been radicalized. They wear beards down to their chests and quote the Koran. They don't drink with him anymore. They speak only of God and destiny. They've become jihadists.

We're not fighting nationalists here. We're fighting extremists infected with a virulent form of Islam. They seek not only to destroy us here in Iraq, but to destroy American power and influence everywhere. They revile our culture and want it swept clean, replaced with Sharia law. The cruelties of Taliban rule in Afghanistan showed us all what that meant.

Ware notices he has his audience's complete attention. He takes the opportunity to segue into a discourse on the different groups we are fighting in Fallujah. He talks about Hezbollah, and the type of training the Iranian Revolutionary Guard gives to the insurgents. That leads him into a tactical discussion. He compares the insurgents who fought in Samarra to those in Najaf. He speaks of the Iranian influence on Sunni Wahhabis. He goes on to explain how Hezbollah-trained squads sometimes carry nothing but RPGs and move without detection. When they attack, they volley-fire their RPGs, then fan out as they retreat. These are all the things Fitts and I have talked about for months, have heard through the infantry grapevine. But I am impressed to hear the same things from a journalist.

And then there are the insurgents' ambush tactics. Ware has seen or heard of them all. He explains how they'll probe an American unit just to get a response. Then the probing element will break contact and withdraw with the hope that the Americans will chase them. If the Americans do give chase, they'll run smack into a horseshoe-shaped or L-shaped ambush and get blown away.

In Fallujah, we face an insurgent global all-star team. It includes Chechen snipers, Filipino machine gunners, Pakistani mortar men, and Saudi suicide bombers. They're all waiting for us down the street.

Ware is an authority on the enemy. He knows more about them than our own intelligence officers. I hang on every word and try to remember everything he tells us. It is the best, most comprehensive discussion I've heard about the enemy since arriving in Iraq.

And it comes from a fucking reporter.

The conversation continues until it is almost dark. Our lieutenant breaks it up by asking me to take a patrol north to check out the house into which the battery-carrying, M16-wielding insurgent ran at lunchtime. We've been tasked by battalion headquarters with doing Battle Damage Assessment (BDA), which I learned to hate in April during the battles in Muqdadiyah.

I gather my squad, and we hit the street. Our plan is to take down another house to the north with a better view of the insurgents' last known position. Above us, Fitts, Lawson, and the gunners provide cover. A Brad is just down the road behind us. We hustle along the splintered asphalt, dodging craters and debris from the blasts.

Just before we get to the house, a barrage of fire stops us cold.

"That fuck is still alive in there!"

That's it. Screw the BDA. I call Staff Sergeant Brown on the radio, and his Brad lumbers up the road to our position. We back off as he pounds the house. Gossard takes careful aim and shoots out all the house's support pillars. The roof collapses and the entire house folds in on itself. Scratch at least one insurgent.

Up the street we see another insurgent sprint across the craggy road surface. We shoot at him and miss. This is one determined son of a bitch. He breaks cover again and slips into a building, where he takes potshots at us from a window.

We withdraw back to our foothold in the three-story house. When we get back, Fitts is still trying to suppress another insurgent to the northeast from the roof.

"Santos!" I shout.

"Yeah, Sarge?"

"Prep a Javelin."

The Javelin is the largest antitank missile we have at our disposal. If we do this right, we may be able to collapse the whole building on the bastard. The Javelin has two different firing settings: one for shooting the missile straight into a target on a flat trajectory, and another that arcs the missile high, to plummet down from above. We settle on the latter. We've never fired one like this before.

Santos preps the Javelin. He moves to the parapet and takes aim.

"I'm ready when you are!"

The Javelin spears the growing darkness with a tail of orange-white flame as it races down the street. Suddenly, it swerves straight up and then plunges down through the roof of the target house. It penetrates deep into the structure before it explodes. Black smoke spools out over the impact site as things inside the house get blasted through the windows.

A torn rag slaps into the street. More pieces crash around it. Debris rains down all over the block. Did we kill him?

His return fire stops, but that doesn't mean anything.

We've gotta go over there for BDA. It isn't worth risking the men.

A dog appears in the street near the heaps of rags that were blown from the house. His lips are curled back, his ears pinned. He's one of hundreds of feral dogs roving Fallujah. We've seen them all around us, but normally, they keep their distance and watch us in silence. He takes a few more steps toward the rags, sniffing the air warily as he moves. His temerity encourages others. Soon, three or four dogs are in the street with the original. I watch them, curious to see what they're doing.

They're feeding.

The rags are the shredded remains of the insurgent. The dogs gnaw and tear at his flesh. One comes up, his snout smeared in gore. They're ravenous. My stomach flutters.

"The dogs are fucking eating that dude," I hear somebody say.

The dogs fill their bellies.

"Well," I manage, holding tight to my stomach, "there's our BDA now."

We stare in horror. Suddenly, a wave of gunfire breaks over us from the south. Private McDaniel's machine gun chatters a reply. We're taking fire from the industrial area again.

We forget the dogs and swing to the southern end of the roof. Across Highway 10, we can see muzzle-flashes winking at us from a run-down warehouse. At least a dozen insurgents are holed up there.

This is actually really foolish of them. They've chosen to get into a fire exchange with a mechanized infantry platoon, using nothing but small-arms fire. Two platoons, actually: First Platoon sees these guys as well, and they've opened up on them.

I walk up to McDaniel, "See that warehouse? I want you to shoot! Shoot! Shoot!"

McDaniel's 240 stutters and bucks. Swanson shows up with his 240 and gets into the fight as well. The warehouse is 450 meters away, really too far for our SAWs and M4s. The machine guns will do the work this time.

I get between them and act as their spotter. "Z!" I shout.

The gunners swing their barrels back and forth, making intersecting Z patterns across the warehouse. They hold their triggers down. The machine guns spew rounds. I help them adjust fire by smacking their shoulders. A smack on the left means ease more to the left. A smack on the head means shoot higher. It is the only way to communicate when the guns are rocking. It is almost impossible to shout over them.

Fewer muzzle flashes wink at us now. Every time McDaniel and Swanson sweep their guns across the windows, the counterfire grows weaker and weaker. It is just like a giant, real-life video game.

The Brads roll up and their Bushmasters go to work. The insurgents in the warehouse are about to get a tutorial on the effects of American firepower. It is awe-inspiring. The 240s tear chunks out of the warehouse. The 25 mike-mike rounds blast holes and send shrapnel spinning deep into the building's interior. We lace the evening sky with streaming red tracers. The streaks lace across and through each other, forming what looks like an intricate laser light show.

Sergeant Juhasz gets into the act. He seizes his radio and calls in a fire mission. Eighty-one millimeter mortar fire soon falls on the insurgents. Juhasz adjusts, then orders fire for effect. The mortar rounds plunge into the buildings around the warehouse. In seconds, an entire city block is ablaze. Juhasz adjusts fire again. A decrepit building collapses under the barrage.

And then, just as the last shreds of daylight are pulled over the horizon, Team Tank rolls down Highway 10. Each Abrams cruises arrogantly. They are the baddest motherfuckers in this valley, and they fear no evil. They're on their way west on a mission of their own and just happened to drive into our firefight. Obligingly, they pause to help us out. The tanks train their turrets to the south. Their 120mm tubes spew flames. The warehouse is smothered by smoke and fire. One by one, the four tanks take their shots before driving on into the city.

When the last one departs, the enemy is silent. Those who survived break contact. Juhasz stops the mortar barrage. First Platoon ceases fire. Once again, we're bathed in the beauty of a silent battlefield. Our ears ring, but the quiet is more than welcome. All of us are hard of hearing now, thanks to all the heavy weapons we've been around these past twenty-four hours.

I look over at Ware. He's filmed much of the firefight from a position between our machine gunners and the wall. He hasn't hesitated to expose himself. Yuri is the same way. They'll do almost anything to capture the action.

We stay alert and keep security up at every corner of our rooftops. Yet as the evening grows long, the enemy stays clear of our position. Just before midnight, we get word that Lieutenant Colonel Newell has hot chow waiting for us at the cloverleaf. Cantrell sends two soldiers from each squad and a pair of Bradleys to go pick up the food.

While we wait for them to return, I take a few minutes to try to clean myself up. We've got precious little water, so tonight I make do with a whore's bath.

Later, I return to the second-floor roof to listen to Michael Ware regale the men with more stories of the insurgents he's met. The Brads return, and the soldiers get their food. Lieutenant Meno, Fitts, Lawson, and I wait. A good leader never eats before his men, no matter what the situation.

Ware and Yuri dig in. Stuckert comes by and hands me a meal, then moves on down the roof.

"Hey, did you hear that the sergeant major got killed?"

I freeze. Food forgotten, I turn to see Stuckert talking to a couple of the other Joes.

". . . Killed by a sniper, man."

What?

I explode with fury. "STUCKERT!" I scream. He cringes, but turns to me.

"Yeah, Sergeant Bell?"

"Listen, you fat piece of fucking shit: What the fuck are you talking about? You don't know dick about what is going on outside this rooftop. You don't know that he's fucking dead, got it?"

"Sarge, I heard some support guys talking about Sergeant Major Faulkenburg dying while I was at the cloverleaf," he says weakly.

I lose it. All self-control out the window, I lay into Stuckert. As I scream and shout at him, my mouth froths, and I spray him with spit. Yuri and Ware stare at me with shocked expressions on their faces. If they weren't so hungry, I'm sure they'd beat a retreat off the roof.

"I hear you mention his name again, Stuckert, so help me fucking God, I will take your soul. You hear me? You're spreading rumors and fucking gossip. You don't know shit!"

I've never been this angry in my life. I want to throttle the kid. I want to beat him raw. I want to inflict the kind of pain on him that his words have just inflicted on me. It's because I know they're true. And right now, I can't handle that.

"Sorry, Sergeant Bell. That's just what I heard." Stuckert's face is beat red. He looks terrorized. I'm still warming up.

"You don't get paid to inform the masses. You get paid to shoot a fucking SAW. Is that clear? You do your job and stay outta my lane, you understand me, you piece of fucking shit? You don't know shit about Sergeant Major. And you certainly don't go telling Joe about dead Ramrods, you ignorant fuck."

I know I've gone too far, but I can't hold anything back. I'm reeling. I'm praying against the evidence the news isn't true. By the time I'm done, I've pushed every one of Stuckert's buttons, and he looks utterly broken. I know I will regret that later. Right now, I just don't care.

Downstairs, Cantrell has heard my rant from the commander's hatch of his Bradley. He keys his radio and calls for me. I leave Stuckert and storm downstairs. When I get to the street, Cantrell drops his ramp. I see Fitts inside.

Oh fuck no. Fuck no.

Cantrell slides into the back of the Brad with Fitts. He motions me inside and raises the ramp. When we have leaders' meetings like this, I always feel like a part of a secret club, and the back of the Brad becomes our own portable Bat Cave.

Cantrell points at my uniform and says, "You got to get another top, Sergeant Bell. That one is about filthied, wouldn't you say?"

I look down at myself. My desert uniform top is smeared with Pratt's dried blood, dirt, and grime. "I don't know, Sarge, I think this has got a couple more days."

Cantrell looks me in the eyes, "First Sergeant Smith told me that Ramrod Seven was killed at the breach."

There. It's out. My Sergeant Major is dead.

Fitts looks at my uniform and says, "Sarge, I can't get this dude to shower at Normandy. He ain't touching shit while we're out here."

Fitts is trying to distract me. I keep my expression blank.

I fucking loved that man.

"Try to keep cleaner," Cantrell adds. I nod.

He was bulletproof. How could he get killed?

Cantrell dismisses me. The ramp drops, and Fitts and I jump out into the street.

"Look, Bell, try and get some sleep. We got three hours," Fitts says.

I nod. I don't trust myself to speak. We walk into the house in silence, and I go find a place to lie down.

The muj start to mortar us. I lie in the dark, listening to the explosions around us as I try to fall asleep. I cannot shut off my brain. I am physically exhausted and desperately need to get some rest, but my mind won't allow it.

Somewhere in the night, the feral dogs snarl and growl between mortar volleys. They're fighting over another morsel of food. Human meat. I try not to listen.

Faulkenburg's dead.

The Iraqis helped to load him into an M113 medevac track right after he got shot. The track raced him to our battalion aid station at the cloverleaf east of Fallujah, but it was too late. He died before he fell into the street. The bullet exited out the top of his head. He never had a chance.

Our larger-than-life father figure is dead.

Minutes after Faulkenburg's body reached the aid station, a flood of wounded IIF soldiers arrived. Seventeen of them survived their wounds, but three did not. Had it not been for Steve Faulkenburg's last act of bravery, many more would have joined them.

Faulkenburg was our first Angel, the first American to die by enemy fire in the Second Battle of Fallujah.

Was Faulkenburg's body the one I saw in the street last night at the breach? Was he among the dead I saw the Iraqis cover up and carry away? Did I witness his last moments and not even realize it?

That thought leaves me stricken with grief. I know now is not the time to mourn. We have a battle to win, and I must repress the pain to be able to do my job. My mind torments me with images of Faulkenburg in that street. At times like these, a good imagination becomes your worst enemy.

If they can kill Sergeant Major Faulkenburg, how have I survived? He was so much more skilled than I, so much more experienced than almost every other soldier out here. Is this more about luck than skill? If it is, we're all only one bullet away from Faulkenburg's undeserved fate.

I dwell on that for a while, and ache with vulnerability. Life seems so perilous, so fragile now—I just don't understand how he can die while I survive. For the first time since we entered the city, I am forced to recognize my own mortality. In doing so, I get a glimpse of what Fitts must have been going through all along.

Does Fitts face these thoughts every night? April 9 must still prey on him in the darkness. I'm sorry I ever ragged him about it.

The mortars fall. The man-eating dogs bay. The night never ends.

CHAPTER FOURTEEN

Better Homes and Gardens

Fallujah
November 10, 2004

Long before sunrise, we begin our third day in the city. As it got cold last night, the men tore down drapes and used them as blankets. Others wrapped themselves up like burritos in filthy area rugs. We passed the night on guard, shivering, anxious, and irritated.

I grab my gear and head out onto the roof to check on things. Two days into the battle, and already our boys are banged up. Gashes adorn every face. Our hands are skinned raw from climbing through the debris of all these ruined buildings. Between the putrefying corpses, the flies, and feral dogs, Fallujah teems with gut-liquefying bacteria. We can't avoid the germs and the majority of the platoon has diarrhea. There were times yesterday that men were shitting while they shot. We're filthy, bone-weary, bruised, and bleeding. Our joints ache, our muscles protest every move.

Today brings a new mission. The Marines have lagged behind us. Ware was right about that. A gap has opened between our right flank and their left one. The insurgents know it is there, and they exploit it to infiltrate our rear. Today, we will countermarch north and thoroughly clear the Askari District while we wait for the Marines to get forward.

Meno briefs us on Captain Sims's plan for the day. We'll go house to house, killing anyone we find and destroying the weapons and ammo we left untouched during our original push to Highway 10.

Just before dawn, the entire company gets on line and begins the drive north into yesterday's stomping grounds. The cold night has left the streets slick with moisture. We slip and slide in our boots as we make our way up the street toward Objective Wolf again. As we countermarch with our Brads and tanks in support, I notice that the dogs follow behind us. When we stop to search a house, they stop as well. I emerge from one building and see a line of them in the street, their tails thumping expectantly on the asphalt. They're waiting for us to provide them with their next meal.

The smell of death is all around us. Insurgent corpses rot in buildings and alleyways. We are under orders to double tap every insurgent we find, no matter what his condition. Yet some are already covered with moss and mold. They're so far gone that even the dogs turn away from them. As we start to clear another block of houses, I spot an insurgent lying against a wall. I shoot him, and my bullets pop his bloated stomach like a balloon. The corpse lets out a long farting sound as the gas inside it escapes. I turn to Sucholas and say, "Excuse me. I've been fighting that back since Baghdad."

"If I let one go like that," Sucholas says, "you would scrape my intestines off the wall."

Throughout the morning, we kick in so many doors that we lose count. Unlike the previous day, we take a deliberate approach to each dwelling. We assume they are all booby-trapped. We move with caution and do not touch anything unnecessarily. It doesn't take us long to find all sorts of devilish traps: bras and panties covering booby-trapped hand grenades, cabinets wired with explosives, mortar rounds under sinks, land mines buried in front and backyards. We negotiate all these hazards and find hundreds of weapons in the process. Everything from World War II American M1 Garand rifles to the latest production SVD sniper rifles straight from Russian factories are left for us to find. We even discover an American Army field manual from 1941 with Arabic notes written in the margins.

It takes us hours to clear three blocks. Fitts and I decide that we could make better time if we split up. He takes one side of the street, my squad takes the other. The Brads stay close, ready to support either or both of us.

In one house, I find a beautiful Czech-made SKS Cold War–era rifle. The former owner had put a 75-round drum magazine on it and kept it in pristine condition. I pick it up and decide to keep it as a present to myself. Today is my twenty-ninth birthday. The SKS goes into Chad Ellis's Bradley for safekeeping.

More houses. More arms caches. We find Iranian FAL rifles, German G3 assault weapons made by Heckler & Koch, shotguns, hunting rifles, and M16s. Fitts has a soldier in his squad named Matthew Woodbury who is a *Guns & Ammo* magazine savant. He's read so much on rifles that he can tell the country of origin by the serial number on the weapon.

We improvise ways to blow up all the stuff we find. Sometimes, we blow it in place with C-4, other times we use the Bradleys to crush mortar tubes, rocket launchers, and rifles. It is very dangerous work. The ordnance is unstable, frequently old, and improperly maintained. At one point, we pull about a dozen rocket-propelled grenades out of a house and load them into a car. Since we're supposed to blow up every automobile we find, this seems like a good way to kill two birds with one stone. We add some mortar shells and stand back. Staff Sergeant Jamie McDaniel's Brad rolls up. In the turret is his Nigerian-born gunner, Sergeant Olakunle Delalu. He is an electrical engineering graduate of Columbia University who joined the army to get American citizenship. Delalu takes aim at the car and unloads on it with a TOW missile. An eyeblink later, the car vaporizes into a ball of flame.

We move on to the next house and find a truck in the driveway. We load it full of the weapons and ammo we find inside the dwelling, then touch it off with an incendiary grenade. The grenade melts the front part of the truck and sets fire to some nearby barrels of gasoline and oil. Soon, the flames spread and four houses catch fire. In one of them, the fire touches off another weapons cache and the subsequent explosion bounces me into a wall.

Later, I wire a pile of grenades, RPGs, and 107mm rockets up to several bricks of C-4. Living with combat engineers for over eight months, we had learned just about every way to blow explosive ordnance imaginable. Yet after I lit the fuse, nothing happened. I creep back to the house and peer inside. Smoke obscures my view. I start to tremble, and I wonder if this is the cautionary story my young soldiers will tell once they become drill sergeants back home. "This is how my squad leader blew himself up in Fallujah. . . ."

I step inside the house and find that the blast caps had come loose. I carry the ordnance to the doorway and leave it there in a big pile. A Brad shoots it up, but the rockets fail to explode. Pissed off now, I drag the stuff over to a nearby bomb crater. I put the C-4 among the rockets again and ask Cory Brown to shoot the entire mess. His gunner laces the cache with HE shells. Nothing happens. He switches to armor piercing, and as soon as the first round hits the cache, the entire pile explodes. Rocket-propelled grenades suddenly sizzle out of the flames. Several tear into the houses across the street and explode. Others fly off in all directions, which sends my squad diving for cover.

When the explosions cease, I hear screaming. A rocket went right into the house Fitts and his men are clearing across the street. Fitts limps out into the courtyard and shouts at me, "What the fuck are you doing?"

"I'm out of blasting caps for the C-4. Are you guys okay?"

"Dude, you almost killed my fucking squad, man. No, we are not okay."

I try to apologize, but Fitts is pissed. The work continues.

All day long, we play with fate as we discover and destroy all these enemy stockpiles. It is dangerous work. I feel like a juvenile delinquent turned loose on a devastated city. Somehow, we manage to avoid blowing anyone up, but it isn't for lack of trying. It is simply luck.

As dusk settles over us, we ache. Backs, arms, calves are tight and sore. We've cleared so many houses, it has all blended together into one long day of door-kicking and cache-blowing. We have yet to see a single live insurgent.

At one point, we stumble across a small cache of about fifteen rocket-propelled grenades. As we debate how to dispose of them, Cantrell calls us on the radio. Lieutenant Iwan needs help. He's run into contact a few blocks to the south. With Sims tied up with First Platoon about four hundred meters up the road, the platoon sergeant tells us to take care of the RPGs. I want to take them with us, but he nixes that idea. I offer to shoot them off with a launcher. He tells me we don't have time. We need to get to Iwan.

I give up and head for my track. Just as I get inside, I hear Knapp screaming at Cantrell on the radio. Cantrell's ordered him to blow the RPGs up with a thermite grenade.

"Sarge," Knapp rails at me, "I am not letting my guys blow up RPGs that way. It is fucking stupid."

I get on the radio and tell Cantrell his idea stinks and I won't risk my men to do it.

"Well, then you do it, hero. I don't give a fuck who does it. If you don't have the nuts, make one of your boys do it. Get someone to do it. Just blow these fuckers up."

I look around in the Bradley. My men are staring at me, waiting for my next move. They're wondering if I'll make them do this crazy stunt.

Fuck it.

I take a thermite grenade and walk over to the bag of RPGs. The Brads get on line, ready to roll out to help Iwan as soon as I'm done. The Bradley commanders get low in their turrets. The ramps close. The men are safe inside.

I put the RPGs into a tub sitting amid the ruins of another house. I look back at Cantrell's Brad and give him the coldest scowl I can manage. "No, Sarge," I say with a raw and raspy voice, "You see this. You watch what happens."

I'm feeling like a martyr. I pull out the incendiary grenade and hold it over the rockets. I pull the pin and white phosphorus spews out like a Diet Coke with a Mentos in it. I've hardly let go of it when the WP burns through one of the RPGs. The rocket touches off and skates off into the neighborhood. It explodes a short distance away. I start running for the Brads even as more rockets sizzle out of the tub.

I've lost my fucking mind.

Ahead, a Brad starts to move down the road. A rocket whirs overhead and blows up in a nearby building. The Brad's ramp drops. Another explosion rocks the ground. I reach the ramp and jump in. I'm safe with my brotherhood now, but I am fucking pissed.

We roll north. The aches, the exhaustion, the pain, scrapes, and spastic shits mean nothing to us. We are infantry. The killing is all.

As we countermarch north, Lieutenant Iwan leads a search and attack mission against the enemy cell he's located. The enemy is about a dozen strong. They are aggressive and disciplined. Iwan's Bradley tries to knock them down with its cannon. In the heat of the fight, the cannon malfunctions, leaving Iwan's track with only its single coaxial machine gun. The insurgents slip away, disappearing into a block of upscale homes in the battalion's rear.

One gutsy insurgent with a bandolier of linked machine-gun rounds slung across his chest becomes separated from the rest of his cell. He takes refuge in a house about four hundred meters north of his buddies. Iwan calls in the battalion scout platoon to dig him out of the house. Three scouts go in through the front door.

As they open the door they are met by a torrent of bullets meted out by a crew-served machine gun. Staff Sergeant Jason Laser goes down, hit in the chest. A second one, Sergeant Andy Karnes, tries to help his wounded comrade, but he gets shot in the side. The machine gunner is unrelenting. A third scout suffers a grazing wound to the stomach.

Sergeant J. C. Matteson spots another insurgent who is about to enter the back door to the house. From the turret of a Humvee, Matteson blows the enemy to bits with a Mark 19 automatic grenade launcher.

Captain Sims reaches the scene just as the insurgent machine gunner starts shouting out the window, "Fuck America!" He moves from room to room in the house to avoid all the fire Sims directs on him.

When bullets don't work, Sims calls up a bulldozer. As it rumbles toward the house, the insurgent peppers it with bullets. Though surrounded by the better part of a mech infantry company, this man will not give up.

While Sims handles the lone gunman, Iwan and Lieutenant

Meno huddle up outside a house our platoon has just cleared half a kilometer away. Iwan tells Meno that tracking down the rest of the cell will be our job. If the other guys are half as committed as the one Sims faces, it'll be one hell of a fight.

Meno outlines a plan. He wants the platoon's Bradleys to cordon off the neighborhood. With a track on every corner, and a tank in support, we will search each house one by one.

Iwan approves the plan, climbs into his Bradley, and moves south to help set up the cordon.

House by house, we start to clear the block. We kick in doors, sweep through rooms, and try to maintain our situational awareness. Despite the threat, it is hard not to get a little complacent from the repetition. We've cleared too many buildings since starting out this morning.

In one house, we find rockets and ammunition. In another, we stumble across a cache of American helmets and old Kevlar flak jackets.

The big Abrams tanks clank forward and roar and rumble, leaving buildings in flaming ruins. We follow in their paths, peering into the hollowed, burning shells. Smoke coils out over the rooftops. We're destroying the best neighborhood in town.

I watch a Bradley and an Abrams open up on a house. A 120mm round explodes inside while the Bradley's cannon shells streak through the wreckage, eventually falling hundreds of meters away.

The area around us suddenly erupts with grenades and machine-gun fire. Those shells landed near some Marines, who have finally reached our area. It is about time they get online with us.

Then again, it is a mixed blessing to have them around. They don't take kindly to the 25mm incoming. Their response sends us diving for cover behind our tracks as .50-caliber machine-gun fire stitches across our street. Rodriguez gets on the radio. The

Marines are not apologetic. We are told that they will return any and all incoming fire, friendly or otherwise.

Not long after, the Marines send a barrage of parachute flares and star clusters over our heads. They are supposed to be moving south parallel to us, on a line some three hundred meters to the west. The coordination needs work. They send up flares at the slightest hint of contact and bathe our neighborhood in brilliant white light. This is the last thing we want. We're fine operating in the dark; we all have night-vision goggles. But the Marines issue them only to their leadership. We own the night; the Marines rent it.

We move to another house and prepare to clear it. A star shell bursts overhead, leaving us perfectly backlit for the enemy. The sudden bloom of light washes out our night vision. For a critical moment, we're exposed and blind. And then they send us scrambling as they commence shooting at our movement underneath their flares. Fucking Marines.

As much as I love to point out their Semper Fi-diocy, I am awed by their cohesive fire. When one Marine fires, so does his entire platoon. Their fire superiority is humbling, as I grab earth to avoid its death. Roll-playing for even two minutes as an insurgent is too long against a platoon or company of Marines. No matter what, you gotta respect that.

We continue on to the next house as the friendly star-shell barrage continues. When we get inside, my squad finds piles of IVs, gauze, and fluid bags. We press on to the next house. This one holds two sets of desert GI boots tucked away in one room. Some of the men find eight complete Iraqi National Guard uniforms.

Four hours later, we are beyond exhausted. I look over at Fitts. His limp is more pronounced.

Knapp spots something ahead in the street. Through the darkness, we see a man lying in the road, a Russian machine gun next to him. Knapp and I open fire. I hit him twice in the back and hear his lungs expel a sudden rush of air. Was it a death rattle? I'm not sure. Knapp puts a round right through his head, and that finishes the job.

We approach the insurgent. He lies on his stomach in a thick pool of his own blood. He must have been hit by a cannon shell from a passing Bradley as he hid inside one of the nearby houses. In his dying moments, he crawled into the street, still dragging his weapon and ammunition. Belts of 7.62mm rounds lie accordioned around him.

It is our job to make sure each insurgent is really dead and not just playing possum. We're supposed to kick apart their legs, then give them a hard boot in the crotch. If they don't flinch, they're dead, and we can search them for booby traps and intel.

I try to kick this insurgent's legs apart, but one is almost entirely gone and the other one is little more than tattered pink flesh and gore. When I try to kick his balls, my boot sinks into his leg cavity. It dawns on me that the guy has no nut sack left.

"Dude," I wonder aloud, "What do you do when the guy has no legs? That wasn't covered in training."

I draw my knife and poke tentatively at his back. I probably should have just buried the blade in him, but I've never used a knife in combat before, and I'm not sure how to do it. I poke at him a couple more times, embarrassed by my lack of skill.

Lawson pulls out a larger knife and slams it home into the guy's back. He looks over at me shaking his head.

"What a day, huh?"

It is obvious that this insurgent is dead. I lift his head up, and Knapp sweeps underneath him. "Clear," he says, and I let the dead man sag back to the pavement. We spike his weapon and leave him for the dogs.

What a day? No shit. Happy birthday.

We continue down the street. Rubble clogs the way, and we

struggle through blocks of masonry, bricks, and chunks of concrete that the tracks have left in their wake. I hear a curse. Ruiz has fallen and turned his ankle. It starts to swell inside his boot.

We move inside a nearby house so our medic can treat Ruiz. Meanwhile, the men break out their MREs and wolf down a few bites. It is the first meal we've eaten all day. Some of the men grab quick catnaps. Fitts and I catch hell from Cantrell, who is in a track on the left side of the cordon. He badgers us over the radio for situation reports. It is deeply irritating. We lie and tell him we're still clearing houses.

A half hour shy of midnight, we move out again. We're weary and our pace lags. The break has flushed the adrenaline out of our systems. The rebound from a combat-induced adrenaline rush is almost as bad as a hangover.

We cross the street and reach a nine-foot wall untouched by bullets or Bradleys. Behind it is a house also left unscathed. The gate, which is just wide enough for a car, stands partly open. The platoon files through it and enters an open courtyard. Four decorative brick columns, each about a man and a half in width, dot the courtyard. They are the only cover between the front door and the nine-foot wall.

I enter behind Fitts and his squad. Some rich Ba'athist must have owned this house. It is square-shaped, with a pillboxlike second story that opens onto a balcony overlooking the garden. The front door is to our left. Two windows into a living room take up the center, flanked by a barred window into a kitchen at the far right.

To the right is a beautifully landscaped garden with palm and date trees. A series of hedges winds around their trunks. It's a pretty nice pad, ripe for *Better Homes and Gardens: Fallujah Edition*. The front door is ornate. We've been kicking in doors all over Iraq since February; I've long since become a door connoisseur. I can tell which ones are flimsy, which ones are thick, and which ones are so secure they will require our man-beast, Sergeant Hall, to demolish.

This door is a composite of sheet metal and steel with a beautiful glass partition inlaid in the middle. I am surprised that a thing of such beauty could survive the carnage we've delivered to the neighborhood.

In a neighborhood that values siege-warfare architecture, whoever built this place knew what he was doing. It's a micro-fortress, a perfect summer getaway for a drug cartel. It's going to be a bitch to clear.

We secure the courtyard. Fitts moves to the front door. I follow and take up a position next to a window. I look inside and see nothing unusual. My instincts aren't tingling, which leads me to believe this place is empty like all the other ones on the block. The men aren't overly concerned either. They spread out in the courtyard and wait for orders.

Fitts stands by the door and waits for his squad to join him. When nobody follows, he gets riled. He waits by the door, and I know he's starting to boil. His mouth bulges with a huge wad of Copenhagen that he cadged off somebody earlier in the evening.

He spits a wad of chaw, then bellows in a tired and horse rasp, "I don't care what squad you're in, get in the motherfucking stack ASAP."

Behind us, the men stir. Misa reaches the door first. The tracer fragment in his cheek has festered overnight and now looks like a giant, burned and bloody boil. It's still oozing black liquid.

Ohle follows Misa and lines up behind him, single file. The Fallujah grime has not been kind to his face either. Beyond the cuts we all have, Ohle's got whiteheads poking through the dirt encrusted on his face. Metcalf gets behind Ohle. Ruiz limps up to the door with Maxfield. Fitts now has his stack. He moves to the rear of it so he can watch the men as they go inside. Misa will lead the way.

Hall prepares to kick in the door, but finds it unlocked. Disappointed, he opens it the old-fashioned way, and Misa charges inside, with the rest of the men still in single file, close behind. Seconds later, most of the platoon, minus Lawson's weapons squad and Lieutenant Meno, follows in the entry team's wake.

I stay outside and keep my eyes on the adjoining living room through a window. This way, I can get eyes on the rooms the rest of the platoon is about to clear. If an enemy is lurking inside, I can put rounds into the bad guys before the men are exposed.

Through the window, I can see the platoon's SureFire lights bouncing off the walls and ceilings as the men start clearing the room. They don't need me covering now, so I move toward the front door to join up with them.

Inside the house, Misa and Ohle lead the entry team through a foyer and into the living room. There's a closed door on the far wall. Ohle brazenly throws it open.

An instant later, red tracers stripe the darkness around Ohle. He doesn't flinch at the surprise gunfire. Instead, he swings his SAW to his shoulder, flips the safety off, and unloads a burst. It's no use. Unable to see the enemy, Ohle is going to die if he stays in that doorway. Misa grabs him from behind and pulls him out of the line of fire. Ohle's finger remains tight on the trigger, and his SAW unleashes a rainbow of tracers into the next room and up into the ceiling of the living room as he spins out of balance in Misa's grasp.

Jumping back to the window I can see Ohle's bullets arcing into the ceiling of the living room. They ricochet crazily in all directions. More tracers bounce around, fired by the insurgents in the next room. Unsure of what's going on, I run through the front door. Just as I get inside, a rash of gunfire tears into the foyer. Overhead, a chandelier explodes in a shower of glass and metal. I throw myself against the wall between the foyer and the living room.

I'm totally confused. I assume Fitts and his men are reconning by fire, but it's gotten a little out of control. Our own tracers are boomeranging around our heads, sending chips of plaster, brick, and concrete spinning through the room.

"Cease fucking fire! What are you doing?" I yell. My voice is rough and sandpapery. After all the excitement of the mosque fight the day before, my vocal chords are shot. My words come rasping out. I sound like Demi Moore.

"CEASE FUCKING FIRE," Sergeant Hall echoes my command.

A hoarse voice rises from the living room, "NO! Don't cease fire! Continue to fucking fire!"

"They're shooting at us," Ohle yells back. He is unable to move.

The shooting continues. Tracers tic-tac-toe through the foyer and living room, zipping off the walls, ceiling, and cement floor. We're in a beehive.

I need to get a handle on the situation. I shout again, "Cease fucking fire! What are we shooting at?"

I look through the door leading into the living room and see the platoon pinned against one wall. Ohle, Misa, Fitts, and the rest of the men are bleeding from dozens of wounds caused by the flying chunks of concrete and masonry. What is going on?

Fitts sees me. "Hey, Bell," he says, "Why don't you tell the fuckers on the other side of this wall to cease fire?"

Oh my God. We're in contact. It dawns on me just how precarious our position is now. Fitts watches the light go on in my head and nods at me. "Yeah, bro."

The bulk of our two squads are trapped inside the living room.

The insurgents are dug into positions in a central stairwell, just inside one door off the foyer and with a clear shot through another door to the living room, the door that Ohle opened. They can shoot through that doorway and kill anyone making a run for the foyer, since our guys are behind the far wall of the living room. They have a bowling-alley-wide field of fire into the living room, and a pie-shaped one into the foyer. They have plenty of ammunition and are not afraid to use it.

I peek through the foyer doorway to their stairwell and make out two figures. They're hunkered down behind a pair of three-foot-high concrete Jersey barriers with little more than their heads and shoulders exposed. They've created a veritable bunker smack in the middle of the house. One of the insurgents holds an AK-47 against each shoulder with the barrels resting on one barrier. The other mans a Russian belt-fed PKM machine gun perched atop the other barrier.

How on earth did they get those concrete barriers in there? They must weigh a half ton each. Eight men would be hard pressed to lift them.

The house is a prepared kill zone. They wanted us to clear it, and just waited to spring an ambush.

"Watch the roof, watch the fucking roof!" Knapp yells from outside in the courtyard.

I lean back into the foyer just as the wall explodes with sparks. Bullets crack and whine all around us again. Metcalf buckles and falls to the floor. "I'm hit! Oh fuck, I'm hit!" he screams, clutching his stomach.

From below the stairwell comes laughter, and mockery in broken English. *"Ohhhh, I'm heeet!"* one mimics. The comedian and his pal cackle. At the sound of their jeering, the hair on the back of my neck stands up. Every man in the platoon reacts the same way. Eyes are saucers now. Panic is not far away.

Metcalf clutches his hands to his stomach. A bullet grazed

him under his body armor. The others aren't much better off. Hands are lacerated; knuckles are slick with grime and blood.

The two under the stairs open up again. The living room and foyer fill with dancing tracers. They sizzle and hiss and start little blazes in piles of refuse and paper lying on the floor in both rooms. The living-room wall, which provides our only cover from the stairwell bunker, starts to give way. The automatic fire blows bricks clear out of it. Other bricks jut out, still intact but knocked from their original position by the enemy bullets.

Three bricks pop out of the wall directly over Fitts's head. A fissure furrows up the wall from floor to ceiling. We don't have much time. When the wall gives way, my platoon will face a massacre.

Outside, machine gunner Jamison McDaniel lies prone in the courtyard. He is totally exposed to whomever is shooting out of the kitchen window. Bullets spark all around him. But the kid is an iceberg. Ignoring the bullets, he shoulders his 240 and tears off a blistering burst of return fire. It is an incongruous sight; McDaniel is nineteen but could pass as a middle schooler. The baby-faced gunner is just rocking on the 240. More bullets gouge the ground around him, but he stays on the trigger. His display of courage swells my heart. In the chaos of battle, the true strength of the human spirit will sometimes emerge. This is one of those moments.

In this duel of machine guns, hundreds of bullets fly back and forth. Sergeant Jose Rodriguez, Meno's radio guy, gets hit. He goes down and cries for help. Lieutenant Meno grabs him by the arm and flings him into an outhouse at the back of the courtyard. For the moment, he is out of the fight.

McDaniel's big machine gun has thoroughly redecorated the kitchen. It's a pockmarked ruin. The counterfire proves too much for the insurgents, who break contact. Unaware he's driven off the threat, McDaniel continues to hammer away.

His bullets tear the cabinets apart, destroying dishes and glass. Some hit the common wall with the living room, knocking even more bricks loose. We can't get him to stop.

From under the stairwell, the insurgents unleash a fresh volley at us. The living room is full of angry tracers again. Through the gloom I see Fitts. We're on opposite sides of the enemy's field of fire. He's trapped. I'm not. Partially lit by the flickering fires burning around the room, he examines the bricks sticking out of the wall above his head. He lets out a frustrated sigh. Then he rolls his eyes right and locks on me.

"Hey, Bell," he says, "Bro, I need you. I need you in a bad way."

CHAPTER FIFTEEN

"The Power of Christ Compels You"

Fitts never shows fear. Even after he got shot three times in April, he displayed less concern than a civilian with a splinter in his thumb. That day, as he bled from both arms and a leg, he still kept his head about him, focusing on the mission before his serious wounds.

Now Fitts has that scrunched-up look he gets when the medics are about to give us our tetanus shots. It is the closest to fear I've ever seen in him. If I dwell on that look, I know it will unnerve me.

Should the rest of the platoon see it, it might be enough to push the boys over the edge. They're on the border of panic already. The darkness, the smoke, and the reddish glow from the small piles of burning trash are macabre.

"I need you, bro," Fitts says again.

"Alright, alright . . . alright," I reply, stalling for time as I try to get my brain in gear long enough to think of a way out of this mess. My mind starts ticking off options.

Obviously, we can't call in an air strike. We have no way to call it, and air-to-surface bombs would smoke the whole compound, including us. Same with an artillery fire mission. A tank or a Bradley would be of no use now, not as long as we're stuck inside the house.

This ambush is the product of study, an enemy who has thoroughly analyzed our strengths and weaknesses. They've created a fighting position that negates our advantages of firepower and mobility. All we can do is fight them at point-blank range with the weapons in our hands.

I thought we were ready for everything. We're not ready for this.

Over in the far corner of the living room, Misa stirs. He pulls out a grenade.

"Frag out. Frag out," he shouts.

This mortifies Fitts. "No," he hisses. Misa freezes. Fitts continues, "They'll bowl that bitch right back at us. You've got no idea where they're at."

Misa is undeterred. He peers around the doorway and reports, "I see them . . . I see where they're at."

Sergeant Hugh Hall sees Ware and Yuri and tells them, "Get behind something, man!"

"Is anyone hit?" Doc Abernathy calls from outside.

"Lemme frag out," Misa will not let this go.

Fitts will have none of it. "You don't know how many fucking dudes are in here. Don't frag out. Put it away." Misa abandons the grenade idea.

Another flurry of bullets laces the living room. The tracers cleave the smoky air, sending tendrils spinning off into the darkness and briefly clearing the air in the doorway.

I risk a look into the stairwell room. In the fire's crimson glow, I spot one of the insurgents. He's crouched behind the Jersey barriers holding an AK in each hand. He's grinning like a fiend, and I notice his perfectly straight, white teeth.

How the fuck is that possible? We've got field dentists, a health plan, and all the trappings of modern medicine, and our teeth look like caramel popcorn. Apparently, these cocksuckers don't like Red Man.

I duck back into the foyer. Misa's aborted plan gives me an idea. A few days before we assaulted Fallujah, Staff Sergeant Hector Diaz, our supply NCO, traded some shit with Special Forces to get me a flash-bang grenade. It has a two-second fuse, and will stun anyone who is unfortunate enough to be around when it goes off. I could throw it and stun the insurgents long enough for everyone to escape. I mull this over while fingering the flash-bang's cylindrical tube. It looks like an oversized roll of Kodak film. I've never used one of these things before, and that gives me pause. If I fuck up, I could flash out the entire platoon and incapacitate myself and my own men. That's a pretty big risk. I abandon the flash-bang idea.

I'm running out of ideas. We can't flank them. They're covering the outside of the house, and the back door opens into the stairwell room five feet from the Jersey barriers. Getting around behind them is not an option.

The enemy designed this trap to force us into a head-on, stand-up fight. Okay then, we'll play their game.

I peek around the wall into the living room. Metcalf remains on the ground, checking himself and his wound. Clouds of smoke now obscure most of their details, but from their postures I can tell who's who. I know everything about these men, and I can tell they aren't far from reaching a breaking point.

I know there's only one option, exactly what the fuckers under the stairs want.

"Give me a 240 gunner and a SAW," I shout.

Ohle slides me his SAW and I immediately suppress the corner of the room without looking. The bolt locks back. I am out of ammo.

"Give me another weapon system. I need another SAW and a fucking 240," I scream in frustration.

"Get a fucking 240 up here, man," Hall screams outside.

A second later, McDaniel flies into the foyer through the front door. Simultaneously, I make eye contact with Specialist Mathieu. At thirty-seven, his body has taken a pounding in Iraq, and he has to work twice as hard to keep up with his eighteen-year-old peers. After 9/11, he left a good job as a medical technician at a major hospital to join the Army. That move dumped him in a significantly lower tax bracket, a fact that caused a strain on his family and eventual divorce from his wife. His patriotism cost him his family.

We are his family now. Through the gloom and smoke I can read his features, I can see his divot chin that makes him look a bit like John Travolta. He's ready to do whatever I need. Across the living room, he waits for my order.

"Mathieu, toss me your SAW."

He holds out his hands as I fling my M4 across the kill zone to him. My rifle has no night optics, just the three-power telescopic sight that I got from Pratt. It's useless for night fighting and close-quarters combat. The SAW is the weapon for this fight.

Mathieu hurls the SAW right into my arms. The damn thing weighs over twenty pounds loaded, but he threw it as if it were a toy.

"Sarge," he calls to me, "it's loaded with 200 in the drum."

"Sweet."

Two hundred 5.56mm bullets. Should be enough.

Fitts watches the exchange with intensity. "What're you doing? What're you doing?" he asks.

"Dude, on me," I reply. "Pull out. Australian Peel and pull out. On me. Everyone go but Misa. Misa, you stay. Last man. So I know."

"I'm last man. I'm last man," Misa echoes.

I hear firing outside. Tracers blast through the kitchen window, blowing out the glass and shredding the iron bars beyond.

There's a third insurgent in the kitchen, and he pours machine-gun fire into Lawson's weapons squad covering the outside of the house from the courtyard.

Six feet from the kitchen window, Swanson throws himself behind one of the courtyard's decorative columns. A blizzard of metal and glass fragments scythe his face and arms. He slumps against the pillar, drops his M240 machine gun and throws his hands to his face. A cone of fire just misses Sergeant Hugh Hall, who falls to the ground as rounds whiz and impact all around him.

"My face! My eyes! Goddamnit!" Swanson is in misery.

"You alright man? You look hit." Mick Ware is holding up Swanson.

"I'm good. I'm good. Where's my weapon? Give me my weapon."

Swanson is far from good. His eyes are almost swollen shut, and his face drips blood from numerous wounds. The rest of the men look spent. They've got fresh gashes crisscrossing older cuts and scrapes. Each of these new injuries bleeds freely. Their faces are smoke-stained and bloody. Some pause to pick glass and metal fragments out of each other's faces. Blood splatters the street. Doc Abernathy moves from man to man, gauzing and taping wounds. This is a huge cluster fuck.

"I got fucking shrapnel all across my fucking back," shouts Hall.

Hall has had enough. He can't tell what is going on inside the house.

"Hey, who the FUCK is shooting, man?"

"It's someone in there," yells Flannery from inside the house.

"It's the fucking hajjis inside." Knapp is equally frustrated and helpless to do anything from where he is pinned down.

"My fucking face. Christ." Swanson is rolling on the ground.

"DOC! DOC!" Lawson screams for Abernathy.

The fuckers under the stairs find this hilarious. Their hellish laughter echoes through the house. They mock us once more, "*Ohhhh, my feece, my feece!*"

"Hey, you hear that shit? They are fucking with our injured. They are FUCKING WITH OUR INJURED," I scream over to Fitts.

"Hey, Sarge, fuck them."

"No man. FUCK THEM. FUCK THESE FAGGOTS. Listen to 'em fucking with us."

"Hey motherfucker, I don't give a shit about them. You need to focus on this shit here," Fitts screams back to me.

"Nah, FUCK YOU!" I shout back at the insurgents. They say something in return, but I don't understand it. "Huh, bitch? You wanna fuck with us? You fucking bitch. *Kelp.*" Dog. I am starting to flip out and Fitts sees this.

"Let's just stop. Hold on." Fitts is trying to calm me down. He looks over at his guys and says, "We're going to get the fuck out."

"Roger that," somebody replies.

Misa's getting anxious. "Ready. You ready?" he calls to me.

"Hold the fuck on," I reply, my voice hoarse and raspy. I feel everyone's eyes on me. In two lifetimes I could never feel so much pressure.

Chastised, Misa replies, "Whenever you're ready, Sarge."

I know I have to move, but my nerves are jangling and my mind races furiously. A thousand thoughts tumble at once through my mind. They get jammed up, piling on top of each other so that all I get are unintelligible fragments. My palms are slick with sweat. I've got to breathe. I've got to relax and get ready for what I must do.

The power of Christ compels you.

What? Of all the thoughts to get through the logjam in my brain, this one pops out of nowhere. Just before going to Fallujah, I had watched the latest version of *The Exorcist*. Now that memorable line from the movie—the mantra of the priests as they battle Satan—sticks in my head like a bad song lyric. Well, if this is to be my dying thought, at least it's not some vapid Madison Avenue marketing slogan. My brain could have picked "Drop the chalupa."

The power of Christ compels you. The power of Christ compels you.

I've got to do this thing. I take a long breath. The air is stagnant, full of smoke and body odor. I try not to gag. Another deep breath. The foul air acts like a slap in the face. I'm back in control, alert and aware.

I'm ready. I've got total clarity and am of singular purpose. I whisper a short prayer and stand up.

"GO! GO! GO! GO! GET OUT!" I scream at the top of my lungs.

At a crouch, I move up the wall and cross into the living room, the SAW leveled, my finger tense on the trigger. A few quick strides and I step into the doorway to the stairwell room. I'm in the fatal funnel.

CHAPTER SIXTEEN

The Failed Test of Manhood

My sudden appearance catches the enemy off guard. I expect the AKs to open up again as soon as I expose myself. But they don't. Instead, I squeeze the trigger and hold it down. Hellfire starts flying toward the enemy. Mathieu's SAW is impeccably clean and well maintained, and I am confident that it will not jam.

The insurgents under the stairs react with discipline and speed. The one on the left hammers the doorway with both AKs. The other mans the PKM, and I can see his weapon chewing through its ammo belt.

Bullets bash into the wall to my left. The door-frame splinters. Tracers hiss this way and that, bouncing off the bricks and ceiling. I'm in a firestorm, totally exposed. I'm amazed I haven't been hit.

I sidestep through the doorway and to the left, trying to get a section of the stairwell between me and the enemy for at least a little cover. I hold my own trigger down, abandoning any pretense of disciplined fire. The SAW booms and goes cyclic, spitting bullets at an incredible rate. They carve chunks out of the Jersey barriers. Bits of concrete spin crazily around the room.

I stay on the trigger. More bullets slam into the Jersey barriers and penetrate to their hard foam centers. Hunks of the foam pop out of the holes I've made and cartwheel through the room. The fuckers under the stairs still fire back, but they are wildly inaccurate. Their tracers ricochet in dizzying patterns—*wall, ceiling, floor, wall.*

My SAW's barrel acts like a torch, illuminating the room with rapid-fire muzzle flashes. I've got a much better view now. I can see my straight-teethed assailants staring malevolently at me as they shoot. I sweep the SAW toward one and really hammer at him. He ducks to avoid getting his head blown off. I've got him pinned.

I may not be able to speak with canonical authority on the power of Christ, but I know a compelling weapon when I see one. An M249 SAW is like a bullwhip. I swing it at the other insurgent. My rounds—725 a minute—slap into the wall, the stairs, and the barriers. He dives for cover. Both of them are on the defensive now, pinned and unable to fight back.

In the living room behind me, Fitts barks orders and the platoon kicks into action. They peel off from the wall one by one and sprint across the room into the foyer. Within seconds, they clear the house and weave through the gauntlet of the courtyard out to the street.

My men are safe.

Trigger still depressed, my mind races. I've suppressed the enemy. Now I should kill them. My heart urges me forward around the stairwell.

Get out there. Clear the room and juice these guys.

I try to step forward, but my feet won't move. My legs feel like they're chained to the floor. I can't advance the ten feet needed to end the fight.

Don't be a bitch. Move forward. Do not nut up.

I strain against my own body. I cannot move. The SAW's bolt clacks back and forth as it chews through my ammo supply.

Okay, I probably have about a hundred and ten rounds left. What if I make a push and get on the stairs?

No. My body still refuses. My heart rages.

I "Z" the SAW along the barriers. More foam explodes out to cascade onto the floor. It looks like snowfall in hell in the fire-lit gloom.

Okay, I've got probably less than a hundred rounds left. It's time to move. Get forward. Finish this. Finish this now.

I push. I swear. My legs won't budge. The enemy remains unhurt, hiding behind the ripped-up barriers.

I can't do it. My heart seethes with contempt. Then my SAW runs away from me. Sometimes, with that weapon, once you go cyclic you can't stop it. I ease off the trigger but it remains locked back. The bolt charges on its own. The gun spews at least fifty more rounds, then clunks on an empty chamber. I'm out of ammunition.

I'm still in the stairwell room. Any second, the fuckers under the stairs will pop their heads back up, see that I'm an open target, and finish me. My legs suddenly free up. I've got to get out. *Run. RUN.*

I spin right and bolt through the doorway, thinking McDaniel and his 240 will be in the foyer to cover my escape. I don't see Misa anywhere. But both the living room and foyer are empty. I charge through both and out the front door. As I fly into the courtyard, an automatic weapon clatters.

"Give me another automatic weapon," I scream, still standing in the courtyard.

"Yo, pull back," Fitts yells.

"I need 203s. Give me some 203 fire."

Bullets crack over my left shoulder and hit the outer wall in front of me. I keep running, my legs pumping furiously. And then I'm through the gate and with my men. Misa appears at the gate and throws me to the side of the outside wall on the street.

"I got you. You're good, man," he says to me.

We're safe. The wall should shield us from the machine gun in the kitchen and give us time to reorganize. The platoon is scattered all over the place. Some of the men hug the wall on the left side of the gate, some are on the right. Others mill about uncertainly. Everyone is shouting. Above the din, Fitts tries to count heads. He wants to be sure nobody has been left behind.

"Team leaders report," I shout.

From down the street, Misa replies first, even though he's one of Fitts's guys, "I've got Ruiz and Sucholas."

"What the fuck? Give me a goddamned up on your guys."

Somebody else shouts, "I've got Metcalf, Flannery, and Ohle. Metcalf is up. We're green."

Around me, I've got two of Fitts's soldiers, one of mine, and one man from Lawson's weapons squad.

Fitts barks orders, trying to piece together a fire team from the disorganized mess the platoon has become. Everyone is talking over each other.

"Where they at?"

"I need a heads-up. Gimme a fucking heads-up."

"Bring those Bradleys up here," Fitts barks.

Knapp tosses a frag over the wall. *PFOMPT!*

I grab another drum of ammunition for my SAW. I grab Maxfield and Stuckert.

"Hey, SAW gunners suppress."

All three light machine guns lay into the roof line of the house.

"Here's what we are gonna do—" Fitts is cut off by all the confusion.

I try to cut in, "Is anyone hurt? Is anyone still in the house?" Nobody answers.

"Did anyone get shot on the way out?"

No answer. Everyone's still absorbed with their own issues.

"I need to know, goddamnit. Do you all have your shit?"

Fitts gathers part of the platoon. He intends to clear and occupy the two houses across the street, to gain a vantage point over the enemy. He points at one house that has three stories. "We'll get up there and lay down a base of fire!" Fitts is doing it by the book.

My shouting does no good. Nobody answers me. I start to pace, growing more furious with myself. There's no escaping this: I cut and ran. When shit got hot, I ran. I'm an NCO. I'm supposed to lead by example.

What the hell kind of example was that?

"Give me my fucking rifle. Who has my fucking rifle?" I am livid with myself.

I gave up the SAW, now I need a weapon. Mathieu shows up in front of me. He hands me my M4 and says, "There's a malfunction with your M4. It's jammed. It looks like something hit the trigger well."

He stands there in the street and gives me a detailed report on my weapon. Bullets are still zipping overhead every now and then. We're in a battle, and Mathieu is trying painfully hard to be thorough. But I've got other things to worry about. I interrupt him, "Mathieu, go get me a PEQ-2 Alpha!"

This is an infrared targeting system that fits atop our rifles. All you need to do is point the infrared laser at something and pull the trigger. You can even shoot from the hip, it doesn't matter. The bullets will tear holes in whatever the laser pinpoints. Even better, it can only be seen while wearing night-vision goggles. This way, the enemy won't know he's lased. For close-quarters fighting, this beats an iron sight or a red-dot scope hands down. It allows for speed, maneuverability, stealth, and quick firing.

Santos materializes out of the night and hands me his M16. The weapon is long and heavy and it has a full stock. Seated on the gun's rail is the laser sight I want. Nestled under the barrel is the blunt, reassuring presence of Santos's grenade launcher. This makes the weapon even heavier and more cumbersome, both detrimental in a close-quarters firefight.

I take the M16 and a thought occurs to me. If I go back into the house and die, the enemy will get my weapon and ammunition. I remember the insurgent we killed yesterday who had an M16.

I wonder what happened to the American who owned that rifle.

I start handing my extra magazines to Santos and Mathieu. I usually carry fifteen mags in the pouches on the right side of my chest. I keep three for myself. The others go to the men. If I die inside the house, the enemy will not get much ammo off my dead body.

The crack of a machine gun splinters our sense of safety. I watch Stuckert sink his head into his hands as he throws himself against the wall. A line of bullets gouge fragments out of the wall above his head. Stuckert looks up, pissed. He suddenly pivots out into the street. SAW shouldered, he scans for a target. An AK on semiauto blasts a few rounds at him. Bullet sparks flare in the street around him. He's undeterred. He takes aim on the rooftops and uncorks a long, angry burst.

"Why don't you fucking die already?" he shouts as his SAW bucks against him.

I key my radio, "Get a Bradley up here now." We need support. The fuckers are trying to pin us down on the goddamned street. I'm beyond furious; I feel responsible. Had I closed the deal inside the house, they would not be shooting at my men. If somebody dies now, it will be my fault. I should have crossed that stairwell room, stuck the SAW into the space between the stairs and the Jersey barriers, and just unloaded. I'd imagined that scenario a hundred times in training. I had prayed to be tested like that. I should have handled things differently. A true leader would have.

Bullets sweep the street again. A rash of sparks surges around me and several other men. Fitts's group blasts back with grenades and M16s.

"I should've assaulted that faggot by fire. I AM A GOD-DAMNED INFANTRYMAN! WE ARE NOT RUNNING AWAY! Get me a Bradley up here now." I look up and see Sergeant Jose Rodriguez looking at me as if I have lost my mind. Maybe I have. He holds the radio to his now gaping mouth. He says nothing, but I can see fear in his eyes. Is he afraid of the enemy—or me?

I put my face inches from Rodriguez's, "I want a Bradley up here *now.*"

Rodriguez doesn't react. I whack him across his helmet.

Fitts grabs me.

"Hey, chill out, bro. I need a heads-up. We're gonna bring a Brad up here. Don't lose focus on the fact that we got buildings unsecured all around us. We need you to calm the fuck down."

More near misses register off the asphalt.

"Oh fuck, we're all going to die," comes a voice thick with fear and panic.

I've got to end that shit right now. "We're not going to die," I shout into the night, "*they're* going to fucking die. We've got this under control, so just shut the fuck up, check in with your team leaders, and make sure everyone's fucking good."

That puts a clamp on the panic. We've got to fight back. Stuckert has no angle on the enemy. The grenades seem ineffective. We've got to do something else.

A round just misses Private First Class McDaniel.

"Jesus!" someone screams.

"C'mon. Where are they shooting from?"

Another round nearly takes out Stuckert.

"I almost got shot in the fucking head," McDaniel says in disbelief.

Stuckert scans everywhere looking for the man who is trying to kill him. "Where is this fucking dude?"

I step toward a group of soldiers clustered against the wall. "Give me your grenades."

The men start pulling frags off their kits. I turn to Sergeant Knapp and say, "Knapper, you ready? Alley-oop. Hooah?"

"Hooah, Sarge."

Knapp is the only one looking like he's in control at the moment. He sidles up to the wall and waits for me.

Someone tosses me a frag. I pull the tape off the spoon, slip the pin out, and toss the grenade to Knapp. Knapp catches it one-handed and launches it over the wall, aiming at the palm-lined garden inside the courtyard and the roof of the house. His arm is like a cannon. He can throw a football like a pro and blaze a baseball knee-high to the plate from center field. The man is an athlete with confidence to burn. We need that.

BOOM! The grenade explodes somewhere over by the palm grove.

I catch another grenade, prep it, and lob it at Knapp. Effortlessly, he slings it over the wall. His arm is simply amazing. In training, I saw him throw inert grenades fifty, sixty meters. He's a human mortar.

"Get another one ready. Another one. Another one. Another one," I scream in a rage to those around me moving too slow. "You listen to me, you stubborn fucks. Grab whatever you got and toss it to Sergeant Knapp."

We alley-oop three more grenades. He shows no sign of nerves as I throw sizzling frags at him. Had he dropped one, he'd have been done. Instead, he pitches them at the enemy, and for the moment their fire slackens.

Right then, Cantrell's Bradley lumbers up the street. The platoon scatters as the Brad arrives. Some get behind it for cover.

Others move down the wall out of the track's probable line of fire. Fitts divides his group into two maneuver elements. They shotgun the locks off the gates and disappear into the houses across the street.

Cantrell calls to me over the radio. "What do you need?" Shouting over a Bradley's engine is nothing but wasted effort. I make eye contact with my platoon sergeant and ask, "Can you bulldoze the fucking wall?"

Cantrell examines the area. The road is so narrow, the track looks like a monstrous toy, too big for the scenery.

"No way. I can't even maneuver to hit the wall hard enough."

I had wanted the Brad to smash through the wall, drive into the palm grove, and then tear up the side of the building with 25mm shells. Then we could call in a tank and blast the house to dust. That would take care of the fuckers inside for sure.

But it isn't going to go down like that. Sergeant Brad Unterseher, Cantrell's gunner, has a hard time even getting his cannon trained on the house. The outer wall is so tall that it obstructs the track's field of fire. And even if a tank could drive down this narrow road, it wouldn't be able to train its main gun on the house either. The 120mm gun tube is simply too long.

Cantrell comes over the radio, "I see a front room . . . okay, two front rooms."

"Juice 'em."

The turret traverses, his gun barks. The shells explode high and to the side, into the kitchen and living room. Unterseher walks his fire back and forth, seesawing between the two rooms. He pauses as Cantrell sweeps the track free of shell casings, which tumble hot and smoking into the street.

Unterseher pumps almost two hundred shells into the house. Cantrell holds him up and then asks me, "What else can I do?"

"Can you coax the palm grove?"

The M240 machine gun next to the cannon spits lead. I watch the fire tear the trees apart and realize the grove is a lot smaller than I initially thought. There's probably nobody in the palm grove. This isn't working.

I know what must be done, but I'm not ready to do it.

"What else?" Cantrell asks.

I key the mike and tell him to wax the palm grove some more. The M240 unloads again. This is probably pointless, and I realize I'm just stalling.

Cantrell backs the Brad up the street to where he can lay down a curtain of fire on the rooftops. Most of the shells go high, but the incoming shots cease—for the moment anyway.

"What else you got? You think we got them?" Cantrell asks.

Michael Ware hears the question. Over the din of the Brad's engine he shouts, "There's no way he's got 'em. Sergeant Bell, there's no way." Ware had been in the courtyard when the shit hit the fan. He had to dodge the machine-gun fire from the kitchen.

In my heart, I know he's right. But at the same time, there's no point in wasting any more ammunition. The Brad just can't get a kill shot into the house. At best, the barrage drove the insurgents away from the front windows overlooking the courtyard.

"I think we're good," I tell the Brad crew.

We're back to square one.

I start to pace again. Walking back and forth, my inner monologue spills out of my mouth. I'm talking to myself in front of Ware, in front of the men. I'm livid. This whole situation has taken my dignity. I need to find the strength to get it back.

Honor. What an overused word. It's an abstraction. Who can define it? All year in Iraq, I've stood with my men. If they had to fill sandbags until three in the morning, I'd be out there in the dirt and mud with them. I would never give an order, then go relax as they worked. My example is all I have as a noncommissioned officer. I take pride in that. That is my honor.

I've always told my men not to be afraid in combat. When the bullets start flying, they need to man-up and dish it back tenfold. How many times have I drilled this into them? Perhaps telling them to be unafraid is unrealistic. We're all human. Fear walks with us in every battle. Yet we cannot allow fear to dictate to us who we are and how we act. We cannot let it control us. We must master it. That is another essential element of honor.

As I storm around in the street, struggling with myself, Ware regards me curiously. The last thing I want right now is a journalist watching me grapple with my own demons. I turn away and pace back up the street, slipping on a couple of 25mm shell casings in the process. Another spray of sparks flares around me.

Do I have the balls? Do I have the nuts to do what my fucking heart wants me to do?

If I don't go in, they'll have won. How many times have we heard that American soldiers rely on firepower and technology because they lack courage? How many times has our enemy said that man-for-man, they can beat us? That's nothing new. The Germans and Japanese said the same thing in World War II.

Inside that house, I surrendered my honor and my manhood. Now I have to take both back, or live with the fact that they are right about me. That is unacceptable.

I rant and swear with abandon. Down the street, I see Sergeant Knapp taking care of my men like they are his little brothers. I want to cry I am so proud. I love these kids in a way I will never be able to express.

I see their faces. One by one. John Ruiz, Lucas Abernathy, Piotr Sucholas, Alex Stuckert, Victor Santos, Brett Pulley, Tristan Maxfield—they deserve more from me.

I stop pacing and let out a deep, rattling sigh. Only Ware remains near me on the street. Everyone else has moved away. Perhaps my display has convinced them I've gone mad.

But Ware is still here. The journalist. Our platoon's unofficial intel officer. We stare intently at each other.

"Fuck it," I say.

"Fuck it," agrees Ware.

That settles it. I'm going back in.

CHAPTER SEVENTEEN

A Soldier's Prayer

You know things are not right with the world when you share a spiritual moment with a damn journalist. But there it is. Mick Ware and I are standing on the street, digesting the finality of the option we've just chosen. His job is to write the story, not become the story. But he's done just that. He's committed, just as I'm committed. I can see it in his eyes.

It is time to do this thing. I half turn and roar, "Alpha Team, on me!"

And nothing happens. Most of the platoon is either in the two houses across the street, shooting locks and kicking in doors, or pulling security in front of them. Aside from Ware, there is no one around me.

"Bravo Team, on me! Sucholas!" I shout. I'm not sure I can be heard. Fitts's Mossberg shotgun is blasting in the background. Stray shots and random noise fill the street. My voice is almost gone. When I speak, it feels like I'm gargling with gravel.

I hear Maxfield call, "Hey, come on. Sergeant Bell needs us."

Maxy is over at the gate to the three-story house, pulling security. He grabs Ohle and together they run across the street to Ware and me. Maxy had been our company commander's driver because he's mechanically inclined. He hated that gig and was always begging to get into our platoon. We finally made it happen, and he proved himself. The kid's alright.

He's got blood speckled on his face. Sweat streaks the gunk on his cheeks, and he looks like he's got tiger stripes of filth running from his temple to his jaw. His eyes are huge. I wonder if he's just scared or really terrified.

"Sarge," Maxy says as he reaches me, "I'm here if you need me."

"We're going back in."

His eyes get a bit wider.

"Maxy, do you want to do this?"

"Yeah, I wanna do this."

Those eyes betray him. Then it strikes me that my eyes probably look exactly like his. He's fighting the same inner battle that I just fought. I notice that his lip is quivering. It makes me realize mine is, too. We both need a little encouragement.

"Fuck these guys. They're dead."

Maxy and Ohle gape at me.

I warm up. "We *got* this fucking shit, dude. Are you comin' with me? Is that new ammo, asshole?"

Both men nod. I need to put on an Oscar performance here. Terrified or not, I need them to know we're going to be resolute.

"Are you a fucking stud, Maxy? This is what you were born to do, man. You were born for this moment. You were born to kill these evil motherfuckin' terrorists. Let's terrorize them. We're gonna taste them. We're gonna eat their flesh and send them to fucking Lucifer. Do you hear me? Six- to nine-round bursts. Aim low, hit high."

More nods. I turn around to find Staff Sergeant Lawson running toward me.

"Whaddya doin', Bell?" he asks.

"We're going back in."

A ripple of shock flits across his face, then vanishes. He sets his jaw and comes close to me. He's drenched with sweat, and as he speaks, I can see his whole body shivering.

"I'm not going to let you go in there and die alone."

Now it is my turn to be shocked. I thought he'd try to talk me out of it. Instead, he's just set the gold standard for devotion to a brother in arms. In that instant, I feel closer to Lawson than to my own kin.

His words force me to confront a fact that has been hiding in the back of my own mind. We could die. *I* could die. I don't want to face it, but the look in his eyes reinforces the words. He's right. There may be no coming out. I start to shiver, as if every muscle from my toes to my eyelids picked this moment to spasm.

If I die, my death will be something I brought on myself. At least I'll go down fighting in the house, where I should have made my stand the first time. If they shoot me here in the street, I deserve that death without honor. If I get killed inside the house, well, I'll be dying for the right reasons. That is good enough for me.

"Dude, this is fucking insane," is all I manage to say. I want to tell Lawson so much more. I want to tell him what he's just done for me. His words, his loyalty, the bond he's just shown we share. It is unusual in my life, and I want to tell him. I don't know how.

Lawson nods his head. "I know, but I'm not gonna let you die alone."

"You're fucking coming?"

"Absofuckinlutely."

Lawson is the weapons squad leader. He doesn't have any reason to come with me. He's not one of my soldiers. He is my friend, a buddy really. If I survive, I will never forget this.

All the same, that doesn't mean I can't bust his nuts a bit. Humor diffuses the awkward, emotional moments that make infantrymen so uncomfortable.

I lean into him and whisper melodramatically in his ear, "Dude, I'm fucking scared to death."

"I know, man, I am, too," he replies.

I spring the trap: "You're a fucking pussy. Whaddya mean, you're scared?"

He bursts out laughing and the tension breaks for just a moment.

Ware stands next to Lawson, looking grim and resolute.

"Do you know what the fuck you're doing?" I ask him.

Ware nods. There is no wavering in his eyes.

"Look, dude, this ain't no fucking Samarra, pal."

"I'll stay right here."

I'm doubtful, but I've got other things to worry about. Like getting a grenade."

"Maxy, you got a grenade?"

"Yeah, Sarge."

"Good. Get your grenade ready."

"Roger."

We move toward the wall, not far from where Cantrell has parked his Bradley. I grab my radio and tell Cantrell the plan.

"We're gonna frag out and charge this bitch."

Maxy's got a SAW with a collapsible stock strapped to his back. The weapon is twenty pounds of deadweight, and I worry about him throwing a grenade while carrying it.

"Can you toss that fucker with a SAW on your back?" I ask him.

Without hesitating he says, "I can do it."

I want him to throw the grenade over the wall and as close to the house as possible. The blast should cause the insurgents to duck their heads long enough for us to rush into the courtyard. I don't want to get through the gate only to be greeted with a hail of machine-gun fire.

I tell Maxy to chuck the grenade.

He pulls the tape off, unbends the pin, and pulls it out. The spoon flies off, the grenade sizzles. He tosses it awkwardly, the SAW slipping around on his back.

Lawson grabs Maxfield and tosses him to the ground as he screams, *"Oh shit!"*

As soon as I see his release, I know we're in trouble. The throw looks short. I pull Ohle behind the Bradley. The grenade bounces atop the rim of the outer wall, bounces again and teeters on the edge. I'm convinced it's about to fall into the street and blow up, spraying the Brad with shrapnel.

At the last second, it rolls forward off the wall, and lands in the courtyard. *BOOM!* A cloud of dust unfurls.

I notice that the wall is so thick the grenade didn't even buckle it.

Wow. If the whole house is built like that, we're in trouble.

Maxy emerges from behind the Bradley, looking shaken.

I glare over at him, "Nice throw, asshole."

Chagrined, all he can say is, "Sorry."

It is time to go. To Ohle and Maxy, I say, "Charlie's Angels!" This is our platoon's code for forming up into a three-man wedge, weapons at high ready, just like the famous silhouetted trio of babes from the old television show. Ohle takes my left shoulder, Maxfield takes my right. "You stay on my goddamned wing, Hooah? No matter what happens . . . keep steady and fire."

"Hooah," they whisper in unison.

Ware is still with us. I was sure he would opt out of this one. I give him one more chance.

As we move toward the gate I say, "Do you know what the fuck you're doing?"

"Yes, I do," he replies, his Aussie accent particularly thick. I feel the need to test him further. I can't afford his courage to collapse on me.

"What are you doing? You're not fucking coming."

"Okay."

What the hell does that mean?

We move closer to the gate. I pause and look back. Ware is right behind us. The guy is determined, I'll give him that. I look Ware over. He sees this and says, "You can do this. You're a fuckin' stud, mate."

I stop looking at him. To see him put faith in me when I feel like a little bitch is unbearable. It makes me feel like an impostor.

We're going to be running across an open stretch of terrain, probably covered by at least one insurgent with a machine gun. Who knows how many others are on the roof. If we draw fire, the only thing that will save us is the fluidity of our motion. Before we launch our assault, I drill that into my men.

"If we take fire and somebody goes down, no one render aid. I don't care if I'm hit and screaming to Jesus. Leave me. Do not look down. Do not look back. Continue to move forward and shoot. Kill the threat or we all go down."

With wide eyes all around, everyone nods.

"Maxy, Ohle, suppress fire at forty-five degrees on either side. Do not stop. Keep moving. That's our only chance or we'll fucking die."

I take a long sip from my CamelBak. The water is scorching hot, like tea without the flavor. At least it's wet.

I take a step. The motion breaks all reservations and suddenly we're moving. Weapons at high ready, we round the gate and pour into the courtyard. Maxy and Ohle match me stride for stride. Ware is right on my ass. Lawson trails him, his 9mm pistol in hand.

We blitz past the first columns. I've got my eyes on the windows and rooftops. Ohle and Maxy scan the flanks. No fire greets us. I'm stunned by this. A minute ago, these insurgents couldn't wait to kill us in the street. The Brad and our grenade barrage must have forced them deeper into the house.

I'm panting now, my gear rattling as I lead my group to the door. We pass the second set of columns. With hand signals, I tell Ohle and Maxy to take up positions on either end of the house. They reach the corners and cover the sides. I smack Ohle on the helmet and give him a push in the butt. That's my signal for "get prone."

Lawson stops short of the house and covers the windows. He's particularly wary of the kitchen window after the PKM in there nearly killed his entire squad. He eyes it like a cold predator. Should somebody pop up there, both Ohle and Maxy would be sitting ducks. They need Lawson to protect their backs.

I reach the front door. It is standing open, inviting. The insurgents want this battle. It is their turf on their terms. They have all the advantages. Inside the foyer, it is pitch black. The little fires that had been burning have been snuffed out. As I move through the foyer, I notice I'm sloshing through a quarter inch of water. The Bradley's barrage must have blown apart a water tank in the kitchen.

Then the smell assails me. It is really rank in here now. It conjures soggy, rotting fish. The stench is powerful and putrid, and I beat back my gag reflex.

I pause to look behind me. Ware is in the doorway gazing right at me. He nods and has an expression on his face like a father about to watch his son pedal off on his first bike. That really pisses me off. Who the fuck is he?

Then he takes two steps into the room. Now he's right behind me.

I shake my head to show him my seriousness about him coming farther into the house.

I turn away from him and take a look into the living room through my NODs. It is empty. I start to move, but decide to check on Ware one more time. He's at the front door now. He bends down, places his video camera in the foyer and backs out into the courtyard. The red blinking light on the recorder is the only light I can see. Lawson slowly creeps past him into the house, his nine mil at high ready. He touches my shoulder with one hand, letting me know he's right next to me. I slap his hip, a signal for him to get behind me and hug the foyer wall. His presence reassures me, and for a fleeting moment, all the tension that's built up eases just a bit.

I flick the safety off on my M16 as I start to move again. This time, I inch into the back of the living room. For a second, I'm exposed in the insurgent's field of fire as I rush for the common wall with the kitchen. I get to the back corner just as the fuckers under the stairs start whispering to each other. The hushed tones in the darkness are unnerving. I freeze and to try to listen.

What are they up to?

My heart beats so hard it feels ready to come through my chest plate. I drop on all fours and crawl to the stairwell room doorway. Cautiously, I take a peek.

Just as my head pokes around the door frame, a burst of gunfire echoes through the house. Though it came from outside, it still startles me so badly that I jerk backward and nearly lose my balance. My heart kicks into overdrive, pounding so hard I can hear the blood rushing through my ears.

My night-vision goggles reveal little in the room around me. It is so dark, they barely function. The dim green outlines provide a surreal scene. It is hard to focus. My breathing comes quick and shallow. I'm probably hyperventilating.

I look up at the wall I'm using for cover. The insurgents have already shot it up during the earlier fight. Scores of bricks have been blasted to dust by the AK rounds. Pieces of them lie scattered on the living-room floor. This is nominal cover at best.

What a huge fucking mistake. You can't fuck up like this. They'll kill you before you can even get in there after them.

I'm getting light-headed now. Panic grips me. I've chosen the worst place to be in the house. If they open up with that machine gun, the wall will simply crumble around me. If I go through the doorway, well, they're waiting for that.

Okay, I've got to do something that evens the odds a bit. I lean back against the wall and try to think, but my mind is floating. Everything has an ethereal quality. I hear noises all around me. I can't tell what is my imagination and what is real. Am I hallucinating?

Get a grip. Get a fucking grip.

I whack myself on the helmet. I'm still disoriented. It fails to clear my head.

Come on, you've got to get a hold of yourself.

And then, I hear one of the insurgents speak from the stairwell room. He slurs something in Arabic with such preternatural calm that it sounds almost disembodied. The serenity in his voice is so out of place that it jars my nerves. A flood of terror ices my spine, and for a second I'm paralyzed.

The voice says something else. I can't understand it, but it is so tranquil and languid that I suspect he's drugged up.

In the distance, rifles bark. A shotgun blasts. Then I hear Fitts and Hall screaming. Is there an insurgent on the roof keeping them from getting into the courtyard? If so, we really are on our own now. They won't be able to get through the courtyard to us. Since we're inside, they can't use Cantrell's Brad to stitch the roof again.

What have I done to myself? This is crazy.

You're going to die.

My breathing is rapid fire. My head swims. I'm losing all control.

You stupid fuck. You've trapped yourself.

Then comes another voice, strong and confident. "Allahu Akbar!"

God is great? What was that for?

What the fuck are they doing? Is one of those dudes about to strap on a C-4 vest and take us all out? Is he psyching himself up before he detonates?

I have to act. I have to find out what they're doing and put a stop to it. Then I remember the 40mm grenade tucked in the launcher on my M16. That should do the trick. I get up into a crouch, then swing the rifle into the doorway. I don't aim; I just trigger the grenade. The grenade sails across the stairwell room, through the room where the insurgents are, and right out the back door that stands open a few feet to the right of the insurgent's bunker. A second later, I hear an explosion in the palmgrove garden behind the house.

Nice work. I've wasted my only 40mm. Come on, David. You've got to be disciplined.

I pull the M16 out of the doorway and roll back against the wall. As I do, my PEQ-2 gunsight lazes the living room and flares on something against the far wall. I notice a mirror fragment mounted low on the wall. There are others in here as well, strategically placed so the men in the other room can peer around every corner. I also make out something else: stacks of propane tanks lining one wall.

I'm in a room with flammable gas and open flames.

The insurgents can see every move I make. They can anticipate when I'll come through the doorway. That's why they were able to fire so effectively when we were all in here.

But it works both ways. Through the haze, I can see them. The one with the two AKs is young. The one behind the PKM has a well-trimmed beard and wears a wife-beater type of T-shirt.

They sit and softly recite their mantra over and over again.

"Allahu Akbar."

Jesus, that is unnerving.

In one mirror fragment, I watch the younger insurgent lower his AK. He bends down and pulls out what looks like a vest.

Oh my God. He's going to blow us all up with a bomb vest.

I continue to watch. It turns out to be not a vest, but a bag. The young one reaches in and withdraws a yellow-tipped rocket, a reload for an RPG launcher. He fumbles with the warhead. He's trying to arm it.

Right then, I know I'm dead. I'm trapped in the living room just as thoroughly as Fitts and the rest of the platoon had been only a few minutes before. If I run, they'll cut me down before I even get to the foyer. If I stay in place, they'll fire a rocket into the propane tanks stacked against the far wall. That'd probably blow a good portion of the house to pieces. That'll kill me, Lawson, and Ware. Maxy and Ohle will probably die, too.

I don't know if it is the air quality or the fact that I am breathing so quickly, but I'm so light-headed and dizzy now I can't tell what's real and what's running through my mind. My handle on reality is slipping.

I'm confused and wracked by fear, convinced that these are my last few moments. Words spill out of my mouth but I can't tell what I'm saying. Am I even talking aloud, or am I hearing my thoughts?

"Allahu Akbar!"

Oh Jesus.

More words tumble out. What am I saying? I have no idea. What's going on? What am I doing?

Then it dawns on me. I'm talking to God. The realization focuses my mind and for a second all confusion vanishes. I was raised by a churchgoing family. I believe in God. I'm irreverent as hell—I cuss and swear and have no problem killing the enemy. But at the same time, there is a reverence for the Almighty that lies deep inside me. It is one of those paradoxes you find in a lot of combat infantrymen. We're irreverently reverent.

My brain catches up to my words. I'm not praying, not in a conventional sense. I don't plan to ask for anything, and I am not begging for my life. Call it a soldier's prayer, a confession for having lived a life not worthy of His gift.

"Listen. I've been a horrible fucking person. I'm not gonna ask you to forgive me. I'm not gonna ask you to make it quick. I know I deserve to fucking suffer and hurt. I expect that. But I am just telling you that I will die the way I should have lived my fucking life—without fear. I will be completely fearless, and if I say I believe in You, then fuck it. I believe in You. And this is the way I'm going out, faithful and unafraid. They're fanatics. Fine. I'll be a fanatic, too."

I know I don't have much time left. The younger insurgent is still trying to prep the rocket, but any second his fumbling fingers will get it armed.

I try to remember the Twenty-seventh Psalm. It is one of my favorites. The words do not come. Instead, my brain locks on to *The Exorcist* again.

The power of Christ compels you.

From the next room I hear more whispers. "Allahu Akbar."

Suddenly, the movie line doesn't seem so foolish and random any more. They have their God. I have mine.

"The power of Christ compels you." Did I say that aloud? I don't know. I don't care. I seize those words. I embrace them. They become a lifeline. I stake everything on the strength they evoke. I utter them again, louder. I have my own mantra now. It is my talisman, my testament of faith.

"THE POWER OF CHRIST COMPELS YOU!"

"ALLAHU AKBAR! ALLAHU AKBAR!"

In one sudden rush, I carry the fight to my enemy.

CHAPTER EIGHTEEN

Man-to-Man

Somebody must die now. There is no turning back.

I bring my rifle to the ready up position. The M16 feels right; it is exactly what I need right now. Tucked firmly against my shoulder, I have a perfect eye line over the rifle's sights.

Across the room, I see the young insurgent standing behind the barriers. His head is down, still working on the RPG. The kid's gotta be drugged halfway to Neptune.

I take a step into the room; my feet slosh in the water and send ripples across the flooded floor. The M16's barrel pivots and stops when it is pointed at the insurgent's chest. I have the sight picture. My finger is about to end him.

He looks up. He stares at me with terror in his eyes. I know right then that I have surprised him. He doesn't have a chance, and he knows it, too.

"Jew!" he hisses in fear and spite, as if the word can protect him.

Close-quarters combat is instinctual, fought on the most basic and animalistic level of the human brain. Body language, eye contact, the inflection of a voice can turn a fight in a heart-beat. That is what happens here.

I know I've surprised him. His face is a portrait of fear. Instinctively, I know I've won. He knows it, too.

I have you.

I pull the trigger and hit him right in the chest. He staggers back. I take a step to the left to move out of the doorway. The room's carpet is so waterlogged that my boots make a sucking sound with each step.

After a heartbeat's pause, I shoot him again. This time, my bullet goes into his pelvis. He spins completely around and falls across the barrier. Hands splayed, head draped, he gushes blood across the concrete. The water around him turns a milky crimson.

The last thing he expected was a rush through the doorway. That surprise saved my life and doomed his.

I can win this fight. I can do this.

A red heat forms on my face. The back of my neck tingles.

Where's the second guy?

In a nanosecond I flip from confident to borderline panic. I'm in the open, exposed with no chance to return fire before he juices me. He has me cold, just like I had his friend.

My eyes dart to the right. The man with the well-trimmed beard is there, running across the room. My surprise appearance and the death of his friend have panicked him. He tries to flee. As he reaches the kitchen door, I fire two quick shots. I think one hits him in the back below his shoulder, but I can't be sure.

The door swings closed.

I slosh farther into the room, sidling left as I keep my rifle trained on the kitchen door to the right.

I've got to find some cover. If this dude comes out of the kitchen, I'm dead.

The stairway is the only thing that can give me any sort of protection. I head to it, and kneel down a few steps up from the bottom.

Movement in the darkness catches my eye. A shape appears in the living room doorway.

"Who's that?" I cry. I'm spooked and confused.

"It's me, Mick."

"Who?" I rasp. I feel like I'm in a trance. Everything has an ethereal quality. Motion seems fluid and slow. The adrenaline shots my body has taken have left me a little dizzy and nauseated. My stomach flutters. I train my rifle on the living room doorway. One more wrong answer and I fire.

The shadow in the living room answers me, "It's Mick! Mick the journalist!"

This doesn't make any sense to my adrenaline-sotted mind. "Who?" I ask again, and I hear despair in my voice.

"Don't do that, man," says Lawson, who must be somewhere in the living room behind Ware.

Something clunks on the floor upstairs. I glance up to the landing above me. Then I hear the insurgent in the kitchen. My eyes go back to that doorway. I hear a footstep above me. Then another.

There's somebody upstairs.

I could get rushed from two directions at once. I realize how precarious my position is.

And then I glance behind me. Over my left shoulder I see a doorway next to the stairwell.

Oh my God. I have an uncleared room to my rear.

My heart rate goes cyclic. Another surge of sweat soaks my uniform and gloves. I can't cover all three threats at the same time.

I'm in real trouble. Stay calm. You've got to fight your way out of this.

The insurgent in the kitchen recovers his composure. He rallies and kicks open the door. "Fucking Jewish dog!" he spits in broken English as he opens fire. Bullets splinter the stairs and burrow into the ceiling right in front of me. I duck against the wall.

He fires again.

I roll right and get my M16 on him. I trigger a few rounds. He ducks back inside the kitchen.

That's when I see Lawson. He's standing in the doorway to the living room now. He's got his 9mm pistol in one hand, and I watch him slam home a clip.

"Lawson, how many you got left?"

"One," he says morosely.

Lawson looks waxy and gray. His right sleeve looks slick and wet. I wonder if he's been wounded.

"Lawson, you okay?"

"I think I'm hit."

"You're shot?"

Oh fuck. Fuck.

My breathing is ragged. I'm shivering in my sweat. I've got to slow down and think this through.

"Lawson, get out of here. Get me a SAW and a shotgun."

"I'm not going anywhere, Bell."

"Dude, you're shot."

Lawson pauses. "It's not bad. Don't move from here."

I nod. He disappears into the living room.

You're good right here. Just breathe. You're good.

With a sudden rush, the insurgent in the kitchen throws open the door and storms out into the room, searching for a target. He's got a snub-nosed AK in one hand.

Reflexively, my M16 comes up. I feel the stock, cold against my shoulder. I pull the trigger. A fan of blood sprays from his back and spatters the wall behind him. It's an exit wound. My bullet went all the way through him. It spins him off balance. I fire four more times. He falls through the door to the kitchen and disappears.

Cantrell's voice booms into my ear, "Bellavia! Bellavia! Give me a fucking SITREP! Give me a SITREP!"

His voice is so loud it makes me even dizzier.

"Two fuckers down. One RPG!" I shout into my hand mike, attached to my Kevlar's chin strap.

I hear more movement over my head.

The man in the kitchen moans.

I could leave right now. I could run for the living room and get out. I can still survive this.

I can't move. Fear and pride intermingle.

I will not dishonor myself again. I will not let my men see me run again. Ever.

Every sound, every footfall seems magnified. Each one sends an ice pick into my nerves. My survival depends on both instinct and training. I remember Sergeant Major Darrin Bohn, the second-highest-ranking senior noncommissioned officer in our battalion, telling us, "Always recharge your weapon. I don't care if you've only shot four rounds. If you're in combat, you're gonna need 'em."

I've fired a lot of rounds. My M16 feels light, and I realize the magazine is almost empty. I don't know how many shots I have left.

I pull the magazine from my rifle, reach into a pouch on the right side of my vest, and grab a new one.

I hear another thump upstairs.

Someone's coming for me.

The new mag seems light, too. I glance down at it. It's empty. Somehow, I've mixed my empties in with my fresh ones.

Did I count this as a fresh one? Do I have three or two full mags? I don't know.

Something makes a brushing sound, like a jacket swishing against a wall. I can't tell where it came from.

Stay calm. Stay focused.

I hurl the empty mag. It slams into the wall next to the doorway to the living room.

My hand snakes into the ammo pouch. I feel for a full magazine.

A hollow footstep, like a boot on wood, comes from upstairs. Someone's on the stairs, around the corner from the landing.

I withdraw a fresh mag from the pouch—this one's nice and heavy—and slap it home. I slink my bolt forward.

Crouched on the stairs, I wait. Waves of fear rock me. I feel unsteady and totally vulnerable.

You've got to use the fear. Use it. Control it. Don't let it overwhelm you.

A scraping sound echoes through the house. I can't tell where it came from.

I still have an uncleared room behind me.

The hairs on the back of my neck stand straight up. My instincts tingle. I am certain somebody is behind me. If I stay here, I will die. I'll either get hit from the stairs or get shot in the back.

I slip off the stairwell and work along the wall until I reach the doorway. I slide into the back room, back against the wall so I cannot be surprised from behind. I make out a small mattress on the floor and a stand-alone armoire sort of closet on the far wall. I'm in a bedroom.

I hear footsteps on the stairs. Someone is hunting me.

I push myself along the wall until I come to a small alcove. I duck inside.

More footsteps on the stairs. He's close.

Through my radio earpiece, Cantrell's voice suddenly demands, "Goddamnit, Sergeant Bell! What the fuck is going on in there?"

My hearing is bad enough already. Cantrell's yelling in my

ear makes me almost deaf to everything else around me. That could get me killed in a fight like this.

He waits for an answer.

Another footfall on the stairs. I hear a board creak. He's right at the edge of the bedroom door.

I whisper into the radio again, "Two fuckers down, one RPG."

The room is a black hole. The darkness is almost total, and it has swallowed me up. I drop my night vision into position and flick it on. The goggles stutter on and off, then fail. Now I have only my natural senses against whoever is on the stairs. My senses against his.

Unless he has night vision that works. The thought chills me.

"BELLAVIA, GODDAMNIT. . . ." Cantrell is raving now.

I key my hand mike. "I'm really fucking stressed out right now, Sarge. I'm okay, but please just give me some fucking time. Everything's gonna be alright. Just give me some time. I've got two faggots down."

Cantrell launches into another tirade.

That's it. I'm done with the radio. I shut it off and pull the hand mike off my Kevlar. A second later, the radio splashes into the soggy area carpet at my feet. I cannot fight and get screamed at simultaneously. I grip my M16 and crouch in the alcove.

A black form pivots into the doorway. A muzzle flash leaps toward me and strobes the scene. I catch a quick glimpse of the shooter. He's wearing a belt of AK ammo pouches around his belly.

A couple rounds slam into the wall right beside me. If it wasn't for this alcove, I'd be dead.

Before he can get another shot off, I fire my M16. He bucks and jerks as I hit him again and again and again. My finger flies on the trigger, fueled by terror and adrenaline. By the time I ease off, I've hit him in the knees, stomach, and pelvis. He collapses in a heap in the doorway.

A tracer strikes the wall right next to my head.

What the fuck? Where did that come from? Is that one of my own shots ricocheting?

I look around wildly. Another flash. Another lightning streak shoots past me and smacks into the alcove over my head. It's another tracer, and this one came from the far wall.

There's somebody else in the bedroom.

CHAPTER NINETEEN

Blood Oath

Still in a crouch, I inch out along the wall across from the doorway, where the insurgent I've just shot lies motionless in a pool of blood and water.

Where did those two shots come from?

I edge past the mattress. I'm halfway across the room now. Even though it's dark, I can make out my surroundings, and there is nowhere my enemy could be hiding: a mattress on the floor, the empty alcove, not much else. Everything is quiet. I can't even hear the Brads on the street outside. This is the kind of silence that breeds terror. I have to keep control.

I'm almost to the edge of the armoire when I notice two splintered holes in the door.

There's a fucking boogeyman in the closet.

The doors fly open. A form jumps clear: an insurgent with two bandoliers of ammo crisscrossing his chest. He hits the floor amid a tangle of women's clothing that cascades out of the armoire with him. I'm so shocked that I can't even react. He tumbles past me, only an arm's reach away. I suck air in surprise and get a lungful of his pungent body odor. He's as foul and filthy as I am.

As he passes, he senses my presence and I can tell it startles him. He must have thought I was still across the room. He swings his snub-nosed AK-47 up under his right armpit. The barrel sticks out sideways. He's about to fire, but he trips on a dress that is half-in, half-out of the armoire. He goes flying and lands facedown on the mattress just as the armoire starts to teeter behind him.

The armoire tips over and nearly falls on top of him. I duck behind it just as he gets back to his feet and frantically triggers his AK. A wild stream of tracers pierces the darkness. Bullets whine and crack. He runs for it, his weapon still under his armpit, muzzle blazing.

Bullets thump into the armoire with hollow, hammerlike thuds. Each bullet sends a spray of splinters across the back of the room. Suddenly, I feel a sharp pain in my elbow.

Am I shot? Is this a bullet, or just a splinter?

My heart is a hummingbird. I can't focus. I can't even think. Instinct takes over. I get my M16 up over the side of the armoire. The room is a crazy-quilt pattern of darkness and hellish red from the sizzling tracers. I see him.

Steady. Steady.

I squeeze my trigger. The M16 barks. The bullet hits him in the leg. I fire again, but can't tell if I hit him or not. I think I have, but he keeps going. He hits the doorway, spins and sends another burst right over my head. I duck behind the armoire.

And then he's gone.

Hollow footsteps echo through the house. He's running up the stairs. I hear him scream something as he runs.

I'm frozen with terror. Did he just call for help? Are there more insurgents in here? I have no idea how many enemy I face.

My elbow hurts. I'm afraid to look at it, afraid of what I might find.

How did Fitts ever deal with getting shot?

If I have been shot, there's nothing I can do about it right now. The pain is not severe.

You know you will die horribly in here, right? This pain is just a warm-up.

A voice in my head is taunting me. For a minute, I'm stunned by it.

How many bullets can you stand? How many before you just say, "End this. End me." Can you take what Fitts took?

I try to erase those thoughts and focus on the moment. I don't have much luck. The darkness is so complete that my mind plays tricks on me.

Focus on your job. Stay alive.

Faulkenburg. Fitts. Lawson. All shot. You will be next.

FOCUS!

I reach into my ammo pouch and feel for a fresh magazine. There's only one left.

What the fuck was I thinking? Why the fuck did I do this?

"Ohle! Ohle!" I shout. My voice sounds unearthly, like I'm calling from the depths of my own grave. Just hearing myself unnerves me further.

"Ohle! I need ammo."

I don't hear a response. I wait. The darkness smothers me with fear, the silence spearing any hope.

"Sergeant Bell?"

My shoulders sag with relief. They've heard me outside. Somebody will come for sure now.

Fitts, where are you, man? Lawson, I need you. Help me.

I'm casting for any salvation, anything at all.

Shut the fuck up and get a grip. You've got to get a grip. They are still out there, and you will have to do this alone.

A door creaks. I can't tell where it came from. I search the blackness and train my M16 on the doorway.

A moan echoes through the house. It's wracked with pain and utterly despondent.

Something splashes in the stairwell room. Whatever that was, it was close.

Silence. I strain to capture any clue, any bit of noise to tell me what to expect.

Something slides along the wall on the other side of the doorway. I hear breathing. Somebody is close.

"I will kill you and take your dog collar."

It is a malevolent, accented voice, low and totally devoid of fear. Its self-assured tone triggers a memory of the Nicholas Berg beheading video we watched at our base so long ago. It took them twenty-six seconds to decapitate him, and it was horrifying to watch. They were self-assured, too.

Now my imagination conjures a scene: my severed head, a grimy hand pulling my bloody dog tags free.

That's never gonna happen. Never—gonna—happen—.

He's mind-fucking me, this one behind the door. I can't see him. I start to tremble. I fight it, but I can't control my body's physical reaction to this terror.

I can either go to pieces completely, or mind-fuck him back.

"Okay, listen up. I know you are not going to motherfucking stop. You know I am not going to motherfucking stop. *La ta quiome.*"

La ta quiome is my broken Arabic best for "Do not resist."

The enemy behind the door sniggers. He spits a curse in his native language. Sometimes it sounds like Arabic and sometimes it sounds totally different. Could that have been Farsi?

Am I fucking fighting Iranians in here?

"Mommy will never find your body."

His words are like a stiletto to my self-control. My entire body shakes violently. My stomach heaves. I'm verging on hysteria.

"I'll give you one last chance, or I'm gonna kill you! Fuck you, bitch," I sound like a raspy pubescent boy whose voice has just broken.

The man behind the door mutters something. All I under-stand is *"Fajarah,"* which means "evil one."

Wrong. Who is the evil one here, you motherfucker?

"You scared of me, faggot? You little godless whore? *La ta quiome Amerki mooshot wahed."* Do not resist American First Infantry.

I try one more time to recite my best Arabic from my First Infantry Division's *Surviving in Arabic* handbook we received back in Germany.

"Nah noo Amreekee oon. Man al massol?" *We are Americans. Who is in charge?*

A voice calmly whispered from the hallway near the kitchen, "Allah. Al hum da Allah." I immediately recognize this as "God, all blessed God."

Frustrated, I screamed back, "La ta khaf, mujahideen. Al hum da allah." *Do not be afraid, mujahideen. God is blessed.*

This doesn't rattle him. In fact, my words only encourage the one behind the door.

"I'll cut your head off." His accented English is smooth and so cold and calculated that I can tell he thinks he's got the upper hand on me. He thinks he's in control. He's going to take his time.

He speaks a few more words in his native language. They are measured and slow. It still doesn't sound like Arabic. I wonder if I'm hallucinating.

Have I completely fucking flipped out?

I sense movement. I flick my NODs down and give them one more try. This time, they work. In the dim greenish outline of the doorway, I catch a glimpse of a man's shoulder and arm. He's peering inside to look for me. He's given me a shoulder.

Big mistake.

Another overdose of adrenaline surges into my system. I have him.

My infrared laser pins a long white line right on his shoulder. I squeeze the trigger. The M16 shatters the quiet. His shoulder explodes. He shrieks and falls into the doorway. He must have been standing on the last stair, leaning in. Now he's slipped, and he's mine.

I pump four more rounds into him. He tries to shoot me, and he may have gotten a shot off. In the chaos, I can't tell if he's fired, but I can tell who he is. This is the man from under the stairs who ran into the kitchen at the start of the fight. I recognize his wife-beater T-shirt and well-trimmed beard.

I thought I shot you twice already. What the hell?

He lands on the floor, bullets in his shoulder, chest, and stomach.

He's got to be dead this time. Right?

I peer over the side of the armoire. All I see is an indistinct shape flopped on the floor in the doorway. I can't tell if he's moving or not. Right then, I hear another moan from somewhere else in the house. It is hollowed out and dull this time, as if whoever made it is close to death.

I duck behind the armoire to think.

What now? What are you going to do now?

I finger my last full magazine.

Always recharge your shit.

Sergeant Major Darrin Bohn's words ring in my head again. He's our command sergeant major now that Faulkenburg is dead.

Faulkenburg. The thought of him sends a curl of anger through me. I shudder and curse under my breath.

He's fucking dead. Use it. Use the anger and the grief. Use it to kill these guys.

I'm not leaving this house, not until this is finished.

A competing image of my wife and son flash into view. It is Halloween, and my son is dressed in a miniature set of camouflage. He has my name tape Velcroed to his chest. Deanna's getting him ready to go trick-or-treating. She's so damn beautiful—full lips, shoulder-length brown hair, and those green eyes that always devastated me.

They are gonna be so hurt when the contact team knocks on their door.

No, fuck no. I can't think of them. That'll destroy me. If I think about them, I'll lose my nerve and then I'll never get home to them.

I focus on Faulkenburg and I imagine the sight of his broken body in the street. I think about Rosales, Sprayberry, Garyantes, Prewitt, and Vandayburg—all the men we've lost. Rage boils.

That's right. Use it. Feed it in. Turn it to hate. Use it. It is your fuel. Use it.

I take a deep breath and hold it. My nerves are flayed from the whipsaw of emotions. I know I don't have much left, but I am not going to quit. I can't.

I rise up from behind the armoire. The darkness is total; the tracers have burned themselves out.

Deanna. Evan. I'm sorry. I can't leave this fight. This is what I am. A warrior. It is my blood oath. If I turn my back on that again, I will be nothing and I can't face that.

I creep around the mattress, M16 at the ready. When I reach the doorway, I nearly slip. The water here is deeper and cloudy, probably from blood.

Neither corpse is in the doorway. I study the floor. Dark slicks of blood trail off into the stairwell room. It looks like one or both of them crawled into the kitchen.

Do I go finish them off and face the threat of somebody coming down the stairs again? I could get shot in the back as I go into the kitchen. Or do I go upstairs and face the bandolier-wearing Boogeyman from the closet? He's up there, somewhere in the darkness, waiting for me to do just that.

Or do I leave, get the rest of the squad and do this right.

No! I brought this on myself. I have to finish it.

Lawson is wounded. He's wounded because I didn't finish this the first time. I will not risk another man.

Fuck it.

I step through the doorway and onto the stairs. Eyes on the landing, I drop my current magazine out of the M16. I catch it and sling it into my pouch, then search for my last fresh one. I seize it and slam it home. The new mag makes a metallic *snick* as it snaps into place. I've got twenty-nine rounds in the mag and one in the pipe.

I begin to climb the stairs. There's no turning back now.

The image of my boy in his costume tumbles through my mind again. I hear his little voice in my head. It is the last thing he said to me on the phone before I left for Fallujah.

"I am going to save you, Daddy."

I'm sorry, buddy. I love you. I'm so sorry.

CHAPTER TWENTY

The Last Caress

A desolate soul, bereft of hope, climbs the stairs. There is nothing left in me; I feel the emptiness like a weight on my chest.

I take another step and pause. I hear nothing but the racing of my own heart and the rush of blood through my ears. Maybe he isn't waiting for me. Maybe the house is clear.

I take another step and pause. Suddenly I become aware of the sounds of the night outside the house. I hear shouting. An AC-130 Spectre rumbles overhead, searching for targets. The throb of the Bradley's engine rises from the street. Voices step all over each other and melt together in a confusion of babble.

I'm dimly aware that Fitts is firing his shotgun. I hear two blasts. I have no idea where he is, or how far away.

I take another step. Two more to go and I'm at the landing.

Like a savage animal, I sniff the air. A pungent scent hits my nostrils. It is the Boogeyman. His appalling stench lingers in the air here. He's close.

I take another step with my right foot, only to slip on a slick puddle of blood. My head bobs down and I fight to retain my balance. Just then, a muzzle blast erupts right above my head, not a yard in front of me. The flame spouting from the AK casts flickering shadows on the stairwell wall. I see the shape of the Boogeyman outlined there, his shadow wielding its rifle in my direction. I feel the bullet whir right over my Kevlar. It jars my teeth.

I should be dead. That should have killed me. If I hadn't slipped on his blood, I'd have a bullet hole in my forehead.

In a half crouch, I sling the M16 up and fire a wild shot at the landing. My bullet embeds itself in the far wall. But in the light of my muzzle, I see his face. I've missed him, but I see his eyes. They're full of fear. He's afraid, and that emboldens me.

"You're gonna fucking die, dude."

He runs for it. I hear him clatter up the second flight of stairs.

I move to the landing and follow him around to the next flight of stairs. Smoke swirls trail in my wake. We've filled the stairwell with cordite and gunpowder.

A slip of one foot saved my life.

I can't possibly have any luck left now. The top of the stairs awaits. All I see is darkness.

I see a contact team at my door back home in New York. They're dressed in Class As and look appropriately sober. My wife is tearing up in the doorway, Evan clinging to her without understanding the moment.

I am hallucinating.

I see a sea of tombstones. My mother stands at one, lost and alone. Born November 10, died November 10. Her youngest gone.

How would Evan react? Would he grow up embittered and confused? Would he wonder why his father chose a foreign shore and a fight with strangers over being his dad? Deanna has always been bitter about that. After Kosovo, I could have come home. I chose to go to Iraq. I remember her parting words: "You've chosen the army over us."

Maybe I have. But how could I have let my soldiers go without me? What kind of man would do that? I had to be there with them, to take care of somebody else's son, somebody else's husband. I had to make sure they came home.

I hear movement up ahead. A boot scrape and a grunt tell me the insurgent is not far away.

I've hardly seen Evan these past three years. I've missed most of his life.

I hear another grunt. He sounds like he's moving farther away now.

My elbow aches. I try to ignore it. I refuse to check the wound, still afraid of what I might find.

I take a step into the blackness. The toe of my boot slides up the next stair and finds footing. I'm three from the top now. I still can't see anything. I try my night vision again. Nothing. This will have to be done with bare eyes.

How long will they mourn? Will Evan even care? Or will he just hate me for never being a part of his life?

Stop it. Get a handle on yourself.

Where will I be buried?

This morbid, evil voice wants me to die. It baits me. It wants me to fail. Why am I so self-destructive? Is it guilt? Is it that I don't think I deserve to live?

Fuck it. This has to stop.

I hesitate on the last stair. For a second I clear my head completely. A deep breath fills my lungs. The night air is cold and fouled with so many terrible smells from the house. Blood. Rotting fish and stagnant water. Filthy bodies. Smoke and sulfur. Am I sure I'm not in hell?

A shredder. I see a shredder.

With careful deliberation, in my mind's eye I feed every image and every memory of my family into the shredder. The tattered pieces fall out the bottom.

No more of this. It stops here.

I'm on the second floor now. There's a door to a rooftop balcony at my side. Another doorway looms down the hall. My enemy is in there.

I have a grenade. One frag. It is upside down inside the pouch on my body armor. I know this is the time to use it. I should have used it going up the stairs, but I wasn't thinking clearly.

I pull the tape off, extract the pin, and hold the spoon down. I inch along the hallway to the door. This is the most vulnerable moment. He's probably waiting on the other side, ready to shoot whatever part of my body I give him, exactly as I did to his buddy downstairs in the bedroom.

I peer inside anyway.

He's standing in the middle of an L-shaped room, a dark figure swathed in blackness. I cannot see his face. He's just a form, a shadow. A wraith.

I hold the grenade to my right ear and release the spoon.

PFFTT.

One . . . two . . . three. . . .

I throw the grenade and see it strike him right on the head. He recoils from it as the grenade spins off behind him and disappears. I duck into the hallway and back away from the door.

Boom! In these tight confines, the blast is shattering. My ears ring. Smoke boils from the room. I hear a grunt, then a moan.

I got him.

I spin into the room, M16 steadied on my shoulder.

He is lying on the floor, a chunk of flesh torn from his right forearm.

I'm about to fire and kill him when I smell propane. It gives me pause. I look around the room for the source. In one corner, a pile of foam sleeping mats are smoldering. Oily black smoke leaches off them. Tendrils wick along the ceiling and intermingle. Soon, the room will be full of smoke.

Two propane tanks rest at my feet. Stacks of them line the wall. The entire room is nothing more than a giant bomb.

If I trigger my M16, will the tracer set the propane off? I have no idea. I can't risk it.

The wounded Boogeyman stirs. He's flat on his back, but he still holds his AK in one hand.

I step forward and slam the barrel of my rifle down on his head. He grunts and suddenly swings his AK up. Its barrel slams into my jaw and I feel a tooth break. I reel from the blow, but before I can do anything he backhands me with the AK. This time, the wooden handgrip glances off the bridge of my nose. I taste blood.

I back off and wield my M16 like a baseball bat. Then I step back toward him and swing with everything I've got. The front sight post catches him in the side of the head. I wind up to hit him again, thinking that at the very least I've stunned him. As I get ready to swing, his leg flies up from the floor and slams into my crotch.

I stagger backward, pain radiating from my groin. The pain drives me into a fury. I realize I've dropped my rifle. I can't see where it fell; the smoke is getting thicker, and it is so acrid my eyes start to water and burn.

I leap at my enemy. Before he can respond I land right on top of his chest. A rush of air bursts from his mouth. I've knocked the wind out of him. I tear at my body armor and get it opened. With my right hand on the sleeve that holds my five-pound front armor plate, I grab the insurgent's hair and ram his head forward, jamming his chin into his chest. He's pinned in place now. All I have to do is finish him.

I beat him with the inside of my armor plate. I smash it against his face again and again and again until blood flows all over the inside of my shirt. He kicks and flails and screams. Every scream gets cut off by another blow from the plate. He struggles under me. An arm lashes out. Fingers scratch my face. I ram the plate harder into him. He keens and howls, yet he refuses to submit.

Somebody answers him in Arabic. The voice comes from the roof above us.

Oh my God. My back is to the door, I don't know where my weapon is, and there's more coming down.

"Shut the fuck up!" I bash his face again. Blood flows over my left hand and I lose my grip on his hair. His head snaps back against the floor. In an instant, his fists are pummeling me. I rock from his counterblows. He lands one on my injured jaw and the pain nearly blinds me. He connects with my nose, and blood and snot pour down my throat. I spit blood between my teeth and scream with him. The two of us sound like caged dogs locked in a death match.

We are.

He hits me again, and I nearly fall off him. Somehow, I hold on. I've got to slow him down or he'll get the upper hand. I punch him in the face; my fist meets gristle. Then I remember my helmet. I've still got my helmet on.

I yank my Kevlar off my head. My night-vision goggles go flying into the room. I don't need them anyway. With both hands I invert the helmet and crack his face with it. He shrieks with pain. I bring it up again, but he's swinging his head from side to side and I don't aim my next blow well. The helmet glances off his shoulder and hits the floor. I can see that he's older than the others in the house. His hair is flecked with gray and he's got age lines creasing his face.

"Esqut! Esqut! Esqut!" I am hysterical now as I try to tell him to shut up in Arabic.

He screams on. I hear footsteps on the roof. I do not have long.

The Kevlar comes down again. This time I connect. It's a

crushing blow to his face. Blood splashes both of us. We're slick it with. He grabs my hair and tries to punch me again. I bash his face yet again with the Kevlar.

"*Terra era me!*" That's my broken Arabic for "stop or I'll shoot."

I'm not sure what I expected to accomplish with that. He claws and scratches at me. My elbow burns. My jaw, mouth, and nose spew blood.

My voice isn't human any more.

Neither is his. We've become our base, animal selves, with only survival instincts to keep us going.

I slap one bloodied hand over his mouth and jam all my weight down on it. For the moment, it muffles his calls for help.

"*Es teslem! Es teslem! Es teslem!*" I'm almost crying now as I tell him in Arabic to surrender.

He thrashes and kicks.

"*La ta quiome!*" My voice is just about gone.

He lashes out at me. He lands some blows, but my left hand never leaves his mouth. My right hand comes up. I see his eyes grow wide. He tries to shake his head, but I've pinned it in place. Like a claw, my right hand clutches his throat. I feel his Adam's apple in my grasp. I squeeze, squeeze, squeeze.

A choked scream—or was it a plea? I can't tell. He kicks and bucks. His hands beat against me. I can't get enough pressure on him. He's still strong, still in the fight despite everything I've done.

I cannot break his throat. I don't have the strength. But I can't take my left hand off his mouth. If I do, he'll call for his buddy on the roof again.

"*Esqut, esqut,*" I whisper. *Shut up.*

He opens his mouth under my hand. For a second I think this is over. He's going to surrender. Then a ripping pain sears through my arm.

He clamped his teeth on the side of my thumb near the knuckle, and now he tears at it, trying to pull meat from bone. As he rages against my right hand, his Adam's apple still in my clutch, I feel one of his hands move under me. Suddenly, a pistol cracks in the room. A puff of gunsmoke rolls over us. The bullet hits the wall in front of me.

Where did that come from? Does he have a sidearm?

I cuff him across the face with my torn left hand. He rides the blow and somehow breaks my choke hold on him. I bludgeon his face. He tears at mine.

We share a single question of survival: Which one of us has the stronger will to live?

I gouge his left eye with my right index finger. I am astonished to discover that the human eye is not so much a firm ball as a soft, pliable sack. I try with all my might to send my finger all the way through. He wails like a child. It unnerves me, and I lose the stomach for this dirty trick. I withdraw my finger. Something metallic hits the cold concrete flooring. It is the same hand cannon that almost took my head off. His interest in trying to grab it opens a window of opportunity for me.

As he reaches for his pistol, I slam my left fist as hard as I can down onto his collarbone. He swings wildly at me again. My helmet's gone now. I have no idea where my M16 is. I've got nothing but my hands left. And they're not enough. We will struggle and exhaust each other until the stalemate is broken by whoever's friends show up first.

I feel my strength ebbing. I don't have much left. He kicks at me, throwing his whole body into it. I've got to end this. But I don't know how.

"Surrender!"

I'm ignored. He fights on, and I can sense he's encouraged. He's close to getting free of me. I swallow hard and gag. My mouth is full of blood, and I don't know whose. Both of us are slick with it; we have been bleeding all over each other. I taste bile through the blood. My body's maxed out. I don't know what to do.

Somebody shouts something. I listen for Arabic. I think I hear, "Are you okay?" and "God!"

The man beneath me tries to answer but I cork him with another fist to his face. He takes it and jabs weakly back at me. Blood sprays from his face and speckles onto mine. My grip on him loosens. One more push, and he'll be free.

Suddenly I remember the night of the breach, when Santos and Stuckert were caught in the wire. I used my Gerber knife to try and cut them free, and when I was done, I clipped it to my belt. I had just used it earlier to poke the dead guy outside in the street.

My belt. I have a knife on my belt.

I sit up, putting my weight onto his chest. Slowly I get to my feet. My legs are spread, my center of gravity low. I reach for my belt just as he comes up after me. His face rams my crotch. I feel his teeth clamp onto me.

Oh Fuck.

I pummel down on his head, but he grinds his teeth harder. Searing agony, pain I never knew I could survive rakes across my nervous system. It threatens to take my consciousness. I struggle against it, but I am weak.

It takes a monumental effort to unhitch the Gerber from my belt. I use it as a bludgeon. At first, my blows are pathetic. They land on his head and do nothing to dissuade him. He growls and screams and holds down his bite. I'm almost paralyzed with the pain. It blasts every nerve, every sinew. My brain is overloaded.

Finally, suddenly, I become a madman.

My arm comes up over my head, then chops down with every bit of power I have left. It sends the Gerber's handle thundering down onto my enemy's head. Stunned, he sags back onto the floor.

I can feel warm liquid trickling from my crotch down my legs, but I can't think about it right now. I flick the Gerber open. The blade locks in place.

I pounce on him. My body splays over his and I drive the knife right under his collarbone. My first thrust hits solid meat. The blade stops, and my hand slips off the handle and slides down the blade, slicing my pinkie finger. I grab the handle again and squeeze it hard. The blade sinks into him, and he wails with terror and pain.

The blade finally sinks all the way to the handle.

I push and thrust it, hoping to get it under the collarbone and sever an artery in his neck. He fights, but I can feel he's weakening by the second.

I lunge at him, putting all my weight behind the blade. We're chin to chin now, and his sour breath is hot on my face. His eyes swim with hate and terror. They're wide and dark and rimmed with blood. His face is covered with cuts and gouges. His mouth is curled into a grimace. His teeth are bared. It reminds me of the dogs I'd seen the day before.

The knife finally nicks an artery. We both hear a soft liquidy spurting sound. He tries to look down, but I've pinned him with the weight of my own body. My torn left hand has a killer's grip on his forehead. He can't move.

I'm bathed in warmth from neck to chest. I can't see it, but I know it is his blood. His eyes lose their luster. The hate evaporates. His right hand grabs a tuft of my hair. He pulls and yanks at it and tries to get his other hand up, but he is feeble.

"Just stop! Stop . . . Just stop! *Rajahan hudna,*" I plead. Please truce. We both know it is just a matter of time.

He gurgles a response drowned in blood.

His left hand grabs my open body armor. He pulls at the nothing inside my vest. His fingers scratch weakly against my ribs. It won't be long.

I keep my weight on the knife and push down around the wound in staccato waves, like Satan's version of CPR.

His eyes show nothing but fear now. He knows he's going to die. His face is inches from mine, and I see him regard me for a split second. At the end, he says, "Please."

"Surrender!" I cry. I'm almost in tears.

"No . . ." he manages weakly.

His face goes slack. His right hand slips from my hair. It hangs in the air for a moment, then with one last spasm of strength, he brings it to my cheek. It lingers there, and as I look into his dying eyes, he caresses the side of my face.

His hand runs gently from my cheek to my jaw, then falls to the floor.

He takes a last ragged breath, and his eyes go dim, still staring into mine.

CHAPTER TWENTY-ONE

A Smoke on Borrowed Time

Tears blur my vision. I can hardly see him now, but he looks peaceful.

Why did he touch me like that at the end?

He was forgiving me.

He was no boogeyman. He was a man in a closet. His blood is sticky on my skin. It loses its heat, and soon I'm shivering as it dries on me.

Every part of my body aches with pain. My crotch is the worst. It is almost unbearable, and for a moment I do nothing but lie there, holding myself, shivering uncontrollably.

Karma is a motherfuck. This is what I get for laughing at Pratt. This is my reward for all those jokes.

I don't know how bad it is. I don't want to know. All I know is that if the men find out, I will become the laughingstock of the entire army. I'll forever be known as the NCO who had his dick bit by a bad guy. The John Wayne Bobbitt of the infantry. *Fuck.*

I try to wipe the tears from my eyes, but manage only to smear more blood into them. They burn, and I'm almost blind. I try to wipe my face with a patch of shirt above my sleeve, but that's soaked with blood as well. I've got no way to get my eyesight back.

I reach down inside my pants. I feel a ragged wound, then another. Two harsh teethmarks, but I am intact. I manage a long sigh of relief. It is not as bad as it could have been.

A desperate man, fighting for his life, will do anything to survive. Never forget that.

I wipe my eyes again. This time, I get one clear. Good enough. I look around the room. The man I've killed lies next to me, his arms splayed, legs out. Not far from one hand is his AK-47. My M16 lies nearby. I reach over and pick it up. I get to one knee and jam the stock onto the floor, using the rifle as a crutch.

My stomach churns. I feel like I'm going to throw up. I put my head down and breathe slowly until the nausea passes. I get to my feet. Outside the house, I hear a commotion. I don't know what's going on, and the sounds are too jumbled to give me any clue.

Is that my platoon?

I stumble to the doorway. I'm dizzy and light-headed. A zombie: alive but barely functioning.

What I thought was a hallway is really a foyer, and at the end of it, there's another door that I hadn't noticed when I first came up the stairs.

Now what? Do I open that door and clear the rest of the floor?

I don't have anything left. I'm not going to do it.

As I stand there, too spent to move, a noise crashes over my head. I look up just in time to see a man in green military fatigues jump off the roof over me and land almost on top of me. He's the one who had been calling out to his buddy.

I'm so startled I slip and fall back on my ass. He is surprised, too. He hits the patio floor and drops his AK. I bring my M16 up just as he reaches for his rifle. The dregs of my body's adrenaline supply shoots into my system. He turns to run away toward the wall that leads two stories down to the palm grove. I hit him with two shots in the lower back.

My bolt clicks and locks back. I'm out of ammo. He makes no noise but starts getting up. I can't get into another hand-to-hand fight, I don't have the strength. I push myself back into the smoldering room and dive for the dead guy's AK. It is set on automatic fire. I swing around and pull the trigger as I lunge back into the hall. The AK burps a short burst, then goes silent. I'm out of ammo. From less than two meters away, I've completely missed him.

I remember I've got a few half-empty mags left in my pouch. I roll back into the smoky room with the dead insurgent and grab my M16. With my back to the wounded insurgent, I slam a mag home and release the bolt forward. Two quick steps and I turn to face him on the roof.

The insurgent has moved to the edge of a shrapnel-scarred patio with a yellow water tank. He is dragging his AK by the strap. He's unsteady on his feet and I can tell he's seriously wounded. It looks like he's about to jump off the roof. I notice a puddle of blood near him.

I empty my magazine into him. I see my bullets hit home as strings of flesh from his thigh spin out. I squeeze the trigger again and again until the bolt clicks. Even then, I can't stop.

The insurgent, bloody and torn, pitches forward headfirst and falls from the roof. I hear him land in the garden below with a wet thud. Blue-gray smoke drifts up from my M16's barrel. I stand on the rooftop and watch it dissipate into the night air.

Slowly, I ease over to the edge of the roof and look down. There's an imprint in the vegetation where the insurgent landed below me. I can see his sneakers in the dark, folded grotesquely over his head. A deep belch from a SAW knocks bark and branches off the palm trees that surround him. His legs collapse onto the ground.

Must have been Ohle or Maxfield. That had to have killed him. If not, we'll finish him later.

I turn and limp for the door to the foyer. One shotgun blast shakes the house, then another. A 9mm pistol cracks, followed by a chattering M4. Fitts and Lawson. Misa and Hall. They're downstairs now. I don't want to be standing in the open. I know if it were me, I would shoot anything without a helmet, especially in the shadows.

I sit down in the corner, away from the stairway. I pull out a Marlboro Red. My lips are distended and swollen. I don't care. I light the cigarette and take a long drag, and stare at the drying blood caked under my fingernails. I reach over and pull a chunk of the wardrobe's wood, no more than a supersized splinter, out of my arm above the elbow.

What a fucking day.

Hollow footsteps. Somebody's on the stairs. I take another drag and exhale. The smoke lingers in the air.

My throat is raw, like I have a strep infection.

"Hey."

"Sergeant Bell, Sergeant Bell, where are you?"

It's Lawson.

"Up here," I manage.

"Sergeant Bell, are you okay? Why didn't you stay downstairs? Are you okay, man?"

"Yeah, I'm good. I'm good."

It's a lie. I wonder if I will ever be good again.

CHAPTER TWENTY-TWO

Nut to Butt in Body Bags

Afternoon, November 17, 2004
Cloverleaf east of Fallujah

Seven days later, we emerge from the Battle of Fallujah filthy,
encrusted with dirt, and stinking. We are less than human, just
ragged outlines of what we once had been. Ten days of constant
house-to-house combat, no showers, no respite. Here at the
cloverleaf, we are anomalies among the tidy uniforms and pol-
ished boots of what the late Colonel David Hackworth once
called Rear Echelon Mother Fuckers, REMFs.

Our uniforms are covered with dried gore, blood, grime,
concrete dust, and smoke stains. All of us have brown slicks of
diarrhea pasting our pants to our backsides. We're so sick that
some of us can hardly walk.

We haven't shaved since November 8. We look like bedrag-
gled castaways with whiskers and wild, red-rimmed eyes. Fitts is
the hairiest; he looks like an unwashed and blood-spattered
Grizzly Adams.

As we exit our Bradleys, every step is a challenge. *You're not
going to keel over in front of all these REMFs, are you?*

Our stomachs churn. Our asses feel scorched. We have gouges and cuts and nicks and bruises one atop the other. Our faces are a swollen mess. We've got infections everywhere and the pus to show for it. We are done.

First Sergeant Peter Smith of Alpha Company has arranged hot chow for us. We have been longing for a warm meal, craving it. We don't even care what it tastes like. Our last hot meal was on the eleventh, and we need to fill our bellies. Our stomachs gurgle and spin. We are simultaneously famished and nauseated, and even though we know whatever we eat will just feed our diarrhea, we don't care.

We stagger toward the mess area. Our reeking funk sends all REMFs swinging from our path. At least it's good for something.

The last few days have been brutal on all of us. Our executive officer, Lieutenant Edward Iwan, is dead. A rocket almost tore him in two at the stomach while he was bending down in his Brad's turret to hand a reporter his equipment. At first he was somehow able to cling to life. First Sergeant Peter Smith, Sergeant Eric Dove, and Lieutenant Colonel Newell helped medevac him to our battalion aid station, where our surgeon, Major Lisa DeWitt, personally drove him to the Marine hospital at our base in Fallujah. When she got there, the surgeons said his type of wounds were always fatal. She begged until they agreed to look at him. Though his vital organs were crushed and bowels ruptured, Iwan still had a pulse. That galvanized the Marine doctors, who wheeled him into surgery and fought frantically for forty-five minutes to save him. Lieutenant Iwan's sheer force of will kept his heart beating long after anyone else's would. But in the end, there was no hope. Our beloved executive officer died on the operating table.

Even though Iwan was gone, his Bradley crew's firepower was desperately needed back into what quickly became a full-blown battle after they left on November 12. Sergeant Tyler Colly,

Iwan's gunner, was only inches away when the horrific scene played out in front of him. He was the first to render aid to our mortally wounded executive officer, and now had begun the unenviable task of cleaning the gruesome aftermath from the inside of the turret. Colly was preparing to do this when an arm grabbed him and pulled him from the back of the Bradley. Soapy water splashed over the Bradley's floor panels and back troop bench. Chaplain Ric Brown placed the bucket down and looked into Colly's eyes, instantly recognizing what this young NCO had been through.

"Come on, Sergeant. You got enough to deal with. You can get back out there. Just let me do this for you," he told Colly.

For the next thirty minutes, Iwan's driver, Private Matthew Carswell, and Tyler Colly reflected in complete silence on what had just happened and the unknown of what would lie ahead. In the distance they could hear the familiar clamor of a street battle and the near tinny scrub of the interior of their vehicle, as Chaplain Brown chose the most ghoulish task for himself, so that young men could focus on the difficult mission at hand. Ric Brown, the only semblance of decency in a city surrounded by misery.

Chaplain Brown now walks over to talk to Colly and the rest of the crew as they park next to the rest area of A company as they wait to eat. The mess area is just a big open stretch of desert next to the cloverleaf. The REMFs beat us to our food. They stand happily in line, chatting and gossiping and laughing. Their uniforms are meticulously clean.

We stare in hatred as they eat the meals prepared for us. None of us has the strength to protest. Morosely, we flop into the powdery dirt. I lie on my back next to Ruiz, whose hearing is totally gone now as a result of all the AT4s he's fired these past days. I doubt he'll ever get it completely back. He pulls off one gunk-and-shit-smeared boot. His sock radiates a stench that should be banned by the Rules of Land Warfare. He peels it off and casts it aside. His feet are black and speckled with angry red sores. Yellow-orange fluid leaches from under his toenails. We haven't been able to take our boots off for days.

A few nights ago, we'd just fallen asleep when Misa started screaming to someone outside our commandeered building. In broken English he shattered the silence of the night with, "Put your helmet on, dude. Your helmet!"

Just as Fitts was ready to shut him up, AK rounds zipped in and around the room we were in. Misa answered with an exaggerated belch from the M240 Bravo machine gun we had set up for overwatch. Four insurgents, dressed in American uniform tops and blue jeans, had actually stacked up on the outer wall surrounding our house. Using a preparatory hand squeeze signal, they charged into the courtyard, rifles blazing.

Misa quickly shredded one. The others paused, then fled back into the street where Sergeant First Class Matthew Phelps's tank cut them down with his .50 caliber machine gun.

The incident underscored our constant need for readiness, even when we had the opportunity to grab a few minutes sleep. This meant sleeping with our boots on, no matter what damage it caused our feet over time.

It isn't too much to ask for hot chow, is it? We've been reduced to viewing life's basic necessities as precious luxuries. These REMFs don't understand. Nobody who hasn't been through all this with us ever will. The gap between those who fight and those who support has never been wider.

Sergeant First Class Cantrell storms past on a mission to raise hell over the food. These last seven days, Cantrell has fought with unique fury. I respect him now as never before. He may scream and yell during a firefight, but he proved he'd do anything for us when the shit is on.

The morning after my house fight, as we faced yet another dug-in position, this time a factory complex, my squad stood on the roof of a garage under heavy fire. Cantrell came to our rescue. He handled his Bradley like a battering ram and smashed right through the exterior wall of the factory. He drove into the heart of the complex, Bushmaster belching high-explosive rounds. The big gun raked the buildings we would have otherwise been forced to assault in close combat. A flame bloomed, then another. In seconds, the entire complex was ablaze, thanks to Cantrell's strafing run.

From the rooftop, we listened to the screams of insurgents as they burned alive. We stayed there and listened until the flames finally drove us off the rooftop.

Now while Cantrell looks for someone to yell at for the sake of our food, one of our guys gets to his feet and half-runs, half-staggers to a nearby Bradley. He gets behind it, and I hear him dry heave. I look over to see who it is, but I can't tell. As I'm craning, somebody else loses control of his bowels. When I turn back, there's a puddle of pudding-like diarrhea, slick with bloody mucus, steaming in the dirt next to me.

I'm too exhausted to move away.

We've been shitting like this for days. For me, it started after the house fight on the tenth. My groin burned from my injuries there, and I alternated between covering the wounds with Neosporin and wiping my leaking ass with strips torn from my T-shirt. Finally, desperate to stop the dripping, I tore another strip off and stuffed it into my anus.

At times, the diarrhea left us so dehydrated that Doc Abernathy had to give us IV fluids between firefights. He had us swallow all sorts of pills to stop us up, but nothing worked.

Doc's lying limp on the other side of Ruiz now. He looks around and reminds us, "Remember to wash your hands before you eat."

What the hell for? Could we get any sicker?

Doc, too, had proved himself to me in the past few days.

On the twelfth, the insurgents nearly annihilated us in a six-hour gunfight. J.C. Matteson, one of our scouts, died when an RPG hit him in the gunner's hatch of a Humvee. Not long before, Lieutenant Iwan went down. As the fighting raged, our platoon took down another large building and moved to the second floor. Once we got up there, we found that most of the exterior walls had been blown away. We were exposed from every direction, and the insurgents quickly capitalized on our mistake. Machine-gun and sniper fire hit us from two directions. We fought back with every weapon, but we had no hope of gaining fire superiority. The insurgents overwhelmed us and pinned part of the platoon down.

Doc had a lot of medical work to do that day. Tristan Maxfield had just wounded an insurgent when an RPG nearly tore his foot and ankle off. Without missing a beat, John Ruiz jumped up and dashed to Maxfield's side. As bullets flew all around him, Ruiz shielded Maxfield's head with his own body. A split second later, Doc slid over and started to treat Maxfield. He exposed himself repeatedly to the incoming fire while he worked.

Maxfield ignored the pain, ignored the fact that some muj shithead had just changed his life forever. All he said was, "Doc, roll me over! Roll me on my stomach!"

Puzzled, Doc eased Maxfield onto his chest. Maxy grabbed his weapon and returned to the fight, even as Doc Abernathy fought to staunch his torn and bleeding wounds.

These men look like average guys. On November 12, I saw the greatness of their spirits. They rose to the challenge and they fought selflessly for one another. Despite the terror of those long hours trapped on that building, I have never felt closer to a group of human beings. We stood together, and we shined.

Now, as I'm still pondering Doc's polite suggestions that we wash our hands, a staff sergeant I've never seen before strides up to our platoon. He's got more cool-guy shit dangling off his uniform than a Navy SEAL. He raises his hand and beckons to us. I see he's wearing a Nomex glove with the trigger finger cut out. His nails are clean.

I'll be stunned if this bag of shit has fired a weapon since boot camp.

An advanced combat sight sits atop his M4. We could have used more of those, especially during our battle on the second floor of that ruined building on the twelfth.

He regards us through brand-new Wiley X ballistic sunglasses; the holy grail of combat gear. His face wrinkles with disgust when he catches a whiff of our stench. A brand-new pair of metal handcuffs dangles off his belt. The cuffs catch the sunlight with bright gleams.

"Who is this? Billy the fucking Kid?" I whisper to Fitts.

"What unit is this?" he demands harshly.

Nobody responds. This pisses him off.

"Soldier!" he barks at me. "What outfit is this?" He sounds like a tough-guy wannabe.

"Excuse me?"

"What outfit you in?"

"That's fucking Staff Sergeant, guy."

He ignores that. "What unit is this?"

I'm ready to bitch-slap him until he squeals. Instead, Lieutenant Meno stares at this turd and says, "*Sergeant,* this is 2-2 Alpha." Our platoon leader talks like a badass now, which, after the second-floor battle, he is. Meno killed more than his share that day. The divide between officers and NCOs is usually impenetrable, but Meno broke it. He is one of us. A brother.

Billy the Kid refuses to fuck off. Fitts sits up, and demands, "Hey dick, what do you need?"

"General Batiste is coming. Danger Six wants to thank each of you personally for what you've done."

Outstanding. Somebody cut my face so I'll have a scar and will always be able to remember this day.

He waits for a reaction. I suppose he wants a cheer, or an "Oh boy!" from us. We're not having any of it. All we want is chow and a few hours of sleep. Our lives have whittled down to these two needs. Anything else is simply an obstacle.

Knapp speaks up next. "If Danger Six brings tacos, I'll carry him around this bitch like we just won the Super Bowl." We all break out laughing. Our visitor is not amused.

Billy the Kid tries again. He takes a few reluctant steps toward us. His handcuffs jangle on his body armor. "Danger Six is coming. You men need to get cleaned up for him."

Does this mean I need to put a fresh strip of T-shirt up my blistered ass?

The soldier behind the Bradley dry heaves again. Fitts lies back down into the dirt. We ignore our visitor. The breeze blows the stench of fresh vomit over us, and Billy the Kid makes himself scarce.

Ruiz starts powdering his mangled feet. I've got shit on one side of me, puke on the other. And our general wants to come and talk to us.

I can't take this anymore.

I close my eyes and lie back in the morning sun. In the distance, the REMFs smoke and joke while eating our food. They seem to be talking about some NBA basketball game highlights on ESPN's *SportsCenter*.

A figure blocks my sun. I open my eyes to an upside-down silhouette of a man. I cannot see who it is.

"What's up?"

The man bends forward to look down at me. I see he is a major.

"Danger Six is in the AO (area of operation)," he says dramatically. I notice he's got his rank on the front of his pristine helmet. He also has the classic mark of an REMF: there's no night-vision mount on his Kevlar.

"You men need to get up and shave. He's got the *Army Times* with him, and he's got *Stars and Stripes.*"

We gawk at him like he's a martian. He sees our reaction and decides to scold us, "I know you men have been in the bush, but we're all in the army and we need to uphold the standards, Hooah?"

Nobody responds. *In the bush? Does this fucker think we're in Vietnam?*

The major opens his mouth to say something, but Fitts cuts him off. "What the fuck? You're fucking kidding, right?"

I'm so congested and my hearing is so bad that I'm not sure if he's talking to me or the entire platoon. I sit up and look around, trying to contain my fury.

Then I see him. A hundred meters away, Staff Sergeant Lockwald, our guitar-strumming, berm-blowing engineer, is talking with General Batiste.

Lockwald looks freshly shaved.

You've gotta be kidding. We spent last night sleeping nut to butt in body bags to stay warm. Now we're supposed to shave so the general can have a photo op?

Lockwald isn't the same man who opened the breach at the start of our assault. For one thing, the man who never wanted to take a human life found himself covering a road when a wave of insurgents rushed past, on their way to our precarious second-floor position. He faced a choice. Should he abandon his principles or let the Third Platoon's dismounts get blindsided by thirty insurgents?

He racked the bolt on his Ma Deuce and knocked them down like bowling pins.

For another, the next morning, his half-joking wish came true. Captain Sims was done fucking around, and he ordered Lockwald and his band of engineers to fire a MICLIC down our target street. For blocks in all directions, windows shattered, buildings shook. Debris fell. The concussion wave killed dozens of insurgents. When we went through the neighborhood, we found them twisted in awful ways. In one house, I discovered a man who succumbed while clawing his own face and eyes. The concussion wave turned some of them almost inside out.

Lockwald shakes hands with General Batiste. They share a few words before the general moves on to another engineer.

"Hey, Fitts?"

"Yeah, bro?"

"They made all the engineers shave."

Fitts spits a wad of chew into the dirt. "I can't fucking take this shit."

The major rejoins General Batiste's brass-heavy entourage.

My stomach is grumbling. I look down and my belly is inflated with gas.

If I stand up, I'll blow through the T-shirt strip and it'll be Mount St. Anus again. I will coat my boots with a lava flow of feces.

We are all giant germ bombs. We detonate periodically. None of us has the strength to do anything more than lie in the dirt in our own filth.

"Fitts."

"Bell."

"All I want is some fucking Imodium or Pepto or something to clog me up. Then I want some food and sleep."

"With ya."

Behind us, the soldier dry heaves one final time, then collapses back into our group.

Knapp blows a wad of snot into the dirt. He's got a fever and his throat is a bright crimson.

Our new sergeant major walks up to us. "What did that major want?" he asks.

When we tell him, Sergeant Major Bohn looks at us with incredulity. "He didn't really say that, did he?"

"Yes he did, Sergeant Major."

First Sergeant Smith gets wind of this as well. He comes tearing across the mess area cursing in German. His entire bald head is bright red. I've never seen him so livid. Sergeant Major Bohn goes to intercept him, but Captain Doug Walter collars him first.

Captain Walter. Our old Alpha Company commander.

He's one of us again because of yet another loss. On the day after our second-floor siege, Captain Sims moved up to the next block and entered a house. We heard shots ring out. Sims went down. He'd walked into a prepared ambush. Two others were hit as well: at point-blank range, Joey Seyford took an AK round in the shoulder and another in the leg. Seyford stayed in the fight and drove off two insurgents. Air Force Staff Sergeant Greg Overbay, assigned to Alpha Company as a Joint Tactical Air Controller, was also shot in the house. Sergeant Travis Barreto pulled the men to safety and one of our interpreters, Sammy, ended up shooting an insurgent during the fray.

Sammy, a former Republican Guard weapons' sergeant, felt especially close to what he considered his own commander, Sean Sims. As Barreto carried Seyford and helped Overbay out of the house, Sammy lifted heavy fuel drums so that the American soldiers could cross over the walls to be evacuated.

As they evaluated their wounded, Sammy was an emotional wreck. Tears streaming down his cheeks, Sammy knew what none of the other soldiers giving aid to the two wounded soldiers had yet to realize. Captain Sims had died inside that house.

Not since Vietnam had a unit lost so many leaders in one battle. Our immediate chain of command, Lieutenant Meno excepted, had fallen to enemy fire. Iwan. Sims. And our most senior enlisted man, Faulkenburg.

Captain Walter, who was living in Sims's room at the base to protect his stuff from roving pillagers, caught a Blackhawk and flew to Fallujah to take over Alpha Company. Sims was his best friend, and he grieved more than anyone.

"Fuck the photos! Fuck shaving!" I hear First Sergeant Smith scream to Captain Walter. Sergeant Major Bohn is with them now. He nods his head. Smith is still livid, "All they want is fucking food, sir. Enough of the bullshit. They don't know what these kids have been through."

Before Doug Walter arrived to lead A company, First Sergeant Peter Smith became the acting commander. During a time of great stress, with his company reeling from all the tragic losses, Smith became a steady presence and brought his company to fight only fifteen minutes after losing Sean Sims.

General Batiste is not far away, talking with another engineer. Unless he's as deaf as we are, he can't possibly miss what's going on. He ignores it.

Wow. This is awesome. First Sergeant Smith is about to snap. Our leadership is fighting for us.

But they lose. We are ordered to shave and try to clean up as best we can.

I find a beat-up travel razor powered by a couple of AA batteries and go to work. My beard is so thick, it's like hacking blackberry bushes with a stick. I twist and tear chunks of hair out. By the time I'm done, I've ripped open old cuts all over my face. New ones crisscross the old. I get to my feet with the rest of the platoon. Our faces are splotched with blood from dozens of nicks and cuts. Normally, this would be no cause for worry. But here in Fallujah, they'll be infected before morning.

I glance down at my body armor. It is still stained with the Boogeyman's blood. After Lawson came up and found me on the rooftop, we checked the house and pulled the bodies out. Fitts and Lawson later found a sixth insurgent in a room upstairs behind the door I didn't clear. They shotgunned him through a hole in the wall.

In the kitchen, we found drugs and U.S. Army–issue autoinjectors. They had been full of atropine and epinephrine. The muj inside the house had shot the drug directly into their hearts. It acted like PCP—angel dust—and kept them going long after my bullets should have killed them.

In another section of that house, I found a pouch with a Hezbollah insignia. At least some of the six men inside were Shia, not the radical Sunni we were told were so prevalent in the al Qaeda–dominated Anbar Province. Somebody else found documents from the Palestinian Authority amid the debris upstairs. Three flat stones called turbas were found under a Koran in a velvet cloth. Shiite Muslims place their foreheads on these stones when they prostrate themselves in prayer.

As I stare at the bloodstains on my body armor, I think about how those men died. The young ones were committed and they fought hard, especially the one in the wife-beater T-shirt who ran from the Jersey barriers to the kitchen at the start of the fight. I shot him two separate times, and he still came after me when I was trapped in the bedroom.

I find it ironic that the oldest of the bunch, the Boogeyman, hid in the armoire while his cell fought to the death. Then, when he felt trapped, he made a break for it and tried to run away. In the end, he pleaded for his life.

The young ones were more committed. They've been indoctrinated since childhood and are radicalized beyond reason. They will go willingly when their leaders stay back and order them to their deaths.

I wonder if this place is beyond hope.

General Batiste is coming toward us now. His shiny major

lackey hangs back over one shoulder. Photographers and army reporters cluster around him. At this moment, at this place, General Batiste is a rock star.

I wish Mick Ware could see this. He and Yuri left us on the morning of the twelfth. Before going, Ware handed me his sat phone and told me to call my wife.

"Let the men call their families first," I replied.

One by one, the men took turns talking to their loved ones. I went last. I took the phone and tried to dial with shaking hands.

The phone rang back in New York. Deanna answered.

She knew it was me. "David! Where are you?"

"I'm safe," I said. I wonder what she's been doing as all this has gone on.

"I've been watching the news. Are you in Fallujah?"

I couldn't tell her that without violating operational security. Yet I wanted to tell her everything. I didn't have time and I didn't know how. How do you tell the love of your life that you smelled a man's breath as you drove the life from him?

"My heart is killing me," she exclaimed. "Every time I watch the news, I can't stand it. Where are you? Tell me! You're in Fallujah, right?"

"No," I manage. "I'm near it. We're okay."

"I have had a horrible feeling. Something's wrong, isn't it?"

As I replay the conversation now, I marvel at how she could sense that.

A minute later, my little boy took the phone, "Daddy, make sure you fight bad guys!"

"Okay, buddy. I love you."

"Fight bad guys!"

"Okay, Evan. I love you."

"I love you, too, Daddy."

And then, their voices were gone.

• • •

General Batiste shakes Meno's hand. The two men chat, and as I watch them, Evan's words return to me again. Maybe it is time to stop being a soldier and go home to be a father. And a husband for Deanna.

I'm not sure how.

General Batiste turns to Pulley. He surreptitiously reads his name tape before shaking his hand. "Private Pulley, I've heard good things about you, son."

Cameras click and whir. We're in the middle of a brass and grunt pony show.

The major appears in front of me. Despite my stench, he leans forward and whispers, "Hey soldier, give me your email address, and I'll send you photos of you with Danger Six."

"Sir, that would be david at eatabagofshit dot com."

Fitts starts smiling. I realize we've come full circle. I am just like him now, intolerant of bullshit.

Anger flares across the major's face. He sucks air, then says almost to himself, "We're in Fallujah. I'm with the *infantry*. Just handle it."

An hour later, we're sent back into the fight.

Broken Promises

Summer 2006

In the summer of 2005, I left the army and returned to civilian life. It was the toughest decision I ever had to make. I loved being an NCO, and I missed it every day.

After I returned home, I witnessed another battle raging on the television over Iraq. From Washington, the rancor and defeatism over the war shocked me. As other veterans of the Global War on Terror started to trickle home, we shared the feelings of the disenfranchised. We who sacrificed were being ignored by the World War II and Vietnam generations now holding seats of power in our government. I joined Wade Zirkle in forming Vets for Freedom, a nonpartisan political action committee dedicated to supporting our troops in both Iraq and Afghanistan. I want to believe the war is a noble effort, but I fear it may end ignobly.

Most Americans had no idea what was really going on in Iraq in 2004. Some didn't want to know. For years we have been spoiled by one-sided, sterile air wars. That kind of warfare has more in common with PlayStation games than with Hue City or Seoul in 1950. Or Fallujah in 2004.

Even those who read the paper or watched the evening news didn't get it. The reason for that was clear: the type of reporting in Iraq left much to be desired. The Michael Wares of the war were few and far between. The majority of the journalists covering Iraq stayed in the Baghdad hotels, where Arab stringers with dubious motives fed them their raw material.

In most mainstream news agencies today, we read stories and see images that stem from foreign national stringers without journalistic schooling. Rarely do these stringers get a prominent byline. The home-front audience has no idea of their ethnic, political, or religious bias. Oftentimes, the footage we see of IEDs blowing up is actually filmed by the insurgent cell that triggered the blast. Then the nightly news plays the video at six and eleven. The line between good and evil is now permanently smudged in Iraq.

I refused to sit on the sidelines of this fight, not after all that had happened to my unit in Diyala and Fallujah. In June 2006, I returned to Iraq to bear witness to the fighting in Anbar Province. This time, I came to Iraq as a journalist, determined to tell the truth about what I'd seen. I was there as a correspondent for the *Weekly Standard*, which gave me the credentials to cover Iraq from the point of view of someone who had been there before.

I spent most of my time in Ramadi, where I embedded with both American and Iraqi army units. There, I found what Ware and the other reporters who were with us in Fallujah discovered: soldiers don't like journalists. After all the negative stories, after beating Abu Ghraib to death on the front page of every American newspaper, the average soldier does not trust anyone associated with the media. The warrior class, bleeding in Iraq, has been painted with two brushes: that of the victim and that of the felon. They appreciate neither.

As I went out on patrol with these men, I realized how out of place I was. Despite having been a combat infantryman, in this context, without my own unit to lead, I was alone. If something were to happen to me, no one would really care. I was just a whore chasing a story.

I didn't belong. I never realized how much I missed Fitts and the boys until that moment. They had been the focal point of my life for so long that when I did go home in 2005, my departure from the army left a hole inside me. I tried to fill it with the trip back to Iraq, but instead I made it worse.

I saw Fitts in Kuwait a few days before I returned to Iraq. In 2005, he volunteered to go to Baghdad and train Iraqi commandos. He went out on dozens of missions with them over ten months. As I got in theater in June 2006, his second tour was complete and he was ready to return to Germany. I found him in Kuwait, busily spitting dip into the sand while he sat with his peers and swapped stories of their exploits in Baghdad. I joined them, and for one brief moment I felt like I was one of them again. He and I talked about the old days. Of course, he had to show everyone his scars from April 9. But as we reminisced, I realized I'd probably never see Fitts again. He's made the Army his home and career.

It was a bittersweet thought. There are never happy endings in the Army. There is no closure, not with friends or enemies. I can't say that I ever expected to see Captain Sims or Lieutenant Iwan or Command Sergeant Major Faulkenburg again after I left the service. But Fitts meant more to me, and now I had to realize that that part of my life was behind me forever. The comradeship we shared would never be experienced again.

Several weeks later, with my reporter duties done, I made a lone journey to Fallujah. I moved through the morning sun and tried not to attract too much attention to myself.

I started at the house overlooking Highway 10. It was here that Pratt was wounded. As I stared up at it, I wondered if there were still bloodstains on the roof. I couldn't check; somebody was living in the house. Next door, the house that had been there was little more than rubble. I climbed inside it and the old memories started to flow back. Two years ago, we staked our lives in this fight.

I turned and moved north, chomping on a Slim Jim as I traveled. I was heading for the breach site. Before I'd left New York, I had bought a few flowers from a vendor at JFK airport. They'd been with me on this entire trip, wilting in my backpack in the heat of the Middle East. They weren't much, but they would have to serve as my homage to those we lost.

I zigzagged through desolate neighborhoods full of ruined buildings. Hardly a soul graced the streets. The scars of battle were evident everywhere: broken houses, ruined buildings, and bullet-marked walls. The people who remained here lived with these reminders every day. They could not escape the lost families, lost loved ones. Just existing in this half–ghost town required facing these tragedies every day.

I reached the area where Sergeant Major Faulkenburg died. I found no plaque, no memorial in his honor. Instead, I discovered a falafel stand. Its owner and his customers had no idea of the significance of this place. Even if they did know why this was hallowed soil for me, I wondered if they would care.

I pulled one wizened carnation out of my backpack and laid it reverently on the ground. It was the best I could do for a man I loved and respected. Sick with grief and guilt, I tried to say a prayer.

God and I still had much to work out. On that street corner I realized that before I asked for His blessing over this soil, I had to figure out how to ask for forgiveness.

Heart reeling, I turned away from the breach. This trip had been a mistake. I should have never come back.

Yet I continued. Quitting would have been cowardice.

I hiked south to Highway 10 and pushed into the industrial district.

I tried to find the locations where Lieutenant Edward Iwan and Sergeant J. C. Matteson died. When they fell on November 12, our platoon was several blocks away, already locked in a desperate battle on the second floor of that massive factory building, I didn't see Iwan get hit. I learned of Iwan's death from Fitts while we were pinned down by enemy fire. The news enraged me. In a fight, fury and hate are fuel for an infantryman. Iwan's death was like that—fuel for us. After the word spread, we fought like banshees that morning. In a real sense, Iwan helped us one final time, and we were able to survive this ordeal because of the strength our love for him gave us.

My thoughts turn to an article I read in the Jacksonville *Times-Union* after coming home from Iraq. The story focused on a forty-six-year-old Navy chaplain named Father Ron Camarda, who happened to be in the operating room when Major DeWitt convinced the Marine surgeons to try and save Lieutenant Iwan.

Father Camarda assisted the doctors until hope was lost. Finally, they left Lieutenant Iwan in the chaplain's care. Father Camarda gave my XO last rites. Then as his life slipped away, this Catholic priest stroked Lieutenant Iwan's hair and softly sang "Oh Holy Night" to him. When he finished, Father Camarda kissed him and said, "Edward, I love you." In that, he said what all of his fellow brothers of Alpha Company would have wanted to say but never got the chance.

A single tear escaped from the LT; he died as it slipped down his cheek.

In the midst of all the hatred, the killing, and the sheer evil we faced, Lieutenant Edward Iwan faced death surrounded by the last thing I could ever imagine existed in a combat zone. Grace.

After reading the article back home, I could hardly breathe. Now its words returned to me and I thought about Father Camarda, a man of God and a savior to those of us, the the veterans of Fallujah.

I wandered through the streets of this broken city. The industrial district was still little more than rubble even two years later. Not much had been rebuilt. In the end, I made my best guess and put two carnations on the sidewalk for Lieutenant Iwan and our fallen scout.

Edward, I love you.

Those were the last words my XO heard.

I had one carnation left. This one was for Captain Sims.

I walked west, deeper into the industrial district. I came to one intersection and paused to look around. It seemed familiar. I gazed up at the ruins of a building and recognized it as the one we defended during of our fierce battle on the twelfth. It was here that our platoon made its last stand. We would have all been killed or wounded had it not been for Staff Sergeant Fitts that day.

Withering small-arms fire scythed through our building from the west. All of us were hunkered down behind piles of brick, or an interior wall, or whatever we could find. We had more targets than we could handle. We were all killing insurgents, but more flooded toward us to take their places. We were getting overwhelmed. The enemy seemed to almost toy with our desperate situation. A sniper disabled one of our M240 Bravo machine guns, rather than taking the easier head shot on Specialist Joe Swanson.

The volume of incoming fire swelled. Together Sergeant Charles Knapp and Swanson stuck their Kevlar helmets onto poles and raised them up into the open to draw fire. A sniper put three bullets millimeters away from Swanson's in quick succession. His accuracy chilled us.

And then rockets impacted amid our positions with equally expert aim. One streaked into our building and ping-ponged around. It almost killed Sergeant Jose Rodriguez, who braced himself for the impact by closing his eyes and turning away. The rocket was a dud and failed to explode.

We had no choice but to keep firing. A few minutes later, an insurgent broke cover and shot at us from an adjacent alleyway. Sucholas launched two 40mm grenades toward the man, but both missed. He loaded a third grenade into his M203 and fired again. This time, a bright streak shot from his weapon and embedded itself in the insurgent's chest. The sight left us all stunned. Sucholas had accidentally loaded a green star cluster 40mm grenade into his launcher. Composed largely of white phosphorus, the shell burned the frenzied insurgent from the inside out. He fizzled, popped, and screamed for what seemed like an eternity as his death agony was masked by wisps of green smoke.

Finally, Staff Sergeant Jim and our Bradleys broke through the enemy resistance. Fitts knew that they were our only chance, and they needed to be positioned exactly right in the intersection below to do the most damage at the least risk to themselves. The problem was, from inside the building, we couldn't get a good view of the intersection. At the same time, a bottleneck developed in the street between the tanks and the Brads. With the track commanders buttoned up and unable to see, they were having a hard time getting out of each other's way.

Ignoring the fusillade of incoming bullets, Fitts leaned out the second floor of our building. Holding on to a section of intact exterior wall, he dangled himself precariously over the side of the factory, a radio in his free hand. AK rounds cracked and whined all around him. Several impacted on the wall right next to him. He hung himself out there, spotted the logjam in the side street, and talked the vehicle commanders through it. The whole time he spoke to them over his radio, Fitts was the most exposed human in Fallujah.

Staff Sergeant Jim's tank drove into the fight. A rocket-propelled grenade just missed Fitts. Unfazed, Fitts refused to take cover. Instead, he called out targets for Staff Sergeant Jim. His tank surged forward, its 120mm booming. The big Abrams smashed through a compound wall and blasted insurgents into pink sprays of meat and blood with its main gun. Jim's tank became our savior; his crew crushed the counterattack that threatened to take us all down. Mangy man-eating dogs followed behind him and devoured the remains of his victims. At one point, when the tank paused, I saw the mutts licking its tracks.

Later on, an insurgent in a second-floor window fired on Iwan's old Bradley, now commanded by Sergeant First Class John Ryan. It was suicide by Bushmaster cannon. Ryan's gunner, Sergeant Tyler Colly, blew the insurgent clean out of the building. A tangle of electrical wires snared him like a fly in a spiderweb. He hung there, dripping gore on the snapping dogs below. Others shot him down, and when he splattered to the ground, the dogs went berserk.

Six hours into the fight, the few surviving insurgents fled before the armored juggernaut and the fight ended. My young soldiers withstood the worst the enemy could offer and refused to bend. Instead, they stood brother-to-brother and faced the foe together.

It had been a ghastly yet magnificent day of battle. I'd seen my men perform with the utmost devotion. At the same time, I realized that this grisly violence had numbed me. I feared that for the rest of my life, I would never sober to the true reality of its horror.

It all came back to me as I took one last look at the ruined building and the intersection around me. It had been almost two years. Time was short, and I had one last place to visit. I walked on as my emotions played havoc with me. I missed my platoon more than ever now.

At last, I reached the neighborhood where Captain Sims was killed. People milled about in the street. The appearance of a lone westerner caused many to gape at me. It became awkward, and potentially dangerous.

I walked past the compound my squad had been in on the morning of the thirteenth. This was where I'd last seen Captain Sims, and the moment flashed back into my mind.

We'd been clearing houses. When Captain Sims found us, we were taking a breather. Some of us were smoking. A few others had dug into some MREs.

As Captain Sims approached, I figured for sure he would have a comment about our facial hair. Instead he entered our compound looking like George Michael post Wham!

Some horrible human being had taken a giant-sized shit in a bath tub that rested in the front yard of this compound. I attached wires to it as Captain Sims came to the gate.

"Sir, check out this IED we found."

"Dear Lord," he groaned in mock seriousness. "Does he need a dust off or the chaplain?"

We shared a laugh and I noticed Sims's bloodshot eyes. Exhaustion had taken its toll on him. So had Lieutenant Iwan's death.

"Sir, I am sorry for your loss. We all loved him."

"Sergeant Bellavia, we'll deal with it later. But thank you. How is everyone?"

"Good, sir."

"I heard about what happened the other day. That is some Audie Murphy stuff."

I didn't feel that way, so I didn't reply. Captain Sims came a little closer to me, then chided me. "Listen to me. What you did was Hooah, but it was stupid. We can't take crazy chances like that, you understand me? We can't risk any more loss. You have to use your head. You and Fitts are important to these men and you need to stay in this fight."

"Yes sir."

Another block ahead had to be cleared. We started to gather our gear to go and do it. Captain Sims shook his head. "You men rest. You deserve it. I'll take care of this."

"Are you sure, sir?" Fitts asked as he stood at the gate to the compound.

"First platoon spent the night next to a cache. I'm gonna get some photos. Eventually we are gonna have to blow all this in place. You guys earned a rest."

It was a touching moment. In Fallujah, in our worst moments, Captain Sean Sims had grown into a leader beyond all our wildest expectations.

Not five minutes later, he was shot dead inside a house.

On the same street two years later, I just could not go on. Three hundred meters from the house he died in, my last carnation fell to the sidewalk. I mumbled one last prayer.

My mission was done, and I felt cold and empty. The closure that had lured me to Fallujah in the first place continued to elude me. There will be no closure with the war still ongoing. I guess I just wanted to find a city worthy of the men who bled and died to liberate it. I wanted to see something of value, something that gave it all meaning. I don't pretend to know how the war will be judged by history.

I started to walk away when I felt movement behind me. In that instant, like the old days, my instincts kicked in. Somebody was watching me, and I had to get out of there. Without a weapon, I was an easy target. In my rush to put some distance between me and whatever the threat was, I almost crashed into a woman in black as she came around a corner. I noticed she carried a mat with stringy weeds on her head. Our near collision startled both of us, but I hurried on and failed to even apologize.

Then I heard her footsteps stop. I turned, and saw her regarding my carnation. She stared at it for a long minute before looking back to study my face in the early morning light.

My shoulders sagged. I could not even feign a smile for this woman. Instead, I turned up the street to leave her and this miserable city behind. I took a few steps. Behind me, nothing broke the stillness of the morning. I expected to hear the swish-swish of her sandals again walking on the side of the road. But there was nothing. Curious, I glanced over my shoulder again. She was kneeling in front of my flower.

Tenderly, she placed her own weeds alongside my cheap carnation. She touched her heart, then the ground, and uttered a prayer. She kissed her hand and touched her heart again. My mouth fell open. She looked over at me, and as our eyes met again, my heart broke. All the emotions, all the bottled-up angst and grief I'd pretended didn't exist suddenly broke free. Tears rushed down my cheeks, and I began to sob uncontrollably. I covered my face in complete shame, but I knew the woman still watched me.

She regarded me sadly. For a moment I thought she would attempt to console me. Instead, she nodded, turned, and ambled away, an anonymous elderly woman lost in a city I unapologetically helped destroy.

I slipped off into an abandoned home a street away, embarrassed and surprised by my own meltdown on that Fallujah street. I sat and stared at the front gate. I have no idea how long I sat there, wracked with guilt for surviving. I lost track of time, lost track of where I was. Finally, I moved outside the gate in an attempt to find that woman again. I looked up to see an empty street.

I was alone.

She left without knowing the gift she'd given me.

She wasn't the reason I came to fight in Iraq. But she reminded me of the importance of why we fight. The soil in Fallujah and all of Iraq has been consecrated with the blood of our dead. And her reverence reminded me of that. Fallujah will never be just another battlefield. This old woman showed me that my time in Fallujah was a life-altering privilege. It was here that we fought for hope. It was here that we fought to end the reign of terror that had descended on the innocents of a city.

Through it all, I witnessed the best of the human condition—the loyalty, the self-sacrifice, the love that the brotherhood of arms evokes. I realized then that I am complete for having experienced that. Those who died gave their lives for their brothers. They gave their lives for a noble ideal: that freedom from tyranny and oppression is a basic human right. We were the force to do that, and my brothers paid the price.

I stood up and headed for the street again, tears gone now. I had work to do, a fight to continue. But I knew this: as long as I honored these men each day, I would have a second chance at redemption.

At last, I understood.

Coming home from Iraq one last time in the summer of 2006, I sat in the airliner as it winged its way west and wondered about my future. I still wonder about it. I'm no longer a soldier. I'm no longer an NCO. I am not part of America's warrior class anymore. What am I?

I need to be a family man. My son needs me. My wife needs me. But the transition from infantryman to father and husband has been anything but easy. It started with a lack of understanding on both sides. For that, I am responsible. How can I share all that I've experienced with my son and wife? How can I get them to see what it meant to me to be with these men when they needed me most?

When it comes down to it, I haven't been there for my wife or my son. I don't blame them for being bitter, but that hasn't made things any easier.

The flight attendant brought me a drink. I sipped it and stared out the window at the vast Atlantic Ocean below us.

Captain Doug Walter gave me three weeks of leave to see Evan and Deanna after our nine-month deployment to Kosovo in 2003. It was the first time I even had a chance to be a father, and I loved every moment shared with Evan. Then I volunteered for Iraq, and all the goodwill and love we built during those twenty-five days seemed burned away by that decision. I went to Iraq to be with my men. Evan and Deanna saw that decision only as a rejection. As abandonment.

Things got even tougher. In the summer of 2004, I was supposed to come home on leave and be back in New York in time for our town's Fourth of July fireworks show. In emails and phone calls from Iraq, I'd promised them both we'd watch the pyrotechnics together. Then we'd see a minor-league baseball game, go to the zoo, and eat cotton candy. Through June, I could sense their excitement as my leave drew close. Evan talked nonstop about seeing his daddy again. Deanna's enthusiasm and love shined through every conversation.

The day before I was supposed to leave for Kuwait, insurgents attacked my platoon in downtown Muqdadiyah. We ended up in a sustained, close-quarters battle for several hours at the police station before we finally gained control of the fight. As a result, the convoy that was supposed to take me to the airfield was delayed by a day. I missed the Fourth of July.

I hopped on the first thing smoking back to Kuwait, but when I called home to tell them I was off schedule, Evan was crushed. He wouldn't be able to watch fireworks with his dad. I'd broken another promise. Deanna's excitement evaporated as she watched how the delay hurt our little boy.

It went from bad to worse.

The next day, while I was in Kuwait, an IED nearly killed my medic, Sergeant Robert Bonner, and one of our snipers, Staff Sergeant Carlos Pokos. I couldn't get much information about their conditions. I'd heard Bonner lost both legs and was clinging to life. Pokos was messed up as well, but I couldn't find out what happened to him. I was frantic to get more details. Would they live? Were they going home? Had they been airlifted to the Landstuhl army hospital in Germany? Or were they still in country?

In my search for information, another plane left without me. I took an ass-chewing in Kuwait for that, but it was nothing compared to what happened when I called home again. Deanna and Evan went from crushed and disappointed to bitterly angry. I'd screwed up with them again.

Three days later, on July 7, 2004, I saw Evan for only the second time in two years. I got off the plane at the Buffalo airport, still dressed in my desert camouflage uniform. Deanna regarded me coldly with that *you're an asshole* look she's got down pat and uses when I most deserve it. Evan hid behind her pant legs. When I reached for him, he recoiled.

My own son was afraid of me.

Deanna guided him to me, and I hugged him. He did his best to minimize the contact between the two of us, as if he was hugging a stranger. It was devastating to me. Of course he'd react this way. *I* was *a stranger*. He only recognized me from the photos Deanna taped next to his bed. His memory was empty of any time with his father.

I spent that leave building bridges with my son and wife. We did go to the zoo. We did eat cotton candy together as Evan sat on my shoulder and giggled at all the silly things I said for his benefit. By the end of those two weeks, we had bonded. He'd remember me now, I was sure of it.

But then I had to leave. Evan knew what was happening. The bad guys waited. Dad needed to go fight them. Yet this was the first real time I had been a stable presence in his life, and he didn't want to let go of that.

He hid my car keys. My hat disappeared. My overnight bag vanished. He did everything he could think of to delay my departure. When none of it worked, he sobbed. The little boy sobs turned to sheer despair from a four-year-old. Leaving him in that state was one of the most painful experiences of my life.

After Iraq, I knew I had to make a decision. I could either be an infantryman or a father and a husband. I could not do both. I wrestled with it, agonizing over which to choose and which to give up. Being a noncommissioned officer was everything to me. Wearing the blue cord of the infantry meant even more.

In February of 2005, Task Force 2-2 left Iraq and returned to Germany. We got back on Valentine's Day. When we got off the plane, the men were mobbed by their wives or German girl-friends, and I walked through a sea of soldiers and women passionately sharing this homecoming with long kisses and tender embraces.

There was nobody there for me. That night, I sat in the barracks and watched all the single nineteen-year-olds get ready for a night on the town. By eight, they had all left to meet girls and drink. I spent the evening watching German TV in an empty barracks. Out of combat, this would be my life: hollow, lonely, devoid of love.

Two weeks later, I arrived at the Buffalo airport again. Evan recognized me, but he was standoffish and cautious at first. I had to win him back all over again. This time, it was different. He was five now, and through the leave I began to see all the things I had missed. He was in T-ball. Somebody else had taught him how to throw a baseball. Somebody else bought him his first mitt. I had never even played catch with him.

His grandfather had shown him how to ride a bike. Inside, I was furious. These were my duties—sacred ones a father must do as part of his son's rite of passage. I had failed him again by being absent when he needed me. If I stayed in the army, what else would I miss?

Everything.

We spent March playing family again, but the clock ticked down and soon I had to return to Germany. As my departure time drew near, Evan started hiding my things again. The tears came and wouldn't stop. These brief interludes, however they balmed my own conscience, were nothing but torture for this little boy who only wanted a dad.

I left the army and came home for good in the summer of 2005. When Deanna and Evan met me at the airport this time, Evan asked me, "Daddy, do you have to fight any more bad guys?"

"No, buddy. No more bad guys. No more trips. I'm done."

"Done with the bad guys?"

I smiled and hugged him, "Done with the bad guys. Done with the army. I'm home now."

Except, I wasn't done. A year went by and this chance to go to Iraq and seek answers cropped up. When I made the decision to go, I told Evan only that I had to go on a three-week business trip. He seemed okay with that, mainly since we'd spent the last ten months tight as any father and son. I was finally starting to find my groove. I was even coaching his soccer team that spring.

At one of the last practices, I asked my assistant coach to take over the team while I was in Ramadi and Fallujah. He said he'd be happy to do that; then he called a team meeting and told everyone he'd be running the team while I was in Iraq.

Evan heard this and fell apart. I'd betrayed him again, and this time he was not ready to forgive.

"You're going to Iraq, Daddy?" he demanded. I nodded my head, unable to speak.

"What?! You said you were done going to Iraq. You said you were done fighting bad guys."

The bond we built together hung in the balance. I was losing him. And I had no answers, no defense. Maybe someday he would understand why I needed to do this, but not now.

When I left for Iraq in early June, he barely even spoke to me.

I stared out the plane's window for a while before finally falling asleep in my seat. The flight attendants left me alone, but my slumber was restless and full of anxious dreams. In the back of my mind, I wondered if I'd pushed things too far, done too much damage this time.

An hour later, we made our final approach into Buffalo from JFK in New York. The plane circled, then touched down. I was moments from facing . . . what? Will Evan be hostile? Will he fear me like he did all those other times I came home?

The passengers deplane and head up the gate. I stay in my seat perhaps longer than I should. Almost the last one off, I grab my overnight bag and walk for the terminal. Each step brings more trepidation.

Have I lost him again?

I see Evan and Deanna waiting for me on the other side of the security gates. Evan's face is bereft of expression. I can hardly hold the tears back.

Deanna offers a warm hug and a passionate kiss. I want so desperately to make this work. I need her to know how much I love her. Despite everything, despite who I am and how I react, I love her with such depth that I gave up the one thing that made me feel useful and important for her, and for our son. I am no longer a soldier. This is my gift for them. But is it too late? And do they see it as a gift?

Evan stares at me.

I try to hug him. He takes a step back. I pause, my heart in my throat. I've got to reach out to him, let myself be vulnerable. I find the courage, but he backs up again.

"You can't go to Iraq anymore."

"I know."

He looks up at Deanna, then back to me. "Did you fight bad guys? You told me you weren't." His voice is suspicious, full of accusation. He doesn't trust me, and I don't blame him for that.

"No, Evan. I didn't fight bad guys."

I can't bring myself to tell him the complete truth. I want so desperately to go back into this fight. I miss it every day. I always felt I could change the world with a rifle in my hands and our flag on my shoulder.

"Did you get shot?" he looks me over, apparently searching for bullet wounds.

I grin a little. "No, Bud, I didn't get shot."

"People get shot in Iraq."

"Yes, they do." It strikes me then that Evan for the first time has a grasp on the dangers that are faced over there. He's six now, and the world is coming into focus for him.

"People get shot, Daddy. They *die*. Bad guys kill them."

I think of Edward Iwan and Sean Sims. "Yeah, I know they do, Evan."

He takes a tentative step toward me. Deanna's holding her breath. So am I. He sharpens his gaze and looks me right in the eyes. I can't remember the last time he's done this.

"You know why you didn't get shot?"

I'm surprised by the strength of his tone. He's trying to be tough with me. All I can do is shake my head.

"'Cause I saved you, 'kay? It was *me*."

I start to laugh, but I see he is utterly serious. I humor him. "You did. You saved me. Give me a big hug. I love you."

He steps into my arms and I crush him close. But he's not finished. "No more going to Iraq. Iraq is done, got it?"

I start to cry.

"Bad guys are done. They lost." His voice is even stronger. He's lecturing me, showing me what he needs. I'm so proud he's found the courage to do this; all I can do is hold him. He's making it clear he will not be victimized by my comings and goings anymore. He's drawn the line.

I chose family this time. I chose Evan.

He really did save me.

I break our embrace and kiss his forehead.

"I love you, Daddy."

His eyes start to water, but he ignores the tears. He's being tough. He's being proud. He's being *my son*.

We turn, hand in hand, and depart the terminal as a family.

Spring 2007

The old woman in Fallujah, the final reunion with Evan and Deanna at the airport, these twin moments brought me to where I am today. Evan no longer tells people I fight bad guys for a living. When asked, he tells his friends that his dad talks on the phone a lot and vacuums on occasion. I smile and laugh and go back to working on this book. I wrote it so someday, when he is old enough, he will understand his father at last. And perhaps he'll share that insight with his younger brother. Four months after I came back from Iraq for the last time, Deanna broke the news that she was pregnant.

I am a father now above all else. I've embraced my new life and made my peace with the old one. I will always be unapologetic for what it took to beat our enemies in Iraq and win my battles. I sleep through the night. God and I have had our heart-to-heart.

I don't have the nightmares that I read other veterans are having. None of my old friends do either. I don't dream about seven-foot insurgents chasing me down Iraqi streets. And yet I think about Iraq almost every day of my life. Almost every dream I have is about Iraq, but none of them are bad. There will constantly be regret, sorrow for those we lost, but never nightmares. I will always hate war, but will be forever proud of mine.

When the wind blows just right, sometimes I close my eyes and still envision a heat-scorched stretch of highway. There is a watchtower burning in the distance. It is Highway South Five, the checkpoint we couldn't save from destruction back in Muqdadiyah almost three years ago. My platoon stands on both sides of the road. Bullets are heard in the distance, but there isn't any danger. Each soldier I pass stares at me for what seems like an eternity. Their faces are covered in sweat and soot. They just stare at me expressionless and move to the side as I pass. Fitss spits dip juice onto the road. Captain Sean Sims and Doug Walter look up at me from their map. Sergeant Major fixes his boot lace. And Lieutenant Ed Iwan nods at me. As the smoke from the burning checkpoint billows up from behind, the images from my past get smaller and smaller. Until, finally, all is open road.

I have permission to move on.

For now, I look forward to the time when Evan and his younger brother can play together. I see them in the backyard, both clad in boy-sized desert camo, low-crawling through the grass as they ambush neighborhood kids, playing the bad guys, and save the day. Each attack executed to the pinnacle of absolute doctrinal perfection, a perfection that only a well-rehersed combat element can unleash. Evan cooks off the pine cone grenade as his brother lays down plunging suppressive fire.

Each boy will have his own Bellavia nametape on his chest. Each face camouflaged in tiger stripes. Evan, after all, means "little warrior." As for my youngest son, Aiden, he carries the middle name of an unsung but still great American hero: Edward Iwan.

Aiden Edward Bellavia.

May he grow to be half the patriot of his namesake.

Appendix

They sacrificed so that we may all live without interruption from comfort.

Our fallen warriors:

PFC Nicole M Frye	16 Feb 2004
PFC Jason C. Ludlam	19 Mar 2004
SPC Adam D. Froehlich	25 Mar 2004
SPC Isaac M. Nieves	08 Apr 2004
SPC Allen J. Vandayburg	09 Apr 2004
SGT William C. Eckhart	10 Apr 2004
SSG Victor A. Rosales	13 Apr 2004
PFC Martin W. Kondor	29 Apr 2004
1LT Christopher J. Kenny	03 May 2004
PFC Lyndon A. Marcus	03 May 2004
SGT Gregory L. Wahl	03 May 2004
SGT Marvin R. Sprayberry III	03 May 2004
SPC James J. Holmes	08 May 2004
SSG Joseph P. Garyantes	18 May 2004
CPT Humayun S. M. Khan	08 Jun 2004
PFC Jason N. Lynch	18 Jun 2004
CPT Christopher S. Cash	24 Jun 2004
SPC Daniel A. Desens	24 Jun 2004

SPC Michael A. Martinez	08 Sep 2004
SGT Tyler D. Prewitt	24 Sep 2004
SGT Charles J. Webb	03 Nov 2004
CSM Steven W. Faulkenburg	09 Nov 2004
1LT Edward D. Iwan	12 Nov 2004
SGT James C. Matteson	12 Nov 2004
CPT Sean P. Sims	13 Nov 2004
SGT Jack Bryant, Jr.	20 Nov 2004
SGT Trinidad R. Martinez-Luis	28 Nov 2004
SPC Erik W. Hayes	29 Nov 2004
PFC Gunnar D. Becker	13 Jan 2005
SPC Viktar V. Yolkin	24 Jan 2005
SGT Javier Marin, Jr.	24 Jan 2005
SGT Michael Carlson	24 Jan 2005
PFC Jesus A. Leon-Perez	24 Jan 2005
SSG Joseph W. Stevens	24 Jan 2005
PFC Kevin M. Luna	27 Jan 2005
SFC David J. Salie	14 Feb 2005
SPC Justin B. Carter	16 Feb 2005
SSG Garth D. Sizemore	17 Oct 2006
SSG Leon Hickmon	21 Oct 2006
SGT Willsun M. Mock	22 Oct 2006
SGT Jason C. Denfrund	25 Dec 2006

Brief Glossary of Terms

Abrams: The M1A2 Abrams is the U.S. Army's main battle tank. Equipped with a 120mm gun, a .50 caliber and two 7.62mm machine guns, and reactive armor, it is the finest armored vehicle in the world today.

AK-47: The most widely used rifle in the world. This is the standard assault rifle of the Islamist insurgent in Iraq and Afghanistan. The 7.62mm AK-47 is tough, durable, and can be fired in both full auto and single-shot mode.

AT4: Light antitank weapon armed with the 84mm high-explosive antitank (HEAT) warhead. Although not designed to do so, the M136 AT4 was used in Iraqi Freedom as a tool to destroy built-up enemy positions.

Bradley: The Bradley Fighting Vehicle is both an armored infantry transport and a tracked, heavy-support weapon. It is equipped with a 25mm cannon mounted in a fully transversable turret, an M240C 7.62mm machine gun, and wire-guided anti-tank missiles. It can carry a squad plus of infantry inside its rear bay and is the standard vehicle for every mechanized infantry unit in the U.S. Army.

Cyclic: Firing an infantry weapon fully automatic for a considerable period of time. Usually, such weapons are fired in short, disciplined bursts to ensure accuracy and ammunition conservation.

Fatal Funnel: Doorways. In house-to-house, room-to-room fighting, doorways are deadly places for assaulting infantrymen. Going through a doorway leaves the infantryman at his most vulnerable. He cannot get support from his buddies, and the enemy usually has their weapons zeroed on these entrances. During Fallujah, virtually an entire squad from 2–7 Cav went down in one doorway during an ambush.

Frag: A fragmentation hand grenade has a blast radius of five meters.

JDAM: Joint Direct Attack Munition. This is a fancy way of saying "Smart Bomb." Air-launched by Navy or Air Force planes, the JDAM guides itself to the target based on global positioning system satellite data. It can be dropped in any weather, including fog and low cloud cover. Other smart bombs, such as those guided by lasers, cannot be used in overcast conditions.

M4: A variation of the M16. The M4 carbine has a short barrel, a telescoping stock, and the ability to fire in single-shot or three-round burst mode. It has numerous rail mounts for tactical equipment such as SureFire flashlights, laser targeting systems, and scopes. It is the finest infantry weapon in service today.

M16: The M4's long-barreled, full-stock father, the M16A2 and A4 still equipped much of Task Force 2–2 during Operation Enduring Freedom. Though decades old, it is a remarkably versatile and ergonomic rifle.

M240: The M240 is the new standard U.S. Army 7.62 x 51mm machine gun. Designed to replace the Vietnam-era M60, the 240 looks a little like the German MG-42 of World War II fame. Capable of firing so fast it sounds like a zipper bursting, the 240 is the primary killing weapon for the mechanized infantry.

M249 Squad Automatic Weapon (SAW): The standard U.S. Army light machine gun. Each squad usually has one or two SAW gunners. In Fallujah, we tried to equip most of the platoon with SAWs. Though a fussy weapon—if it isn't spotlessly cleaned on a regular basis, it will jam—the SAW constitutes the bulk of an infantry squad's machine-gun power.

PKM: The PK is a 7.62 x 54mm belt or drum general-purpose Soviet-era machine gun, currently in service by the enemy in Iraq and Afghanistan.

RPK: A Soviet-era drum-fed machine gun that fires 7.62 x 39mm bullets (same as the AK-47). In urban combat, it is a mobile, deadly weapon.

SureFire: A very powerful flashlight that can be mounted on most M16s and M4s. It is a tremendous asset when clearing houses at night. The SureFire provides fantastic illumination—so bright it can blind the enemy.

Tracer: An illuminated bullet that helps infantrymen and tankers to aim their shots. Usually, about one in five bullets in machine-gun ammo is a tracer round. When fired full auto, tracers look almost like laser beams.

Track: A fond expression for an Abrams tank or Bradley Fighting Vehicle.

Unit Organization: Task Force 2–2 was formed from 2nd Battalion, 2nd Infantry, 1st Infantry Division's Third Brigade. The battalion, composed of about 700 men and women, included two infantry maneuver companies of about 140 men each and one tank company, Alpha, Bravo (Tank), Charlie, and the Headquarters and Headquarters Company (HHC), which handled supplies, logistics, and administration duties.

Acknowledgments

David Bellavia

This book would not have been possible without the incredible vision, undying loyalty, and sage wisdom of my agent, Jim Hornfischer. I am truly blessed to have found a stalwart friend with such impeccable integrity. I am grateful in every way for his guidance and support.

I wish to express my profound thanks and gratitude to Bruce Nichols. You are a patient, talented professional, and your vision of this project from day one was the catalyst to achieve the highest standards. Thank you so very much.

Thanks, too, to Kate Jay, Jessica Elkin, Elizabeth Perrella, and all the great people at Free Press and Simon & Schuster.

Mickey Freiberg at ACME Talent Agency displayed the motivation and willingness to endure some difficult terrain during this journey. Thanks for not quitting me.

I am lucky to have a wonderful family, and I can't thank you enough: Mom and Dad, Lucy and Bill Bellavia, Marlene and Ed King, Dan Bellavia, Timmy Bellavia, Rand Bellavia, Joe and Joe Brunacini, Craig Gordon, Paul Spitale, and Bob Mihalko.

I have had so many important influences during my time in the military. Thank you: Eddie Belton, John Gregory, Jerome

De Jean, Captain Grey McCrum, Staff Sergeant Albert Harris, Adam Rissew, Tiffany Passmore, and the VetsForFreedom.org brotherhood of Wade Zirkle, Mark Seavey, Chris Niedziocha, Owen West, and Joe Worley.

Matt Matthews and all the dedicated professionals at the Combat Studies Institute at Fort Leavenworth, Kansas, for having the courage to tell the Army's story in a world full of Anchors. Your help has been incredible, and I am beyond grateful for your assistance.

John Bruning has made this process a joy. His brilliant gifts and steadfast fidelity have helped me beyond words.

Most of all to the family I left behind for over three years while I served my nation. My bride, Deanna, the most complete and perfect woman in the world, I love you so much for giving me this life. Evan and Aiden, being your daddy is the most rewarding job I have ever had. You both make me so proud and so grateful.

John Bruning

The first time I spoke with David on the phone, I felt like I'd found a long-lost friend. More than anything, I will treasure the friendship that bloomed between us as we worked on this project together for almost a year. David, thank you for so many things, but most of all, thank you for trusting me.

I owe a huge debt of gratitude to Jim Hornfischer. It was Jim's idea to hook David and me up, and as we worked together he provided tremendous encouragement and direction. The proposal we created would not have been possible without Jim pushing us and getting the very best out of us. Thank you, Jim. Your support, guidance and trust changed my life. For that I will always be grateful.

Bruce Nichols, your stewardship of our project could not have been better. I have learned so much, and you have been so patient with me that I have felt blessed to have the chance to work with you. I have been part of a tremendous team that all along has made excellence our standard. Bruce, you made all the work a joy. Your editing is in a class by itself. A hearty thank you must also be extended to Elizabeth Perrella, whose cheery demeanor even in the midst of deadline crises always brightened my day

Bob and Laura Archer, your friendship helped make my writing career possible. I still have the pen you gave me eleven years ago when I embarked on this adventure. It has signed every contract. Thank you for everything. Not many writers can call a century-old ballroom in a former Odd Fellows Lodge their office and home away from home.

I owe so much of my career to other people taking chances on me. Eric Hammel, my mentor and friend, you busted my chops and taught me how to be a writer. Pete Salerno, Ryan Howell, Vinni Jacques, Ken Jackola, Shannon Compton, Phil Disney, Alan Ezelle, Phil Larson, John Neibert, Tim Bloom, Brian Hambright, Kris Haney, Doug Jackson, Andy Hellman, Ron Clement, Matt Zedwick, Bill Stout, Tyson Bumgardner, Randy Mitts, Kevin Maries, Rebekah-mae Bruns, Kerry Boggs, and the rest of the Volunteers taught me the basics of what it means to be a noncommissioned officer. In New Orleans, they *showed* me the honor and strength of character such a calling requires. You are all fine NCO's, and I am honored to call you my friends. You will always have my respect and admiration.

Denice and Andy Scott, Allison, Brenda, Larissa, and Olivia Pfaff, thank you for taking care of me throughout this project. You kept me going even when I thought I had nothing left.

Jennifer, Eddie, and Renee, you are my foundation, my reason for being. Thank you for your complete support, your encouragement, and your belief in me. Thank you for understanding during all those nights I had to work. Above all, thank you for loving me and all my quirky, okay obnoxious, ways. With your love, I am truly blessed.

Lastly, to Mary Ann and Larry Beggs, your faith in me and your patience helped make all of this happen. And to think, this all started with a copy of *Red Baron*. I love you both. Thank you for letting me be a part of your family. I hope I have made you proud.

About the Authors

Staff Sergeant David Bellavia spent six years in the U.S. Army and was present at some of the most intense fighting of the Iraq War. He has been awarded the Silver Star and Bronze Star for his actions in Iraq, and was nominated for the Distinguished Service Cross and Medal of Honor for his actions in Fallujah. In 2005, he received the Conspicuous Service Cross (New York State's highest award for military valor) and was inducted into the New York State Veteran's Hall of Fame. He is the cofounder of Vets for Freedom, an advocacy organization of veterans concerned about the politicization of media coverage of military operations in Iraq and Afghanistan. His writing has been published in the *Philadelphia Inquirer, National Review, The Weekly Standard,* and other publications. He lives in western New York.

John Bruning is a prolific military and aviation historian who is the author of six books, including the critically acclaimed *The Devil's Sandbox: With the 2nd Battalion, 162nd Infantry at War in Iraq.* He has also consulted for museums in both the United States and Europe, computer companies such as Sierra Online and Microsoft, and has helped produce more than a dozen historical documentaries.